INTERPERSONAL AND GROUP SKILLS FOR LAW ENFORCEMENT

Terri M. Geerinck
Sir Sandford Fleming College

Prentice Hall Canada Career & Technology
www.phcanada.com

For Rod, my continued inspiration.

For Adelaide and Skyler, who make all things possible.

Canadian Cataloguing in Publication Data

Geerinck, Terri, 1958-
  Interpersonal and group skills for law enforcement

ISBN 0-13-011491-x

1. Law enforcement. 2. Police. 3. Interpersonal communication.
4. Interpersonal communications. 5. Group relations training. 6. Title.

HV7936.P75G43 2000   363.2'3   C99-931525-0

© 2000 Prentice-Hall Canada Inc., Scarborough, Ontario
Pearson Education

ISBN 0-13-011491-x

Vice-President, Editorial Director: Laura Pearson
Acquisitions Editor: David Stover
Developmental Editor: Susan Ratkaj
Copy Editor: Donna Goldman
Proofreader: Lisa Berland
Production Editor: Sarah Dann
Production Coordinator: Peggy Brown
Permissions/Photo Research: Michaele Sinko
Art Director: Mary Opper
Cover Design: Julia Hall
Page Layout: Carol Magee

7 8 9   06 05 04

Printed and bound in Canada

CONTENTS

Preface

This text is designed for policing students who are taking courses on interpersonal relations and working in teams and groups. As frontline workers, officers encounter many different situations that challenge essential communication skills. Dealing with members of the public who may be in great turmoil— with victims of crime, their perpetrators, suspects and other members of the public, demands a wide variety of skills. There are probably few other jobs out there that deal with such a cross section of our Canadian population. No less important, officers also have to work with each other as well as with a variety of other agencies including those in the judicial and penal systems.

In response to these demands, most students such as yourselves will probably take at least one course that will teach you effective communication skills and teamwork for dealing with others. For many, these courses are wrapped into one, such as in Police Foundations Training. This text was written in response to the lack of material designed for policing students in the areas of interpersonal communication skills and teamwork skills and puts these two areas together with an emphasis on application in law enforcement. A wide variety of sources are used in the text, including a large number of sources from law and justice. Some of these sources include research from social psychology, research in psychology, business applications, organizational behaviour, cultural diversity publications, interpersonal and team skills texts and publications and a number of police publications from both Canada and the United States.

Although not a police officer myself, I have been teaching in the area of law and justice for over 10 years. With a background in social work and counselling, I have worked with many officers over the years. For the most part, they are to be commended for their hard work and dedication. I do not foresee policing as becoming an easier job, but rather a more difficult one considering the issues that have surfaced over the last decade. The officers who have visited the college over the last few years point out these issues and reiterate what I have said to my students. Communication is the key to building and sustaining relationships whether it be a brief or long-term encounter.

In policing, how you communicate and how others communicate to you may be the difference between walking away from an encounter or being carried away from it. Thus, this text focuses not only on how you communicate but how others are responding to you. You can assess your current interpersonal communication and then study the chapters, paying special attention to your weaker areas. Areas including diversity, conflict, nonverbal communication, listening, perception and verbal communication are some of the topics in the first part of the book.

The second part of the text concentrates on group and team skills, with a focus on work teams and work groups. Some of these teams are primarily made up of law enforcement personnel, but there will also be other teams that you encounter in community policing. Issues around leadership, problem solving and decision making, change, group make-up and effective and ineffective teams are all discussed from a policing perspective.

I have attempted to make this book as practical as possible without losing the rich research and theoretical background of some of these concepts. Most chapters explore a topic, relate it to policing and offer strategies and suggestions on how to improve in that topic area. As well, each chapter contains a box with a Canadian Perspective as well as interest boxes with a Law and Justice Perspective. The Canadian Perspective boxes allow you to examine current Canadian issues and to assess the impact of these issues on yourself. The Law and Justice Perspective boxes give you the opportunity to see how these skills are actually applied in law enforcement, such as the use of a group problem-solving model currently used by the Ontario Provincial Police. Many skills-based chapters also provide opportunities for skills practice, self-assessment or other "try-it" activities that can be used as a self-study or learning tool or can be used by small groups in the classroom. I firmly believe that these activities will help you improve your skills and help you be a better officer.

The personal and public demands on a police officer will continue to be difficult ones. With recent media attention surrounding ethics, diversity, use of force and recent violent crimes, officers will need effective communication skills to deal with the public. As well, skills to work effectively within police organizations are also critical as services will continue to undergo rapid change to meet the demands of a changing society.

I wish you all the best as you undertake the study with this text. I hope that you continue to grow and to develop in order to become the best officer that you can be in the near future.

Acknowledgements

This book includes efforts from many people, and I wish to thank all of these people who helped in the preparation of this manuscript. While I cannot name them all, I am grateful to all of them.

First, I would like to thank my family for putting up with me while I worked. They gave me the time I needed. Thanks also to my friends who kept me going whenever I got stuck.

Second, I would like to thank my colleagues in the Law and Justice Department at Sir Sandford Fleming College who were invaluable with their information, support and thoughts. My colleagues in Interdisciplinary Studies were also of great help with their understanding and thoughts.

I would also like to thank my third and fourth semester Police Foundations students who continue to teach me about what works and sometimes what doesn't work in Interpersonal and Group Dynamics courses. My group from the fall of 1998 deserves special mention. Many of you will make, and some of you are already, excellent police officers. I should also mention all those past students who continually question and provide valuable insights about this changing world. Many of them are now police officers.

A special note of thanks to Constable Geoff Stark of the Peterborough Lakefield Community Police Service who gave invaluable input on being a police officer and on the kinds of issues that officers face today. He took the time to read and critique the original manuscript. It is officers like Geoff and many others to whom I spoke who point out the need for increased human relations skills in the complex work of community policing. Staff Sergeant Wayne Tucker of the Peterborough Lakefield Community Police Service was invaluable in his assistance for obtaining pictures, as was Senior Constable Brad Filman of the Ontario Provincial Police, Peterborough Detachment. As well, several past and present police officers from the United States also deserve my thanks for giving me permission to use some of their material. The list includes Captain David W. McRoberts, Roland Oulette and Ed Nowicki.

Finally, I would like to also recognize the many tireless and dedicated people at Prentice Hall Canada. This includes David Stover, who continues to keep me writing and whose invaluable insights are a continued source of inspiration. Susan Ratkaj also deserves my thanks as a continued source of guidance in this project. As well, Donna Lubin Goldman and Lisa Berland were tireless in their editing efforts to make this project a success and deserve a special thanks. Sarah Dann also cannot be left out of the picture. She kept her eye on the schedule and made sure we kept to it! There are many others behind the scenes at Prentice Hall Canada who also deserve my thanks and admiration. Keep up the great work!

P a r t

I

INTERPERSONAL COMMUNICATION

INTRODUCTION TO INTERPERSONAL COMMUNICATION

1

LEARNING OUTCOMES

After studying this chapter you should be able to:

1. *Describe the components of the communication process.*

2. *Define interpersonal communication.*

3. *Identify various levels of intimacy and self-disclosure using the Continuum of Interpersonal Communication.*

4. *List the six principles of interpersonal communication.*

5. *Identify reasons why a knowledge of interpersonal and group dynamics is important for personal and career success.*

6. *Identify strategies that will improve your ability to communicate more effectively.*

> *Stop, Police! Drop the knife!*
> *I love you!*
> *I can tell that you're lying by the way you are fidgeting.*

What do all of the above statements have in common? They are about very different topics, but they are all examples of communication. More specifically, they are all verbal human communication, but you can probably read "into" them for more than just verbal content alone. The first statement is **tactical communication** whereby an officer is ordering an individual to put down a weapon. The second statement has a very different tone and is possibly an exclamation of affection. The third statement is a reply to another's statement that is per-

Peterborough Lakefield Community Police Service

Bike patrol offers many opportunities to communicate with the public.

ceived as untruthful. Examination of these three statements illustrates some of the complexity of communication and of interpersonal communication. According to one researcher, while it may be easy and natural to communicate, it is difficult to communicate effectively (Puth, 1994). While you may find it easy to say something to someone, you cannot always be sure that the message will be understood as you intended. For successful interpersonal communication to occur, the meaning of the message must be shared accurately.

This chapter introduces you to the topic of interpersonal communication, which we will be exploring in further detail in the next six chapters. In this chapter, we will define the communication process, examine interpersonal communication, explore the principles of communication, list the ways that this book will help you understand the complexities of interpersonal and group dynamics and identify strategies that can improve your ability to communicate more effectively. Before you proceed with this chapter, assess your current level of interpersonal skills and knowledge with the questionnaire below.

SKILLS PRACTICE:

Interpersonal Skills Assessment

For or each of the following statements, answer true if you think the statement is true or mostly true, and answer false if you think the statement is false or mostly false.

1. Nonverbal communication is the greatest source of information about another person.

2. Active listening should only be used in certain situations.

3. Stereotypes are the same as prototypes.

4. Various vocal cues make up paralanguage.

5. Empathy is different from sympathy.

6. Learning how to speak correctly is the most essential communication skill.

7. Interpreting nonverbal communication is easy once you learn how to do it.

8. One of the problems of rigid thinking is that it leads to static evaluation.

9. Conflict should be avoided.

10. Ethnocentrism reduces prejudice and discrimination.

11. Canada is still a largely masculine culture.

12. Assertive people aggressively pursue their rights.

13. Use I-language to get what you want from others.

14. During a crisis, people often want less personal space.

15. Physical techniques should be used as a last resort in managing a crisis.

Answer key: Give yourself one point if you answered true for questions 1, 2, 4, 5, 8, 11, 15.

Give yourself one point if you answered false for the rest of the questions: 3, 6, 7, 9, 10, 12, 13, 14.

Interpretation: 0-5—This part of the text will assist you in learning the essential skills to improve your current level.

6-10—You have a moderate level of skill, and this part of the text will fill in some of the gaps in your skill level.

11-15—You have a good level of skill. You will be a great asset in class discussions and activities. Pay special attention to the chapters where you feel you need some improvement.

THE COMMUNICATION PROCESS

To understand the communication process, a good starting point is to look at the steps involved in the communication of a message. See Figure 1-1 for a diagram of this process. Communication involves three major steps (Coffee et al., 1994). Be aware that each step is presented ideally here, and in reality each step can have several problems called **interference**, or noise. To fully understand the steps, we can use an example for clarification. Assume that your teenage son wants to stay out at night until 11:30. His normal weekend curfew time is 11:00.

Step One: Encoding. Encoding is a process of organizing ideas into a series of symbols that can be used to deliver the message. Examples of symbols include words and gestures. The words that we choose can strongly influence the effectiveness of the communication. Your son says, "Can I stay out until 11:30 Friday night? There is a late basketball game on TV and I would like to go over to Eddy's house to watch it. His dad will drive me home after."

This is a different message from one in which your son says "I never get to do anything, so I'm going to Eddy's Friday night to watch a basketball game. Are you going to let me or what?"

Step Two: Transmission. The message is transmitted using some form of communication medium such as face-to-face verbal communication, e-mail, telephone or paper. Face-to-face communication allows more nonverbal communication to take place with voice tone, volume, gestures and facial expressions. If your son yells the second request to you, you may perceive that more is going on than a simple request for a change in curfew for a special event.

Step Three: Decoding. This leads us to the third step of decoding where the receiver of the message interprets the message into meaningful information. The receiver attempts to understand what the sender is trying to convey. It is during this step that many communication problems occur. As we try to interpret a message, we can make many mistakes. If your son yells his request, you will most likely perceive that there is more to this message. You may respond with "Why are you shouting at me?" or with "What do you mean you never get to do anything?" This may be the start of an argument about other issues such as parental control.

Decoding the message usually leads to some type of action by the receiver. If your son uses the first type of request, you may say, "Sure, that sounds fine. If Eddy's father can't bring you home, give me a call and I'll come to get you." Your son would probably say this communication experience was successful.

Interference. Unfortunately, not all communication experiences are so successful. Interference, or noise, often distorts or blocks a message and leads to misinterpretation by the receiver. Yelling may be perceived as anger. Your son may not realize he is yelling as he just finished listening to loud music, or maybe he is excited about the basketball game. Even e-mail and paper communication can have interference as we attempt to read between the lines. Has anyone ever said to you that someone's e-mail was bossy or snooty?

Noise is usually divided into three main types (Devito, 1995). **Physical noise** is interference with the physical transmission of a message. An example would be trying to listen to someone in a loud and noisy restaurant. **Psychological noise** is interference that produces barriers in the decoding and processing of information, such as if you are distracted while trying to listen to someone. **Semantic noise** is interference created when the receiver does not decode the message as intended by the sender. If you do not know the meaning of a word, it makes it more difficult to decode the message. Nonverbal communication has great impact on this communication process, as we will see in Chapter 4.

A final note about this process. The diagram shows an arrow going back to the sender from the receiver. Most communication between people is ongoing, with messages being sent back and forth. At any point, problems can occur in the process. These problems may be caused by interference as mentioned above. It should be noted that this interference can also be internal. Our thoughts, personalities, current physiological state, health and other internal characteristics impact on our encoding and decoding of messages. For example, have you ever found it hard to listen to someone when you have a really bad cold? Other sources of interference may be cultural differences, values and beliefs. Some cultures do not maintain eye contact. We may perceive this behaviour as being inattentive or rude. One police officer reported that while working in Toronto, the cultural difference took time to get used to

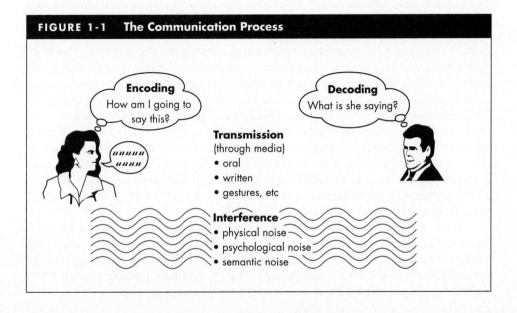

FIGURE 1-1   The Communication Process

as he had been taught to look at those in authority when he was being spoken to by that authority figure. In fact, many of us may have been punished for not demonstrating this behaviour!

INTERPERSONAL COMMUNICATION

We have just finished talking about a model of communication, but what is interpersonal communication? All texts that have a chapter on communication define it in similar ways (Dubrin and Geerinck, 1998; Beebe et al., 1999). Communication is about information, receiving information, thinking or acting upon that information and sending information. **Interpersonal communication** occurs "when we interact simultaneously with another person and mutually influence each other usually for the purpose of managing relationships" (Beebe, et al., 1999, p. 7).

Let's examine this definition more closely. Interpersonal communication is a type of **human communication**. We make sense out of the world and share it with others by using our five basic senses: seeing, hearing, smelling, touching and tasting. We then share our conclusions with others (Beebe et al., 1999). The depth of this sharing differs depending upon the situation and upon whether or not we treat the other person as a unique human being. Therefore, human communication occurs on a **communication continuum** (see Figure 1-2) ranging from impersonal to very intimate.

Impersonal communication occurs when we treat others as objects rather than as "real" people. If I respond to someone simply as a waiter or waitress ("Get me a coffee"), I am responding to him or her only as a role rather than as a person. If I ignore someone who is asking for change on the street, this is also impersonal communication. I may not even acknowledge his or her presence. As we move along the continuum, our communication becomes more personal and takes on more of the characteristics of interpersonal communication. People who frequent the same coffee shop day after day may start to "get to know" the server as a person as the communication gets more personal. Through continued contact, you learn names, interests and even some life experiences of this person. While you may never become "friends," you have moved further away from the impersonal end of the continuum. As a future police officer or other law enforcement worker, think of the kinds of dealings you may have with the public. Policing in a small town as opposed to policing in a large urban centre may lead to friendlier relations. In a small town, you may see and manage the same people on a much more regular basis.

As we move along to more interpersonal communication, the communication becomes more intimate and less formal and includes more personal and self-revealing content. By increasing or decreasing the amount of **self-disclosure**, we increase or decrease the level of intimacy. What happens when someone is too self-disclosing? Choosing a level of self-disclosure can be difficult, and we can become very uncomfortable when we feel someone is telling us more than we want to hear. Sometimes, we also feel uncomfortable when the level of self-disclosure has not been reciprocated. Have you ever felt that you told someone too much? We try to choose the level of self-disclosure that we feel comfortable with and to choose whether we want to maintain a current level of **intimacy**, increase the level of intimacy or decrease the level or degree of intimacy. As we get to know someone and feel closer, intimacy (see Figure 1-2) tends to increase.

The second part of the definition of interpersonal communication is concerned with simultaneous interaction between individuals. In other words, both parties are acting and creating meaning at the same time. Both verbal and nonverbal communication are observed and acted upon. In the third example of communication at the beginning of the chapter, one person is telling another that he or she is lying because of what is being perceived as "fidgeting."

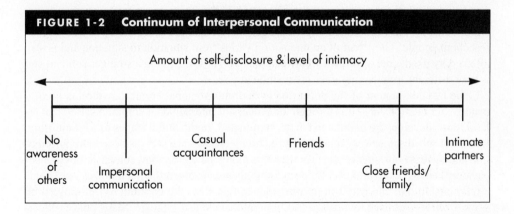

FIGURE 1-2   Continuum of Interpersonal Communication

Amount of self-disclosure & level of intimacy

No awareness of others

Impersonal communication

Casual acquaintances

Friends

Close friends/ family

Intimate partners

SKILLS PRACTICE:

Self-Disclosure: Applying the Continuum of Interpersonal Communication

For each of the following statements, discuss whether the level of self-disclosure was too intimate, not intimate enough, or appropriate. Support your answers. This is a good in-class activity about self-disclosure and intimacy. For added interest, formulate a reply to this person. Did your reply increase, decrease, or maintain the current level of self-disclosure?

1. This is your second class in Interpersonal and Group Dynamics. While on a class break, another student holding a cup of coffee approaches you and sits beside you. You talked very briefly in the last class about the weather and the large amount of work in this course. She says, "I really don't much care for night courses like this. I always worry about leaving my kids with Jimmy. I'm afraid he might start drinking around them or start hitting them again. Do you have any kids?"

2. You have been dating the same person for six months and feel that this is a very serious relationship. It is his or her birthday and you want to announce your love for this person and have already purchased a gold ID bracelet. You had engraved on the back "I love you" with your name. You have made a reservation at a quiet and intimate restaurant, have dressed up, and over dessert you present this person with your gift. You

hand the gift to this person and say, "Happy Birthday! I have something very special to tell you!" He or she opens up the gift, reads the back and says, "This is great! Thank you!" He or she puts the bracelet back in the box and sits back with a cup of coffee and says, "What should we do now?"

3. You are having a really bad day. First, your car would not start and you had to purchase a new battery for it. When you arrived home, you noticed the cat had used your bed instead of the litter box (again), and you received a very large credit card bill. After playing baseball that night and while out with a friend, you say, "I have had one of those days! Between the cat, the car and the bills, I could just explode!!" Your friend replies, "That cat using your bed again? I know what you mean! Sometimes, you question why you ever bothered to get out of bed!"

Mutual influence is the third component of the definition. This means that both parties are affected by the communication exchange. One person accusing the other of lying affects both people. The effect of an interaction varies from situation to situation and is also affected by the degree of intimacy between the two parties. Having a stranger smile at you is very different from having your lover smile at you.

The last component of the definition is that interpersonal communication is used to manage our relationships. It is through the process of interpersonal communication that relationships develop, are maintained or are terminated. In the initial stages of a relationship, we do not self-disclose very much. As attraction increases, we self-disclose more information and increase our interactions. As we move along the continuum, conversations and behaviours become more intimate. By decreasing interaction and reducing intimacy, we "cool" a relationship that can result in termination. In this way, the continuum can move both ways: from less intimate to intimate and from intimate to less intimate. Many police officers have had to reduce interpersonal communication with victims of crime who may reach out for physical comforting that may be inappropriate at a time of crisis and may be classified as unprofessional conduct by the officer.

PRINCIPLES OF INTERPERSONAL COMMUNICATION

Now that you have developed an understanding of interpersonal communication, we will move on to explore the six principles of interpersonal communication (summarized from Wood et al., 1998). An understanding of these principles will help you in developing skills.

1. **We cannot avoid communicating.** As long as others are around you, you cannot help but communicate. No matter what you say (or don't say), people will attempt to interpret your behaviour. We may even be unaware of some of our own communication. For example, you may not be aware of how you are clenching your fists when you are angry, but someone else may observe this behaviour.

2. **Communication is irreversible.** What you say and do has an impact and cannot be undone. Once you say something, it becomes part of that interpersonal relationship. Hopefully, studying this text will help you choose more carefully what you say and how you decide to say it.

3. **Meanings are constructed in interpersonal communication.** Each relationship is unique and the meanings of communication within that relationship are also unique. As relationships develop, meanings are assigned to the ongoing communication in the relationship. One friend may call you crazy and you both laugh about it. However, in another relationship to be called crazy may have a very different meaning and may be nothing to laugh about!

4. **Interpersonal communication develops and sustains relationships.** This is part of our definition of interpersonal communication. To add to this, communication allows us to define and re-define current as well as past relationships. Old boyfriends or girlfriends didn't really mean as much to us as we thought they did now that we have new loves in our lives. Communication also allows us to build futures in relationships. We can ask a potential friend to go bowling next week, and if the reply is positive the relationship has a future for us.

5. **Interpersonal communication is not a cure-all.** While good interpersonal communication skills are essential for working out problems in relationships, these skills will not solve every relationship problem. Also, not all people or cultures support the idea that "things should be talked out."

6. **Interpersonal communication skills can be learned.** We can all become better communicators by learning and practising the skills presented in this text and in related courses.

WHY STUDY INTERPERSONAL COMMUNICATION AND GROUP DYNAMICS?

Many students in programs such as law and justice question why they should study courses on interpersonal communication and group dynamics. Such statements as, "I have done fine so far; why should I learn new strategies and ideas?" or "It's just more psycho-babble" are not uncommon statements heard by this author. Other courses about law, investigative techniques and police powers often hold more appeal for law enforcement students. However, recent research into training for police officers has repeatedly noted the need for well-trained officers who can communicate effectively and who can manage in a diverse and changing society (More, 1985). The notion of better training for officers is gaining momentum in Canada. One example is the new Police Foundations Training in Ontario. In the Law and Justice Perspective box below there is more information on this new initiative. Many officers would also agree that communication is the first and often most effective weapon in any situation that has a potential for escalation. Most crisis intervention starts at a verbal and nonverbal level. Effective communication at this stage may lead to solving the problem at this level. Poor communication at the beginning of a crisis can lead to further escalation and possible injury to the officer.

The number of contacts an officer has illustrates the need for communication. Some of these contacts are with the public (including victims and suspects), other law enforcement and correctional officials, legal representatives (including the Crown attorney and judges) and his or her own team members and partners. The population of Canada is also increasing in diversity (see Chapter 7). All of the aforementioned illustrate the need for effective communication skills both on and off the job.

Although we do not examine groups and teams until later in this text, skills for teams will be addressed here. Many of these skills are similar and work well in teams because teams are also an interpersonal context. Teams and groups also vary in intimacy depending upon the

LAW AND JUSTICE PERSPECTIVE:

Police Foundations Training

In September 1998 a new curriculum was developed in Ontario under the heading Police Foundations Training. This new curriculum was developed by a committee of police professionals and college personnel to standardize training in Ontario for forces across the province. While not officially approved at the time of publication of this edition, the curriculum is being taught at a number of colleges and is using developed vocational learning outcomes. Some of these outcomes have been summarized here for the "Interpersonal and Group Dynamics" course.

The following police foundations vocational outcomes were developed for the Interpersonal and Group Dynamics course:

- Communicate accurately, persuasively and credibly to develop effective working relationships with individuals, groups and multi-disciplinary teams in order to achieve goals.

- Make sound decisions based on an evaluation of situations.

- Apply knowledge of fundamental concepts of psychology, sociology and criminology when interacting with peers, supervisors, other professionals, victims, suspects/offenders and the public.

The following generic outcomes were developed for the course:

- Communicate clearly, concisely and correctly in the written, spoken and visual form that fulfills the purpose and meets the needs of the audiences.

- Interact with others in groups or teams in ways that contribute to effective working relationships and to the achievement of goals.

While not a complete list, the need for effective interpersonal communication skills and teamwork skills is mandated in this new curriculum.

Source: Adapted from Draft Paper, *Police Foundations Training*, 1998; and Draft Outline, *Interpersonal and Group Dynamics*, 1998.

goals of the team or group, how comfortable members are with each other and the **norms** or rules of group behaviour.

HOW THIS BOOK CAN HELP YOU

Increased Knowledge About Interpersonal Communication and Teamwork

Although not a guarantee for skill improvement, knowledge is the beginning of changing your current behaviour. This text includes both individual and team skills that will help you become more successful as you communicate and work with others. The changing role of the police officer will demand better interpersonal skills, an emphasis on a participatory management style and leadership skills that can organize and motivate others (Lunney, 1989). By applying this knowledge to your interpersonal relationships, they can be more satisfying and meaningful.

Increased Self-Knowledge

This text presents psychological information that will help you to get to know yourself better, to become more aware of your strengths and to assist you with identifying personal challenges for self-improvement.

Better Awareness and Understanding of Diversity in Canada

Canada is becoming a very diverse nation. Being aware of this diversity and understanding differences among people with different cultures, backgrounds and lifestyle orientations will reduce barriers to communication and effective team and group work. Many conflicts are caused by cultural differences and values. Increasing your knowledge of cultures and learning effective communication techniques will reduce many of the conflicts that occur as a result of these differences. Continued immigration trends and the federal emphasis on multiculturalism in Canada will continue to be a challenge for employees and officers, particularly in urban areas. In the chapter on diversity we will examine the nature of diversity in Canada and the differences among the cultures and groups.

Knowledge About Team and Group Development

How do groups form? Why are some groups better than others? These are just a couple of the questions that will be answered to better assist you in becoming a productive group or team member. Part of being a team member may be leading the team. An entire chapter will focus on leadership and the skills required for effective leadership. Demographics, economics, patterns of major crime and disorder, and the "new technology" are just some of the challenges that a new police leader will be facing in the twenty-first century (Lunney, 1989).

New Strategies to Manage Conflict, Solve Problems, Make Decisions and Manage Change

Research has pointed the way to effective strategies for handling conflict, solving problems and making decisions that don't involve tossing a coin, arguing or using your best guess. As well, with the numerous changes occurring in policing and in the nation, you need skills to help you understand and manage these changes.

With these goals in mind, let's examine some specific strategies to improve your interpersonal skills. Team skills will be presented in the second half of this text.

STRATEGIES TO IMPROVE YOUR INTERPERSONAL COMMUNICATION SKILLS

Suggested here is a five-part strategy that is expanded upon in the next six chapters (this is an adaptation of Beebe, Beebe and Redmond, 1999; Wood, Sept and Duncan, 1998). Note that some of these were discussed above. This section will highlight and expand on a few of these areas.

Be Knowledgeable

You are already on your journey to increasing your knowledge about interpersonal communication. People who are effective communicators know how communication works. They understand the principles, theories, rules and strategies for more effective interpersonal communication.

Be Skilled

As stated previously, knowledge is the starting point. The old saying "practice makes perfect" applies to learning and using communication skills. You can memorize the steps of a problem-solving model, learn the skills for effective listening and learn about Japanese culture. Such knowledge will have little relevance (other than on a course content test) if you do not apply this knowledge so that it becomes a useful skill. Many students who first learn the steps of active listening report that it feels unnatural to actually try it with another person. Many new skills feel "strange" when you first try them. Use the text exercises to practise new skills so that they start to feel natural. You have probably had two decades or more to develop your current communication skills, so they will not change overnight for you. Developing a skill takes time, patience and practice.

Be Flexible and Open-Minded

Every situation you encounter is unique. As an officer, a person in crisis will demand from you a whole different set of communication skills than a person who is wielding a knife at you. The same set of skills will not work in all situations. Would you say to both people in the above example, "Now, now, calm down" in a quiet tone? Effective communicators examine the situation, the context and other factors (sometimes very quickly!) to establish a relationship at the appropriate level.

Create a Desire for Change

If you feel your skills are perfect or at least decent, you will have very little motivation to try and change those skills. In chapter 2 we will briefly discuss the changes in policing. This discussion may motivate you to realize that changes in police services across the country demand a change in policing style and abilities. Without effective communication skills, your chances of being hired may be reduced. New testing in Police Foundations requires knowledge in psychology and interpersonal and group dynamics. And many courses require not only knowledge but also demonstration of those skills as can be found in the new Police Vocational Outcomes. In general, employers are looking for workers who can demonstrate good interpersonal communication and teamwork skills. See the Canadian Perspective box below for more details on employability skills.

CANADIAN PERSPECTIVE:

Required Skills for Employees in Canada

What are essential skills for workers in Canada as we approach 2000? The Conference Board of Canada has published a brochure that outlines an Employability Skills Profile based on information gathered from a survey of Canadian employers. The skills were classified into three main categories: academic skills, personal management skills and teamwork skills. Here we will explore two of these categories: personal management and teamwork skills. Please note that all the requirements are not listed here. Instead, the ones specific to this type of course are highlighted.

Under the heading of personal management skills, Canadian employers need a person who has self-confidence and self-esteem; a positive attitude toward

CANADIAN PERSPECTIVE: *continued*

learning, growth and personal health; the ability to set goals and priorities in work and personal life, and to recognize and respect for diversity and individual differences.

Under the heading of Teamwork skills, Canadian employers need someone who can work within the culture of a group, plan and make decisions with others and support the outcomes of those decisions, cooperate to achieve group results, use a team approach when neces-

sary and take on effective team leadership when necessary. These are not all of the skills required by Canadian employers, but just a few that will be reviewed in this text. While many of these skills are labelled as "soft skills," in a "hard" job market these may the ones that land you the job.

Source: Adapted from Mary Ann McLaughlin, ED399484 95 "Employability Skills Profile: What Are Employers Looking For?" ERIC Digest. To view the entire document, visit the web site: www2.conferenceboard.ca/nbec/pubs.htm

Be Other-Oriented

In North American society most of us are largely focused on ourselves: our feelings, our beliefs, our problems and our ideas. Like the individual who self-discloses too much about himself or herself, little concern or care is displayed for the other person in a situation. Such self-focus interferes with effectively communicating with others. We may ignore characteristics of the other person, demonstrate poor listening or miss other vital clues that would enhance our ability to communicate effectively. When communicating with others, we need to adapt our messages to make them more easily understood. "Other-oriented communication suggests that we consider the needs, motives, desires and goals of our communication partners while still maintaining our own integrity" (Beebe et al., p. 29). When we become other-oriented, we are not only thinking of ourselves but also about the other person. For example, when talking with a young child, we adjust our words to the level of understanding of the child. If we are speaking to a new Canadian who has difficulty with English, we may simplify our vocabulary or speak more slowly and clearly.

Being other-oriented involves several skills and, according to at least one researcher (Argyle, 1983), these skills can be systematically learned and applied in human interaction. Several of these skills will be discussed further in this book. For instance, examining the development of self-concept and self-esteem, understanding perception and being able to develop accurate perceptions and being able to adapt to others considerably different from you are just a few of these skills to assist in helping you become other-oriented.

Two other skills discussed in work on interpersonal communication to assist in becoming other-oriented are **decentring** and **empathizing** (Beebe et al., 1997). To decentre is to shift the focus from your own thoughts to consciously thinking about the other person's thoughts and feelings. If you are the police officer, what is the other person thinking when you flash your lights to signal him or her to pull over? What would your significant other think if you came home with your belly button pierced? Empathy requires that you also think about how the other person is feeling (although the feelings and thoughts often occur simultaneously). Would your significant other feel happy with your new ring in your belly button or think maybe you have a significant emotional problem? When you stop a vehicle, is the person feeling scared because the car is stolen or angry at the inconvenience?

We try to figure out another person's thoughts or feelings based on our own experiences and knowledge. The more knowledge and experiences you have, the better your educated guess. If you know that your significant other likes novel ideas and strives to be different, your belly button ring may be a success. But you can only gauge this probability based on your experience to date with this person. As an officer, you have had no experience with this person in the vehicle. Here, you have to rely on procedures (how to stop a vehicle) and your own knowledge from past similar experiences. Knowing that traffic stops can be very dangerous, you approach with caution and watch for any signs of unusual activity by the individual (such as reaching under the car seat as you approach). If the person is angry because of the stop, we can empathize with him or her as we all do not like to be detained or inconvenienced. When we discuss nonverbal communication, we will examine empathy in more detail.

Becoming other-oriented helps us to become better communicators as we can try to think and feel what the other person is thinking and feeling. With this knowledge, we can become more tolerant and understanding of another person's perspective. This will be particularly useful in times of conflict or misunderstanding. When we are other-oriented, it is not assumed that we agree with the other person but that we understand "where he or she is coming from." Chapter 7, Conflict Management Skills, will examine this in more detail.

SUMMARY

In this chapter we introduced and explored interpersonal communication. The communication process is a three-step process of encoding, transmitting and decoding information. This process is not always accurate due to interference or noise that can distort communication and lead to misunderstandings between the sender and the receiver. We defined interpersonal communication as interacting and mutually influencing each other in order to manage a relationship. This interpersonal communication takes place along a continuum that varies in the level of self-disclosure and intimacy. On one side of the continuum, communication is impersonal, and at the other extreme, communication is intimate with a high degree of self-disclosure and intimacy.

Six principles of interpersonal communication introduced us to possible ways of improving our interpersonal communication skills and why we should study and improve our skills. Finally, this chapter outlined a five-part strategy to improve skills that will be explored and elaborated upon in future chapters.

JOURNAL AND DISCUSSION QUESTIONS

1. Do you think that all law enforcement workers should have extensive training in interpersonal and team skills? Why or why not?
2 At a presentation on interpersonal communication, the presenter, a police constable with 16 years of training, stated, "Good interpersonal skills are your best weapon." Do you agree or disagree with this statement? Support your answer.
3. Review your own interpersonal skills. What are your strengths? What are your weaknesses? How will this book be useful for your own needs?

WEB SITES

www.selfgrowth.com/index.html

A site devoted to personal growth, self-improvement, self-help and personal power. You can get a free self-improvement newsletter.

www.gov.nf./nlwin/HOME/LGUIDE.HTM

This is the topic page for WorkinfoNET and contains information about jobs and job skills required for today.

www.missouri.edu/~councwww/self_help/topic_1/

A self-help lesson to help improve communication.

REFERENCES

M. Argyle (1983). *The Psychology of Interpersonal Behavior.* London: Penguin.

Steven A. Beebe, Susan J. Beebe, Mark V. Redmond, Terri M. Geerinck, and Carol Milstone (2000, 1997). *Interpersonal Communication: Relating to Others,* Second Canadian edition. Scarborough, ON: Prentice Hall Canada.

Steven A. Beebe, Susan J. Beebe and Mark V. Redmond (1999). *Interpersonal Communication: Relating to Others*. Needham Heights, MA: Allyn and Bacon.

The communication process model is based on several models. An example is Robert E. Coffee, Curtis W. Cook and Phillip L. Hunsaker (1994). *Management and Organizational Behaviour*. Burr Ridge, IL. Irwin, pp. 197–120. See also Joseph A. Devito (1995). *The Interpersonal Communication Book*, 7th edition. United States: Harper Collins.

Joseph A. Devito (1995). *The Interpersonal Communication Book*, 7th edition. United States: Harper Collins.

Andrew J. Dubrin and Terri Geerinck (1998). *Human Relations for Career and Personal Success*, Canadian edition. Scarborough: Prentice Hall.

Robert Lunney (1989). "The Role of the Police Leader in the 21st Century," in Donald J. Loree (Ed.), *Future Issues in Policing: Symposium Proceedings*. Ottawa, ON: Canadian Police College.

J. T. Masterson, S. A. Beebe and N. H. Watson (1989). *Invitation to Effective Speech Communication*. Glenview, IL: Scott, Foresman

H. W. More Jr. (Ed.) (1985). *Critical Issues in Law Enforcement,* 4th edition. Cincinnati: Anderson Publishing Company.

G. Puth (1994). *The Communicating Manager*. Pretoria: Van Schaik.

Julia Wood, Ron Sept and Jane Duncan (1998). *Everyday Encounters: An Introduction to Interpersonal Communication*, first expanded Canadian edition. Toronto, ON: ITP Nelson.

SELF-KNOWLEDGE AND COMMUNICATION

LEARNING OUTCOMES

After studying this chapter you should be able to:

1. Outline Contemporary Policing.
2. Define self-concept, self-esteem and self-presentation and discuss how each relates to communication.
3. Apply Maslow's hierarchy of needs to communication.
4. Explain the additions of diversity and managing technology as human needs.
5. Describe five strategies to improve self-concept and self-esteem.

Casey is a new police officer in a large metropolitan area. She was really excited to finally start work and looked forward to a great career helping the public by protecting people from criminal influences. After two weeks on the job, she is experiencing a real sense of being "let down." She has not apprehended a single criminal or done anything that she considers to be "real" police work! There are reports to be filled out, work to do at a desk, and most of her contact with the public seems to be more like social work. To add insult to injury, she is now being placed temporarily on "school detail" during day shifts, which involves going to community schools to talk about drugs! Her staff sergeant informed her that her youth and great sense of humour would be ideal for the school program. Her self-esteem is plummeting, and she is beginning to question her career choice.

What Casey is experiencing is not uncommon in any kind of work. How you perceive the job and what the job actually entails may not be the same. Most of us who get the chance to choose our careers experience disappointments, and these disappointments can affect our self-concept and lower our self-esteem as we begin to doubt our choices. As individu-

16

Police officers take on many roles in their daily work, including educator.

als, we act and react differently to changes in our lives. As no two people are alike, we have different needs, goals and ideas as to how to communicate and work with others.

Knowing who you are is a vital part of being an effective communicator. Without self-knowledge, you have little awareness of your strengths and limitations. If Casey wants to learn more about her career choice and to be more effective on the job, she will have to learn more about herself. She will have to examine policing and how this profession is changing, learn how to get along with others and communicate with others in a diverse community.

This chapter briefly examines the changing nature of police work. Then, to begin the process of self-knowledge, the "self" and the three components of "self" (self-concept, self-esteem and self-presentation) will be discussed and examined in relation to interpersonal communication. When we express the things that we want or need, we are communicating our needs to others. We will examine how needs influence interpersonal communication. Last, we will discuss strategies to improve our self-concept and self-esteem.

THE CHANGING FACE OF POLICE WORK

The role of the police officer has become a complex one in today's society. A police officer fills more roles than "crime fighter." Other roles include social worker, medic, psychologist, report taker and teacher (Dantzker and Mitchell, 1998). A **role** can be defined in two ways. A role can be a position or a place that you hold in society. Also, a role can be defined as a set of attitudes and beliefs attributed to a position held in a social structure. Often, these roles may be in conflict with each other. For example, as an officer you are called to a store where a "thief" has been apprehended by a convenience store owner. When you get there, the thief is a 10-year-old boy who has stolen a loaf of bread and a jar of peanut butter. It is obvious to you that the child is starving and most likely homeless. What do you do? In Chapter 7 we will explore role conflict as being a source of potential conflict in the complex role of law enforcement. See the Law and Justice Perspective box for more on the conflicting nature of police work.

LAW AND JUSTICE PERSPECTIVE:

Crime Fighter or Social Worker:
Are Police Officer Roles Changing?

The public, perhaps influenced by the media, still perceives police officers as crime fighters who are there to prevent and control criminal behaviour. Numerous studies have found that most calls for service are unrelated to criminal activities (Dantzker and Mitchell, 1998). Calls such as quieting a noisy party, removing bothersome animals, dealing with an unruly teenager, removing someone who has been drinking from a home and other domestic calls are rarely criminal in nature. Many community agencies such as churches or other community support systems that used to deal with such "social issues" are not used as often today. With lack of funding, the school system and public counselling services have cut back on their services, which often leaves individuals little recourse except to feel they can call the police.

There have been many news stories where police have been used in social service situations. One example of this type of situation is police responding to a call about abandoned children left to fend for themselves in an apartment. A recent example in Toronto of a mother pushing her young son into a car and leaving is yet another social service situation that led to police involvement. There are probably many more of these situations in local papers daily. Many members of the public, including police officers themselves, are reluctant to shed the "crime fighter" image. Is "crime fighter" part of an officer's self-concept? Has society assigned this role, and is it now reluctant to change the role to a more complex one involving the social worker role? And is this a fair role for the police officer to adopt? As future law enforcement workers, these questions may be ones that you may need to ask yourself as you continue to pursue a career in law and justice.

With so many social changes, police services themselves have undergone many changes. Police services have been merging and centralizing while still trying to maintain local contacts with the community. Across Canada, there have been many efforts to restructure services in consultation with their respective communities. Therefore, the term community policing has taken a firm hold in Canada. Police services such as the OPP (OPP, 1997) now use the label **"community policing"** to address what services should be offered, what current community problems need addressing and how these services should be implemented for maximum effectiveness. Community policing differs in many ways from the "old-fashioned" reactive policing and, as such, requires different skills. This new "community" or "contemporary policing" is based on a partnership with the community. This is new in that the community and police jointly identify issues and together resolve these issues to mutual satisfaction. Traditionally, policing was more reactive as emergency calls and other complaints were the foundation for service. Today, while still reactive, more proactive and preventative crime measures are being undertaken by a joint force of police and community stakeholders (OPP, 1997).

With this newer emphasis on the community, there is an increasing need for excellent communication skills, teamwork skills and an ability to work with a wide variety of people from the community. Police/community relations programs are becoming popular across Canada. These community programs promote more involvement by the community and make the police more visible and accessible to community members. Many larger urban areas have developed such programs. These include Toronto, Ottawa, Montreal, Halifax, Winnipeg, Fredericton and Victoria. These community programs are also growing in popularity in smaller cities, towns and rural areas.

The first step to becoming effective in such complex work (as are many jobs today) is to discover who you are. In order to be an effective communicator, you need to know yourself. Who you are effects your communication style, your perceptions of a situation and how well you work on a team. Two other areas are also important to gain self-knowledge. The first category is examining your needs. Your needs determine your behaviour, or at least how you would like to behave, and many of our needs are met through interpersonal communication. Second, we need to appreciate the needs of others who may be very different from us. Managing ourselves and communicating effectively in a diverse society is essential for personal and career success. Part of this new and growing diversity is to be able to use the technology that is available to us.

THE SELF

Your "self" consists of three components: **self-concept**, **self-esteem** and **self-presentation.** These three components interact and form the basis of the self. How you communicate is based on your perception of who you are as a person and how you view your profession. For purposes of discussion, we have divided the "self" into three components. But as you read, be aware that all three components interact with each other to form your "self."

Self-Concept

Your self-concept is who you think you are and all your thoughts about you (Philipchalk, 1995). Who we are includes our race, culture, gender, family roles, social roles and our career. A positive self-concept leads to high self-confidence. For instance, if Casey has a positive self-concept she may think that being on "school detail" is a good starting point to demonstrate her good communication skills with youth. If she talks to other officers she may realize that working with schools allows more day-shift opportunities, which many officers would like in order to spend more time with family and friends during more "regular" hours. She may think that good reports back to her superiors may lead to better assignments in the future. On the other hand, a more negative self-concept may lead to self-doubt. She may think that she doesn't really have what it takes to be a good officer and that "school detail" is all she is good for on the service.

Our self-concept arises through interaction and communication with others. In the early years, parents and other primary caregivers have the heaviest influence on our self-concepts. **Reflected appraisal** from others forms a basis for much of our self-concept, particularly in the early years. Reflected appraisal is your view of yourself based on the assessment of others (Philipchalk, 1995). If Casey's parents communicated to her that they viewed her as being smart and capable, then she would have started to view herself as such and this would reflect in her behaviour. Similarly, if others treated her this way (such as teachers, other relatives, friends), she would **internalize** these beliefs as part of her self-concept. Thus, how we receive **feedback** from others can have a great deal of influence on how we view ourselves. Feedback can be defined as information that you receive from others about yourself. When Casey was young her parents may have praised her about how hard she tried when she was learning to ride a bike and how she was so smart to learn the skill so quickly. This early feedback increased her concept of herself as being capable and boosted her self-confidence. Repetition of the same type of feedback has the most influence although this does not preclude a "once only" experience from having a major impact. Some singular experiences such as a traumatic event can have a major impact on the self-concept.

SKILLS PRACTICE:

An Activity Using Reflected Appraisal:
Who Has Been Significant in Your Life?

Take a piece of paper and make three columns. Label the first column: SIGNIFICANT OTHERS IN MY LIFE. Label the second column: WHAT THEY TOLD ME ABOUT ME. Label the third column: HOW IT AFFECTED ME. (See example below.) One person may have told you several things about yourself that had major impact. On the other hand, some people may have given you feedback that had little or no effect. You may be surprised by how many others have influenced us during our lives!

SIGNIFICANT OTHERS	WHAT THEY TOLD ME ABOUT ME	HOW IT AFFECTED ME
Mother	told me I was smart	persist at projects
Baseball coach	said I was good hitter	still love baseball

While reflected appraisal is one process in discovering who we are, **social comparison** arises as we notice differences between ourselves and others (Philipchalk, 1995). Through social comparison, we tend to describe ourselves in terms of how we are different from others. We observe the behaviour of others and compare it to our own abilities, characteristics and behaviours. This process also provides insight into who we are.

And finally, as we get older and more mature, our self-concept increases in complexity. We start to recognize more complex social qualities and psychological qualities (Hart and Damon, 1986). While many of us have positive self-concepts and through these processes have come to know and like ourselves, others have negative self-concepts and beliefs about who they are.

Many people suffer from shyness and social phobias that debilitate them in social situations. In a North American culture that values physical beauty, many people feel they are ugly or too fat or their teeth are not white enough. While we will not deal with these problems in this text, we need to be aware that all of us often have problems with maintaining a positive self-concept and feeling good about who we are. At the end of this chapter, some strategies for improving self-concept may help others to feel better about themselves.

Self-Esteem

The second component of the self is self-esteem. **Self-esteem** is how you feel about who you are (Philipchalk, 1995). People with positive self-esteem feel good about who they are and feel that they are worthwhile (Rinke, 1988). Feeling worthwhile helps to build a positive self-concept. People with high self-esteem feel good about themselves and have a more positive outlook on life. If Casey has high self-esteem, she will remain confident about her career choice and give herself and the job more time before she makes any major decisions.

Think of someone you know who has high self-esteem. How does he or she communicate such esteem? Does that person have a more positive outlook, positive attitudes, and does he or she appear more confident in dealing with others? Now think of someone you feel has low self-esteem. How does he or she communicate lack of self-esteem? While we cannot see attitudes or outlook, they become apparent in our communication with others and in how we present ourselves to others.

Self-Presentation

Self-presentation is the behavioural expression of who we are, what we feel and think about ourselves (Philipchalk, 1995). Self-presentation is the impression that we consciously create and display to others. It includes how we dress, the words we carefully choose, our deliberate body language and other behaviours. In police and other security work, the uniform becomes part of self-presentation, and others will respond to this self-presentation. Some people present themselves in a confident and assertive manner while others are less confident in their self-presentation. At least one researcher suggests that we present ourselves in ways to verify our self-concept (Swann, 1992). We also engage in **strategic self-presentation**, presenting ourselves in such a way as to achieve a specific goal or goals in a relationship (Philipchalk, 1995).

We may present ourselves in such a way in order to get others to like us. We use flattery, compliments, favours, say the right things and demonstrate interest so that the other person will evaluate us positively and like us. Another goal is self-promotion to impress others. We may also present ourselves in ways to gain sympathy and to gain help. You might complain to your roommate that you are not good at finding research material for a paper and hope that he or she will feel sorry for you and maybe find the material for you. Another goal in self-presentation may be to intimidate others. Police officers who use fear tactics and other tactics to make people afraid often present themselves by standing in intimidating positions or by invading another's personal space.

While this may seem phony and contrived, we often work on our self-presentation to achieve a variety of goals, from landing a job to getting a date. However, we are not always conscious of how we present ourselves to others and are not always thinking about how we "look" to others. People also vary as to how much they manipulate their self-presentation and vary in how easily they adjust to a wide variety of situations. Think about how you currently present yourself. What do you consciously do in order to present a certain image such as interested student, caring friend and confident worker? As we learn more about interpersonal communication skills, we will be able to improve how we present ourselves in a professional manner.

Figure 2-1 presents these three components of self. Who you think you are (self-concept), how you feel about those thoughts (self-esteem) and how you present yourself (self-presentation) all impact greatly on how you communicate with others (interpersonal communication).

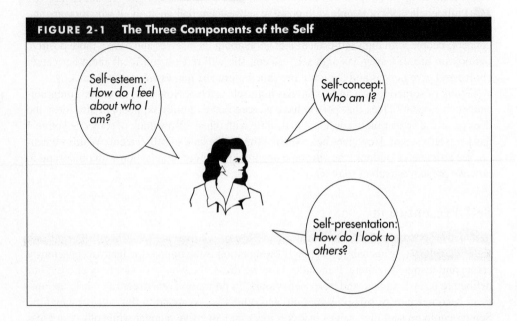

FIGURE 2-1   The Three Components of the Self

Self-esteem: How do I feel about who I am?

Self-concept: Who am I?

Self-presentation: How do I look to others?

NEEDS AND COMMUNICATION

Another aspect of who we are that affects our communication is our needs. As we interact with others, our needs/goals are communicated to others. Meeting needs is one of the main reasons why we interact with others (Wood et al., 1998). If Casey needs reassurance that her career choice is the right one, she may ask a friend to give her feedback. Her friend may say, "Hey, you always wanted to be a cop. And you'll make a great one!"

Abraham Maslow (1954) described human needs as a hierarchy with lower-order needs to be met before we move on to the next levels of needs, which are more abstract and less basic (see Figure 2-2). While Maslow's theory has not always been supported (Williams and Page, 1989), many theories do stress that humans (and animals) seek to meet various needs and various levels of needs. While Maslow's theory is sequential (meet one level of needs before striving to achieve the next level), other ideas and theories are multi-dimensional, and various levels and types of needs can be active at the same time (Greenberg and Baron, 1993). For example, you can be hungry while you are studying hard for an exam, which would be a physiological need (hunger) and an esteem need (need to achieve) operating si-

FIGURE 2-2   Maslow's Hierarchy of Needs

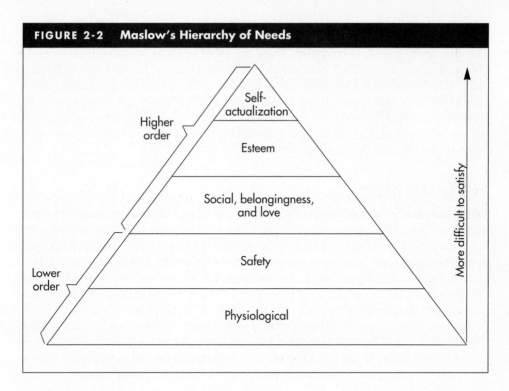

multaneously. Regardless of which theory is correct, we all communicate for assistance to meet various needs. We will use Maslow's theory to illustrate the use of communication to fulfill needs in our everyday lives.

Physical Needs

At the bottom of the "pyramid" are the physiological needs, which include our basic needs such as hunger, thirst and the need for air. Babies alert their caregivers by crying, a basic form of communication. As we mature, we still communicate to fill these basic needs, such as going to the doctor when we feel unwell or having someone fix our furnace so that we can stay warm. We make requests, ask questions and solve problems even at this most basic level. Can you think of an example of how you communicate to meet a physical need?

Safety Needs

The second level, safety needs, are also often met through communication with others. Safety includes such needs as a safe place to live and freedom from harm. Many people may communicate their needs in this area of safety. For example, if someone has been the victim of a break-in at home, his or her safety has been threatened and home no longer feels like the safe haven it was prior to the crime. Upon the advice of the officer or other security personnel, the individual may install a security system in order to feel safe at home.

Belonging Needs

The third level of needs is belonging. These are social needs to be with others: to work, play and live with others. Good relationships with others is essential for happiness, well-being and health. Several studies have pointed out that personal happiness and good relationships keep us healthier and happier (Hojat, 1982; Litwin, 1996). If Casey can develop good and supportive relationships on the job, she will most likely be happier and more positive about being a police officer. She will develop a spirit of community and trust with her co-workers and may make several friends in the service.

Self-Esteem Needs

Self-esteem needs, the fourth level of needs, relate to being valued and respected by those around us. These needs also have a great deal to do with liking and respecting ourselves. As stated earlier, much of our self-esteem relies on feedback from others. This feedback continues throughout our lives as we encounter others personally and professionally. It is through the process of interpersonal communication that we find our value and self-respect. As Casey meets new co-workers, their feedback will be important to her development as a police officer. This feedback may help or hinder her as she struggles in a new career. It is important how we give feedback to others on their performance and behaviour. We need to learn effective feedback skills so that we can critique the behaviour and performance of others in ways that help them change (see Chapter 11 for information on giving feedback). This is preferable to creating a defensive and nonsupportive climate that hinders change.

Self-Actualization Needs

According to Maslow (1954), self-actualization needs are the highest and most difficult level of needs. This level is about self-fulfillment, attainment of true harmony and realization of our unique potential. It is often through our experiences with others that we gain insight into ourselves. Others may see hidden talents and strengths of which we are unaware and point these out to us. A co-worker may notice how good Casey is at calming down victims or perpetrators and may suggest this as a strength. Casey may have been unaware of her unique skill and might have missed a chance at becoming involved in victim services later in her career. As we grow and trust in a relationship, we may also feel confident enough to share our dreams and goals with a person. Obviously, such communication requires support, empathy and a non-defensive climate.

Living in a Diverse Society

In Julia Wood's most recent text (Wood et al., 1998), she adds a sixth level of needs. This level relies on the skills and abilities necessary to live effectively in a very diverse society. Through communication and experiences with others, we can learn about cultures, lifestyles and philosophies that are different from our own. Casey will deal with a broad range of people as an officer, and she will need to develop skills, including communication skills, to manage people with such diverse backgrounds in Canada today. To meet the needs at this level, individuals must learn to respect differences. These differences could include race, ethnicity, religion, sexual orientation, health practices and so forth. Good communication skills will help us to deal with a diverse world. For example, as Casey is a Canadian with a Dutch background, she has learned to look at others when they speak to her. Through contact with some Asian individuals, she will learn that to look at someone in authority is disrespectful.

Mastering Technology as a Special Area in Diversity

One other area of diversity should be mentioned. This is the area of technology. As we head into the twenty-first century, we require more interpersonal communication skills to deal with the incredible array of technology that is available to us. This ranges from the Internet to the new technology with television. We have never been so affected and overwhelmed by the unbelievable amount of technology. For individuals to manage in this era of technology, we need to develop a wide array of skills to cope with such advances. Casey will have to deal effectively with e-mail, the Internet (which has opened up a whole new arena for crime) and computers. As with all new technologies, there are new terms (such as "surfing") to learn, new skills to master and adjustments to be made in the work environment. The Internet has created a new wave of crime opportunities that require police investigation and intervention.

SKILLS PRACTICE:

How Computer Literate Are You?

In Canada and across the globe millions are connecting to the Internet. The impact across many facets of our lives can certainly be outlined by anyone who takes the time to get onto the Internet. A side effect of this wave of change has been a whole new set of terms or lingo to describe experiences of computing today. To be technologically literate requires a whole new vocabulary for the average "surfer." Years ago, if you knew anything about computers you may have been labelled as a computer "nerd." Today, however, many jobs require the ability to use computers and the Internet on a variety of levels ranging from the ability to research material on the "Net" to web design. So, how literate are you with the new vocabulary? Take a minute and find out!

Below are five multiple choice questions about computer knowledge today. See if you are computer literate!

1. What does "FTP" stand for?
   a. First Terminal Position
   b. Fire The Professor
   c. File Transfer Protocol

2. What do you do when you suffer a power surge and you don't have a surge protector?
   a. Bandage your burned fingers
   b. Shop for a new computer
   c. Unplug the machine and then plug it in again

3. What is surfing?
   a. A new word processing package
   b. Exploring and searching on the Internet
   c. A technique for designing a web page

4. What is a search engine?
   a A system to help you purchase a new computer
   b. A trainload of people on a mission
   c A site that helps you search the Net

5. What does HTML stand for?
   a. Hyper Text Markup Language
   b. Higher Technical Memory Language
   c. Hope There's More Lasagna

Answers: 1. c, 2. b, 3. b, 4. c, 5. a

Source: Adapted from *Computer Knowledge Quiz*, Mercury Centre, *San Jose Mercury News*, August 29, 1998. Visit the site at **www.sjmercury.com**

IMPROVING YOUR SELF-CONCEPT AND INCREASING SELF-ESTEEM

We have looked at self-concept, self-esteem, self-presentation and needs. How do these tie in with improving our self-concept and self-esteem? Self-presentation is how we behaviourally present who we believe we are. We express our needs as part of who we are. If you feel you need more friends (a sense of belonging), you will need to come up with a strategy to go out and make new friends. To do this, you require some self-confidence, an understanding of who you are and interpersonal communication skills. While you may feel good about yourself, most of us have problem areas that may need addressing presently or in the near future. For example, some of us are shy, lonely, prone to anger or just wanting to learn more about who we are. Armed with a good self-concept and positive self-esteem, your interpersonal needs are more likely to be met in your career and personal life.

Gain Knowledge to Assist with Personal Change

With information from this chapter and other knowledge about the "self," you will be equipped to make changes. Self-assessments and self-tests that can be accessed from a variety of sources will help pinpoint problem areas. If you are shy, check out the web link at the end of this chapter. The Internet has become a broad source for information on personal growth, health and wellness.

Make a Firm Commitment to Change

How many of us make New Year's resolutions only to break them by the second week in January? Change only happens if we make a firm commitment to that change.

Set Realistic and Specific Goals

One of the major reasons people fail in their attempts to change is that their goals are unrealistic and unclear. If a person is shy, to set a goal of meeting 20 new people soon is not only unrealistic but also unclear. How soon is soon? You may be setting yourself up for failure with unrealistic expectations.

One important goal for changing your self-concept is to first accept who you are and be aware of your strengths as well as your weaknesses. What are some aspects of yourself that will make you a good police officer? Once you have those listed, what is one area of your self-concept that needs to be changed or improved? Start with a small goal that is realistic and that can be accomplished in a short span of time. For example, one of your professors has given you feedback that during an oral presentation you kept your hands in your pockets and shuffled from foot to foot. This appeared very unprofessional. You have decided to change this nervous behaviour at the next presentation. You tell friends and family to tell you to take your hands out of your pockets when they see you do it. You also practice 20 minutes a week, speaking in front of a mirror and maintaining a more professional pose. Accomplishing this one realistic goal will give you self-confidence to set more difficult and long-term goals.

Solicit Support for Change

As the last example illustrated, you also need support for change. Friends and family who are willing to offer feedback, ideas and support will help you on your road to personal change. Unfortunately, not everyone is always pleased when you may be trying to change. You may have to consciously choose people who can assist you or at least support you in your attempt to change. If you are trying to exercise more frequently to pass a fitness test, you may want to start associating with others who have the same goal. In past counselling experience, this author has met individuals who actually try to sabotage another's efforts for change. A good example is when a loved one comes home with a cake when you are trying to change your eating habits to healthier ones!

Don't Get Easily Discouraged

Trying to change personal characteristics, personal behaviours or other major parts of your self-concept is an onerous task. Changing your self-concept is difficult as it requires continuous effort and as it appears that the "self" resists change (Wood et al., 1998). Researchers (such as Rosenberg, 1979) have found that we like consistency and that we want to hold onto our self-image, even one that is negative. Change can be frightening as we are never sure what the outcome may be and whether we will like that outcome.

While others may try to prevent us from changing, we are often our own worst enemy. We engage in **self-sabotage** or in negative self-talk or in other behaviours that sabotage our efforts for change. Don't let small setbacks become excuses for stopping your effort for change. For example, you have decided that you need to manage your aggression better while driving as a way to learn how to better control your temper (see Chapter 3 for information on road rage). You have three excellent trips and are calm through three traffic jams where you were cut off several times. On your fourth trip, you loudly curse and give another driver an obscene nonverbal cue. Rather than telling yourself that you cannot do it, engage in positive self-talk and realize that 75 percent of the time you have controlled your temper! Encourage yourself rather than discourage yourself!

SUMMARY

In this chapter we have started to explore the self. To gain a perspective for this chapter, an overview of changes in policing was introduced that will continue to be explored in future chapters. We examined the self as a process that evolves and changes over our lives and consists of three components: self-concept, self-concept and self-presentation. Through communication with others, including reflected appraisal, and by comparing ourselves with others, we discover and define who we are. We communicate our needs as part of who we are. Meeting these needs helps us to grow and develop into the people we are and want to be in the future. Two newer areas of needs and opportunities for change were discussed: managing in the increasing diversity of this nation and learning to manage the new technology. Finally, we examined some strategies that help us change if we wish to change some aspects of our "selves."

JOURNAL AND DISCUSSION QUESTIONS

1. Many people have a negative self-concept and poor self-esteem. What do you think are the major causes of these negative views of self? What can be done in the early developmental years to improve the self-concept and self-esteem of young children?

2. The new focus on community policing, emphasis on managing diversity and increased formalized training will continue to make changes in how "police business" is carried out. What are some changes that you have currently witnessed in policing? What do you see as future trends in policing? Do you view these changes as positive or negative? Why?

3. Eating disorders such as anorexia nervosa and bulimia have been linked to distorted self-images. Those suffering from anorexia starve themselves in order to attain the perfect body, and those suffering from bulimia engage in a cycle of eating large amounts of food followed by purging. What do you see as some of the causes of these disorders?

WEB SITES

www.shyness.com
A web site devoted to the problems of shyness and social phobia.

www.depression.com
A web site devoted to depression and a wealth of information about this common mental illness.

www.mindbodysoul.
A site devoted to the wellness of the entire person.

www.icomm.ca/cmhacan/english/tentips.htm
From the Canadian Mental Health Association, Ten Tips for Mental Health.

future.sri.com/VALS/ovalshome.html
This is a values and lifestyles test that will categorize your personality type. Although designed for consumer information, it is an interesting test.

REFERENCES

Community Policing *How Do We Do It Manual*, Part 2- Community Partnerships, O.P.P. Community Policing Development Centre, May 1997.

Mark L. Dantzker and Michael P. Mitchell (1998). *Understanding Today's Police.* Scarborough, ON: Prentice Hall Canada.

Andrew J. Dubrin and Terri Geerinck (1998*). Human Relations for Career and Personal Success,* Canadian edition. Scarborough, ON: Prentice Hall Canada.

J. Greenberg and R. A. Baron (1993). *Behavior in Organizations,* 5th edition. Boston: Allyn and Bacon.

D. Hart and W. Damon (1986). "Developmental trends in self-understanding," *Social Cognition*, 4, pp. 388–407.

M. Hojat (1982). "Loneliness as a function of selected personality variables," *Journal of Clinical Psychology*, 38, pp. 136–141.

Frances Litwin (1996). "Careful: That Mood is Catching!" *Better Health Magazine*, volume 2, no. 2.

Abraham Maslow (1954). *Motivation and Personality*. New York: Harper & Row.

Ronald P. Philipchalk (1995). *Invitation to Social Psychology*. United States: Harcourt Brace College Publishers.

Wolf J. Rinke (March 1988). *Maximizing Management Potential by Building Self-Esteem*. "Management Solutions," p.11.

M. Rosenberg (1979). *Conceiving the Self*. New York: Basic Books.

W. B. Swann Jr. (1992). "Seeking "truth", finding despair: Some unhappy consequences of a negative self-concept." *Current Directions in Psychological Science*, 1, pp.15–18.

D. E. Williams and M. M. Page (1989). "A multi-dimensional measure of Maslow's hierarchy of needs." *Journal of Research in Personality*, 23, pp. 763–768.

Julia Wood, Ron Sept and Jane Duncan (1998). *Everyday Encounters: An Introduction to Interpersonal Communication*, Canadian edition. Scarborough: ITP Nelson.

INTERPERSONAL COMMUNICATION AND PERCEPTION

3

LEARNING OUTCOMES

After studying this chapter you should be able to:

1. Define perception and interpersonal perception.
2. List and explain the three stages of perception.
3. Explain the impact of perception on interpersonal communication.
4. Explain attribution theory.
5. Describe errors, barriers and biases in interpersonal perception and attribution.
7. Identify and give an example of five strategies to improve interpersonal perception.

Jim, a police officer with a provincial service, is at the scene of a car accident. No one has been hurt, and there are two witnesses to the accident. One man was walking his dog north up the side of the highway facing the intersection where the accident occurred about an hour earlier. A second witness was driving behind the southbound vehicle and just narrowly missed being in the accident himself. The accident happened when one driver was attempting a left turn from a side road onto the two-lane highway and hit a car travelling south. Jim has separated the two drivers who have already had one heated exchange.

Jim is interviewing the southbound driver first. Immediately, this driver states, "I was just driving down to a friend's house for a visit when she comes right out of the road and hits me!! Lousy woman driver! I'm a real careful driver unlike that nut. I hope you take her license!"

During the second interview, the female driver says, "He had his left turn signal on, and he was driving slowly. He was going to turn. He slowed right down, braked and then for some reason he didn't turn! He was going slow enough that if he had braked more, he would have missed me. He's so old; he shouldn't be allowed to drive anymore!! When I was talk-

Peterborough Lakefield Community Police Service

Both the officer and the person in the vehicle will have differing perceptions of each other.

ing to him, I had to yell at him just so I could be heard. God, old people and their great big cars. Just look at my little beauty over there, wrecked!"

Jim then interviews the witness who was in the car following the "elderly" gentleman. He states, "I don't know if he had his blinker on. The sun was in my eyes. I can tell you that he was driving really slowly. I had to keep putting my brakes on so that I wouldn't rear-end him myself. He was slow poking all the way down the highway. I don't think the old geezer knew where he was going."

The other witness states, "I thought everybody was driving too fast. The gentleman was being tailgated by that young creep there, for one thing! That would be enough to make anybody panic. If you ask me, it was his fault. The old guy did have his blinker on, but I think he was afraid to turn in case he got hit from behind. I know he was slowing down to turn, but he couldn't with that young college punk behind him. If I were you, first thing I'd do is take his driver's license away!"

Obviously, Jim will have to ask many more questions in order to try to find the "truth" about what really happened here. The female driver did pull out into oncoming traffic, and this is a violation of the law. What is not known is what really happened. Was the blinker on? Was the young driver tailgating? Can you pull out into traffic if you feel the other person is going to turn the blinker on and slow down?

All the witnesses have different stories. Are they lying? Maybe? Maybe not? Each person appears to have a different **perception** of the accident. These different viewpoints come from different personal perspectives and perceptions of the sequence of events. For instance, what is driving too slowly? For some, driving too slowly would be to adhere to the legal speed limit. How often have you been passed by a speeding driver when you were already 10 kilometres over the speed limit? And how fast does a car appear to be going as it comes toward you, away from you or past you? Also, there appear to be some distortions as to how the witnesses perceive each other: young and foolish, woman (poor?) driver, and "old."

These differing perceptions will affect the interpersonal communication among these people. How will the young driver treat the older driver with his perception of him as being too old to drive? And how do we view people when we perceive them as "tailgaters" and inconsiderate drivers? You can probably imagine the argument that was taking place prior to the arrival of the officer.

As an officer, you have to try to find the truth, and this may not always be an easy task. How accurate is eyewitness testimony? How accurate are your perceptions during a car accident? Does your personality affect this accuracy?

This chapter introduces the process of perception with particular attention to interpersonal perception and its impact on interpersonal communication. We will define perception and interpersonal perception and examine the three parts of the perception process. Then we will pay particular attention to the processes we use in perceiving others. Next we will discuss errors in person perception. Finally, we will explore five strategies to improve person perception.

THE PERCEPTUAL PROCESS

Perception is a process of selecting, organizing and interpreting information from our five senses. We are continually bombarded by sensations. Stop reading this page, sit back and attend to as many stimuli as possible. If you are sitting in your campus library, what are you experiencing? Can you *hear* others talking, *hear* pages being turned by someone nearby, *smell* anything? What do you *see?* What does the text *feel* like? Obviously, if you paid attention to all of these stimuli, you would never complete reading this chapter! Therefore, we have the capability of selective attention, whereby we attend to some stimuli and not to others.

Interpersonal perception is very similar. Through interpersonal perception we make decisions about who a person is and interpret or give meaning to his or her actions by analyzing and reaching conclusions from incoming stimuli. We make judgments about their characteristics and, like detectives, infer ideas from our observations. If someone is driving too closely behind us, we label it tailgating and may infer that the other person is rude, inconsiderate or maybe just late for an appointment. There are three stages in perception and in interpersonal perception: selecting, organizing and interpreting. It should be noted that for purposes of study, these processes have been discussed as separate categories. In reality, they often act together or in different order as we try to make sense out of the world.

Selecting

During this stage we select the pieces of information to which we are going to pay attention as we cannot pay attention to everything going on around us. Two strategies that help us select information are categorization and simplification (adapted and expanded from Beebe et al., 1999).

We use categorization to reduce the amount of stimuli that is demanding attention. We categorize stimuli in a number of ways. One way is to place stimuli in categories by

proximity, or nearness (Baron et al., 1995). If you see three people standing close together prior to class, you may perceive them as friends. **Similarity** is also used for categorization. We tend to perceive similar items as part of a group, and these similar items share similar characteristics. Classifying women who drive as being incompetent drivers is using the rule of similarity.

This leads to two important ways that we categorize stimuli in our interactions: **prototypes** and **stereotypes**. Prototypes are knowledge structures that represent the best or clearest example of some category. For example, when you think of the word "grandmother," what comes to mind? For many of us, we envision someone with grey hair, with wrinkles in her skin, who wears sensible shoes and bakes wonderful goodies. Few of us conjured up a mental image of a woman on a motor bike (but there are grandmothers who drive motor bikes!). You have many prototypes for a wide variety of categories such as a good teacher, a true friend and the ideal police officer. Once you have placed someone into a prototype, you may automatically attribute qualities and characteristics to this person and communicate with this person based on these attributes. If you have heard that I am a good teacher, you may pay more attention to what I have to say and have already positively evaluated me without meeting me. You may assume that I care about my students, mark papers fairly and take time to listen to students' problems. Obviously, using prototypes is efficient, but it can create problems. It may lead to rigid thinking and treating others in stereotypical ways.

Stereotypes are different from prototypes and are based on over-generalizing characteristics in order to predict the behaviour of the person in a specific category. Stereotyping all elderly drivers as being unable to drive, all women as poor drivers and young drivers as driving too fast, neglects individual differences of these people. Stereotypes are often formed without any interaction with a member from that group. Not all stereotypes are negative, but as we will see in chapter 6, stereotyping can lead to prejudice and discrimination.

Simplification is the most overriding principle of selection. Categorizing is in many ways also an attempt to simplify and reduce the amount of incoming stimuli. When we simplify, we filter out some information that we feel is irrelevant or unimportant. Unfortunately, we may filter out important information as well. Was the sun in the young driver's eyes, or was he simply not paying attention? When we simplify, we ignore some information, distort information and selectively attend to what we feel is important. In an accident, each person has a different idea as to what is important (blinker off or on), how close one car was to another, and he or she may distort the speed of the vehicles (this may not be intentional).

Organizing

Once we have selected the information or stimuli, we need to organize it in some way to make it meaningful to us. There are several strategies we use to assist us in organizing information. One way is to organize information into patterns that are convenient and understandable. These patterns allow for efficient storage of the information in our memory. Stars are organized into patterns of constellations, and cities are organized into streets. We also apply these patterns in interactions with other people. Later in this chapter we will explore scripts, impression formation and implicit personality theory, as these processes help organize our interactions with others into patterns.

Closure is filling in missing pieces or gaps of incoming information. When we have an incomplete picture of another person, we fill in the gaps based on information that we currently have available. We may do this based upon how a person is dressed, how he or she speaks, his or her age or any other relevant information. If an individual is unkempt and is showing up for a job interview in sales, we will probably have many other ideas about this person.

Interpreting

The third stage of perception is interpreting. Once we have selected and organized the stimuli, we are ready to give the information meaning. Based on how we were raised, past experiences and knowledge, we now attribute meaning to the experience or stimuli. We organize information to create unique meanings and interpretations. The Law and Justice box below discusses some perceptions of our RCMP. If the elderly man in our example appears confused and disoriented and cannot remember if his blinker was off or on or which friend he was going to visit, Jim may use more discretion as to whether or not he will charge the other driver with an offence. Jim may have had past experiences with elderly drivers who have lost their way while driving or who have become disoriented due to illness.

LAW AND JUSTICE PERSPECTIVE:

The Mounties and Fighting Crime

When Canadians and foreigners conjure up images of Canada, one of those images is the Royal Canadian Mounted Police. We picture them dressed in their red uniforms, sitting straight-backed on their mounts with the notion that the Mounties "always get their man." Canada has long been admired for its safe and orderly society, and many people still perceive Canada in this way. While Canada is still one of the best places to live in the whole world, according to the United Nations, it is also becoming one of the best places to engage in white-collar or commercial crime! It has been estimated that the annual loss from all varieties of fraud is more than $12 billion a year.

Why this sudden increase of commercial crime? According to a recent article in Maclean's, with government spending cuts and the loss of some of their top investigators, the Mounties cannot keep up with this new wave of crime. Private and corporate firms offer more money and greater opportunities, and many Mounties have "jumped ship" for more lucrative and interesting futures. Glen Harloff, a 21-year veteran with the Mounties who now works as an investigator with Price Waterhouse states that one of the problems is the lack of detachments in the big cities. Rather than increasing salaries or paying living allowances, the Mounties saved money by moving units into smaller towns away from the "real" crime scenes. Also, according to Martin Biegelman, an investigator with the U. S. Postal Inspection Service, Canadian laws hamper agents' ability to conduct effective and quick investigations.

With the loss of highly trained and experienced personnel, cumbersome laws and downsizing of detachments, white-collar criminals may have found a new place for lucrative enterprises. The perception of the Mounties may undergo a significant change in the next few years if measures are not taken to improve their ability to fight such crime.

Source: Paul Palango, "Mountie Misery" *Maclean's*, July 28, 1997. Paul Palango is also the author of *Above the Law* and *The Last Guardians*.

INTERPERSONAL PERCEPTION AND INTERPERSONAL COMMUNICATION

We have already used our example of the traffic stop to illustrate several components involved in perception and interpersonal perception. But one's perception does not take place in a vacuum; it is an interactive process. The same processes that we use to organize and interpret stimuli from the physical world, we also use to interpret behaviour in the world of interpersonal communication. I have ideas about who you are based on my perceptions, and I communicate these ideas to you verbally or nonverbally. You then react (or choose not to react) to these ideas. How others talk to us and behave around us gives us information on how they perceive us. If the young male driver is belligerent to Jim, Jim will form a different impression than if the young driver is courteous and calm. Jim will also be trying to figure out why the person is being angry and belligerent. In fact, he will pay much more attention to this behaviour than if the young person is courteous and calm. Being angry and belligerent to an officer makes an officer prepare for further angry behaviour and may lead to further investigation because this would be classified as unusual behaviour for someone not even involved in the accident.

In the latter case, Jim has become interested in this behaviour and may actively seek further clues as to its cause. When someone does or says something out of the ordinary, we become more active in trying to figure out the underlying causes of the behaviour. We do this by observation and communication. Jim might ask the young person why he is so angry. He may want to "radio" in the license number of his car or use other procedures to assist in finding the cause.

Processes in Perceiving Others

Interpersonal perception relies on organizing and interpreting the information that we have selected in our quest to understand another person. We apply impression formation and implicit personality theories, organize interaction into scripts and form constructs to organize our perceptions. However, we make errors in interpersonal perception. Attribution theory helps us to understand how we finally interpret all of this information concerning another's motives or the reasons for engaging in certain behaviours. As with perception, attribution is not a perfect process, and we make errors here as well. We will deal with each of these separately below.

Impression Formation

As we interact and communicate with others, we form an overall impression of their personalities. We gather information to attribute specific characteristics and, based on these characteristics, assign other characteristics that fit with that impression. However, research has indicated that not all characteristics are given the same "weight" and that once we have identified some characteristics, we fill in the blanks with our own ideas about individuals' other characteristics (Alcock et al., 1996). Classic experiments have demonstrated that we assign some characteristics or traits more importance than others (Asch, 1946; Kelley, 1950). These more heavily weighted traits are referred to as **central traits** because they appear to be related to a wide range of other traits. Traits that do not have these wide relationships are referred to as **peripheral traits**. In Kelley's experiment (1950), the central traits of "warm" and "cold" were varied and assigned to a guest lecturer (in reality, he was part of the experiment). The "cold" lecturer was rated as more unsociable, unpopular, and humourless compared to the "warm" lecturer. In reality, the lectures and the lecturer were identical. The difference was that during the introduction in one condition he was that described as "cold" and in the other introduction as "warm." We fill in the blanks, which is also part of implicit personality theory.

Implicit Personality Theory

Implicit personality theory overlaps with impression formation. With impression formation, we are deriving an overall impression of a person. Using **implicit personality theory**, we are assigning a pattern of characteristics to a person. Like the process of closure and impression formation discussed earlier, we fill in the blanks from our past experiences and knowledge. If we use the example from above, what other characteristics does a "warm" person have? Would you assign them the characteristics of happy, friendly, outgoing, honest, caring, annoying, nosey? Chances are, you would not assign the last two characteristics as they do not "fit" the personality of a "warm" person.

Assigning these characteristics leads to the **halo effect** (Beebe et al., 1999). If we like someone and have formed a positive impression of him or her, this spills over to assigning other positive characteristics. We all know this one from training in how to conduct a successful interview. We present ourselves in the best way possible so that we make a good first impression. Once we have demonstrated a few positive traits and abilities, we hope that this "spills over" into the assignment of other positive traits that eventually lands us the job!

The opposite of the halo effect is the **horn effect**. If we attribute some negative characteristics to an individual and decide we do not like him or her, we assign other negative traits to the individual. If the elderly driver hates "women drivers," he will probably not describe the woman in the accident in glowing terms!

Scripts

Scripts are a sequence of activities that we expect in our interaction with others. These scripts are guides that define what we should say and do in specific situations. They simplify daily interactions and guide and organize the sequence of activities much like the script for a play. Each character knows what the other character is supposed to say and do. For example, you have a script that you use when you come to see a teacher during his or her office hour. If the door is closed, you knock, wait and the teacher says loudly "Come in." You then open the door and continue the conversation. What if the teacher yelled, "Go away"? This does not follow the usual script and would leave most of us a little bewildered! There are scripts that govern dating, going out with friends, greeting casual acquaintances and many other daily situations. Many problems in communication may be a result of someone not following a script. Like the teacher who yelled at you to go away, what happens and how do we feel when the lines are not followed in the "play"? Try the activity below to see if you know some of these social scripts.

SKILLS PRACTICE:

Designing a Script for Social Interaction
(Class or Individual Activity)

Write a brief script for a daily activity. Some ideas are greeting someone you know casually at the mall, going to the dentist to have your teeth cleaned, asking a friend if he or she would like to go out after class for lunch. Make sure that your script includes two characters: you and another person. Share this script with another classmate. Do not give the person his or her lines. Simply outline the situation. For example, tell him or her that you are casual acquaintances who have just run into each other at the mall. Begin your lines (conversation).

Chances are if the other person has also experienced this situation several times, he or she can easily play the part without needing your script. Your lines may have been slightly different, but chances are there will be a number of similarities. This is just one example of the influence of scripts on personal perception and interpersonal communication.

Constructs

Another way that we organize our perceptions of others is to create a set of specific qualities or **constructs**. Constructs are a set of qualities that are bipolar, or opposites of each other, such as good and bad, cold and warm. **Personal constructs** represent specific qualities that allow us to categorize people into one of two groups of polar opposites: friendly or unfriendly, intelligent or unintelligent, extrovert or introvert, funny or serious and so on.

How sophisticated you are in your ability to develop a wide and varied set of personal constructs is referred to as **cognitive complexity**. People with high cognitive complexity are more flexible in their interpretation of complicated information, may have more constructs and are better able to integrate new information into their constructs. People with lower cognitive complexity have difficulty understanding information that does not fit easily into a previous construct (Wood et al., 1998). The more information you have about someone and the more cognitively complex you are, you are better able to interpret his or her messages and/or behaviour.

Attribution Theory

Attribution is the process by which we attempt to identify the causes of others' behaviour (as well as our own behaviour) and is central in interpersonal perception (Feldman, 1998). As we interact with others, we try to "figure out" who they are: their personal qualities and characteristics, their likes and dislikes, their attitudes and ideas about significant events, their beliefs and values. Psychologists and researchers have come up with several models to help us understand attribution.

One model by Kelley (1972) is concerned with identifying the cause of behaviour in social interaction. The three variables of distinctiveness, consensus and consistency are examined to arrive at a conclusion as to the cause of a behaviour. We will not go into great detail with this theory but will point out a few important details that have direct bearing on interpersonal communication and perception.

First, we may look at the actor (the person performing the behaviour of interest) and examine whether this behaviour is unusual or distinctive for this individual. For instance, if the elderly driver in our example has a history of excellent driving and this is his first questionable involvement in an accident (high distinctiveness), Jim may attribute his slow driving to an external cause (fear of a young driver driving too closely). If the witnesses agree that the young driver was tailgating (high consensus), Jim would have more evidence that the elderly driver was afraid of the tailgating, and this caused him not to turn. Consistency refers to an individual reacting to a person the same way over time, and for our example Jim may not have data in this area from witnesses. He may be able to ask the elderly driver if he had been tailgated before and how did he react in the past to such an experience, but it may not shed light on this situation.

A second theory is Weiner's theory of achievement attributions (1974, 1980). Weiner was concerned with how we label our social experiences as successes or failures and suggested a three-step process (Alcock et al., 1996). First, we look at the success or failure according to the dimensions of internal (caused by something inside of the person) or external (caused by something in the situation) factors. Then we decide if this cause is stable (occurs over and over again) or unstable (a one-time event). The third dimension is whether or not the occurrence was under the control of or caused by the person who succeeded or failed. For example, if Jim finds out the young driver has a record of dangerous driving, several accidents and a history of road rage, according to this theory his behaviour (tailgating) is internal, stable and under the individual's control. We might believe that he is a dangerous driver who fails to control his behaviour and was the cause of the accident!

Weiner's theory has some interesting applications to behaviours that we decide are or are not the fault of an individual. One example is alcohol addiction. If we view alcoholism as a disease, we may feel that it is not the fault of the individual, that he or she cannot help himself or herself (internal, stable, out of individual control). We may treat this person very differently if we see this behaviour as his or her own fault (internal, stable, within individual control). If we feel the latter is true, we may feel that the person is weak and with a little bit of effort could control this addiction. Other behaviours that we could examine using this idea of fault or blame include depression, other mental illnesses and other addictions including smoking cigarettes. Are smokers just weak-minded people who fail to control their own behaviour or who suffer from a physical addiction that they cannot control? To what would you attribute this behaviour?

Errors and Biases in Person Perception and Attribution

Now that we have explored how the process of perception, interpersonal perception and attribution occur, we can identify the errors and barriers that interfere with accurate perceptions of others. While this has been a very brief overview of two theories of attribution, what is important is to understand that attribution is not an infallible process. Along the way we make errors and may be biased in our interpretation of events. First, we will examine errors and barriers in perception followed by errors in attribution.

Errors in Selecting

One error in selecting is *that we pay attention to what is obvious and ignore other details.* Information that is easy to pay attention to (remember selective attention) is given more weight than information that may be more difficult to access or understand. For example, appearance is easy to select for attention. If we see someone dressed a certain way, we arrive at certain conclusions and organize and interpret with this small amount of information. We use age, gender, affiliation with certain organizations, career choice and recreational activities to make guesses as to what a person is like. For example, if you learn that a new classmate in your night class is a police officer, you may make some attributions about his or her personality depending upon what you think about police officers.

Part of selection is simplification, but *over-simplification* leads to errors in perception. We prefer simple information as it is easier to make conclusions. Behaviours are complex and people may behave a certain way for a multitude of reasons, but we prefer the simple explanations. As a police officer, you do not want a crime suspect to go into long details about family life and hardship; you want to know whether he or she did it or not.

We also select information that fits our *prototypes* and *other preconceived notions.* If I think that police use excessive force too often, I may notice newspaper articles that illustrate this idea and fail to notice articles of police heroism and acts of kindness. Sometimes we select information that fits with our preconceived notions and ignore or dismiss information that does not fit with those ideas.

Stereotyping and categorizing also lead to poor perception. Labelling people and putting them into categories ignores individual differences. This leads to the assumption that all people in this category act the same, which leads to over-generalizing and assuming similarities that are not really there. If you introduce yourself and say that you are a police officer, how would you feel about the reply, "Oh, so you're one of those guys who likes to beat up on the public."

Errors in Organizing

Stereotyping also occurs as we *organize* information into discreet categories such as good and bad, nice and not-so-nice and other polarized categories. Organizing information into categories also leads to imposing consistency on others' behaviours. Once a person has responded in a certain way to something, we expect this behaviour to repeat itself. If you thank someone profusely for a birthday gift you do not like, such as a specific type of candy, don't be surprised to see it presented to you again and again for every birthday or special occasion!

First impressions do matter, and often these first impressions lead us to organize behaviour to fit those early impressions of an individual. We will later explain behaviour in the light of these early impressions. If a new employee is late the first day of work, later behaviour may be "fitted" into the early impression of not caring about work. What if the next week the employee accidentally breaks something at work? And what if the week after that the employee has to leave work early for a medical appointment?

Errors in Interpreting and Attribution

When we make attributions, we are interpreting behaviour and deciding whether or not a person is behaving in a certain way due to internal dispositions or is responding to the situation.

Making attributions as a way to interpret information also has a number of problems and barriers. Because of the large amount of information on attribution errors, each one has been dealt with separately.

The Fundamental Attribution Error When explaining another person's behaviour, we tend to overestimate dispositional attributions and underestimate situational attributions. This **fundamental attribution error** leads to assigning to behaviour more internal causes such as personality characteristics of the individual. If we notice someone following us too closely in a car, we may assign characteristics such as rude, inconsiderate and irrational and ignore possible situational causes such as the person rushing to the hospital after hearing unpleasant news about a loved one. For more information on "road rage" see the Canadian Perspective feature below.

CANADIAN PERSPECTIVE:

"Road Rage" — Misplaced Anger?

All you have to do today is open up a paper across Canada as well as in other countries to find articles about aggressive and dangerous driving. A term coined from the United States, "road rage," appears to be increasing everywhere. Recent newspaper articles included stabbings (Oshawa, week of December 23, 1998) and dangerous tailgating by an off-duty police officer (Cobourg, week of January 11, 1999). According to the National Traffic Safety Administration, United States, approximately 66 percent of traffic fatalities are caused by aggressive driving behaviours. And it appears that aggressive driving is on the upswing (State Farm Insurance).

In a British article by the Automobile Association Driver Education Foundation, one of the causes of "road rage" is an erroneous perception that another driver is driving aggressively. We may feel that the other driver is invading our "personal space," as a car becomes an extension of this personal space or bubble that we keep around us to mark our territory. Since the territory expands to the space around our vehicle, we may feel anger if another vehicle cuts in, and this may lead to a defensive response such as flashing our lights, tailgating (invading the other's space), following or "chasing" the car or more aggressive behaviour. According to this article, the driver's mood also plays a part, and the driver may displace his or her mood onto the driving event. Also, a survey reported in this article stated that 90 percent of polled motorists had experienced "road rage" incidents, and 60 percent admitted to losing their temper behind the wheel (Joint, AADEF).

It appears then that "road rage" may be a result of a misperception or a misattribution of the other driver's motives, and it is increasing. We label the offending driver with personality traits, such as inconsiderate or dangerous, and we respond in some manner to indicate our opinion of his or her behaviour. We also displace our bad moods onto these often "innocent" drivers. As many articles have pointed out, such as the story about the stabbings in Oshawa (Findlay, December 30, 1998), the "offenders" are not even aware of their behaviour that precipitates the attack. Two other factors seem to be important. First, there are more drivers on the road, and second, commuters in large cities spend well over 40 hours a year in traffic jams (State Farm). Bad moods, flaring tempers, long and irritating waits, invasion of territory and misunderstood intent all seem to be factors in this aggression.

If you think you might be guilty of "road rage," there is an excellent survey that can be found on the Internet (see source below). Do you race with other drivers? Do you curse at other drivers? Do you brake suddenly to punish a tailgater? If you have responded "yes" to any of these questions, you may want to take the full test. And once you have identified yourself as a potential "road rager," visit other web links to learn how to manage this stress.

Some simple tips are to not take poor driving incidents personally. The other driver may be unaware of what he or she did. Don't misattribute the situation or characteristics of the other driver. Stay calm in traffic jams and slow-moving traffic. Practice some stress management techniques such as deep breathing. All of these strategies will help to get you where you are going safely.

Source: Adapted from;

Are you an aggressive driver? Road Rage Test, based on a driver stress test by Dr. John Larson, Institute for Stress Medicine, Norwalk, CT, 1998.

Alan Findlay. *Police track road rage assailants.* The London Free Press, Wednesday, December 30, 1998.

Matthew Joint, Msc Bsc MCIT. *Road Rage.* The Automobile Association Driver Education Association, January 21, 1999. www.aadef.co.nz/roadrage.htm

State Farm Insurance, Claims, Consumer Awareness. "Aggressive driving: Asking for trouble, aggressive driving facts." www.statefarm.com/consumer/crash3.htm

Actor-Versus-Observer Bias While we tend to view others' behaviour as being caused by personality, we tend to view our own behaviour as being caused by situational factors. This tendency is referred to as **actor-versus-observer bias**. Not only do we try to figure out why others are behaving the way they do, we also try to figure out why we behave in certain ways. While we use the fundamental attribution error for others and overestimate personal characteristics in their behaviour, we underestimate personal characteristics in our own behaviour. For example, if a classmate fails the next test in this course, you may attribute it to his or her lack of ability or motivation. If you fail the test, you may attribute it to the unfair and hard marking of the teacher, the number of hours you have had to work recently or to other external causes. Very rarely do we say, "Yes, I failed the test because I have an extremely low IQ!" In a car accident, we may want to blame other drivers rather than our poor driving skills. The actor-versus-observer bias may function to help us preserve our self-esteem. It may be easier to identify situational causes rather than our own lack of caring or selfishness.

Self-Serving Bias The self-serving bias may also help to assist in maintaining self-esteem and is a bias in self-attributions. The **self-serving bias** is attributing success to internal dispositions or traits and attributing failure to external factors beyond personal control, such as the weather, bad luck or the other person's characteristics. It may be easier to blame the elderly driver as driving too slowly rather than the young man stating that he was knowingly tailgating.

Self-Handicapping Strategy The self-handicapping strategy is similar to the self-serving bias except that we set up possible external reasons for failure *prior* to the situation. When people engage in **self-handicapping**, they set up an external cause or excuse for possible failure in the near future. If you are fearful that you may fail a test, you may tell classmates prior to the test that your boss is making you work too many hours and you couldn't find enough time for proper test preparation. If you do fail, you have already stated the reason. On the other hand, if you do pass, you can use the self-serving bias and explain the pass as a result of your great intelligence. Athletes will often complain about track or field conditions prior to competition.

While these conditions may be true, these last two attributional biases can be used for preserving self-esteem. The problem with overusing these biases is that we may unduly inflate our abilities or ignore personal responsibility when we do poorly (Wood et al., 1998).

The Ultimate Attribution Error The **ultimate attribution error** is a combination of biases that we use to interpret the behaviour of people we like or dislike (Philipchalk, 1995). When we like someone, we explain his or her positive behaviour as being dispositional and explain his or her negative behaviour as being caused by the situation. For example, a friend has just been caught shoplifting. How would you explain this behaviour of a good friend who has never done this before? You might explain it by acknowledging that he or she is having a difficult time at home (situational), stress at school (situational), or she did it on a dare (situational). But what if someone you really dislike has been caught shoplifting? Then, according to the ultimate attribution error, we explain the negative behaviour as dispositional and positive behaviour as a response to the situation. She did it because she's sneaky (dispositional), crazy enough to think she could get away with it (dispositional) or stupid (dispositional).

In other words, we make attributions that fit depending upon whether or not we like the other person or, in the case of stereotyping, the membership group. In some ways this is similar to the self-serving bias as we view our own behaviour.

STRATEGIES TO IMPROVE PERSON PERCEPTION

So now that you are aware of all the errors you make in person perception, how do you go about improving your skills to make better and more accurate perceptions? Five strategies are suggested here to help you improve your skills.

Increase Your Knowledge of Perception and Attribution

Reading and understanding the material in this chapter will help you to increase your knowledge of the processes of perception and attribution. You can become more aware of how you use these processes and pinpoint some areas where you may need improvement.

Go Beyond First Impressions and Find the Truth

Don't rely on first impressions. By paying closer attention to people, you may notice many more things than you did at that first impression or meeting. Remember that people may be strategically presenting themselves, and this may not be an accurate presentation of who they really are.

Engage in Perception Checking

Seek out more information about another person. Check out his or her body language, pay more attention to tone of voice and don't ignore the small things. If you are unclear about a behaviour and what it means, ask about it in an appropriate way. If you are honestly seeking clarification, most people will not react with anger. For example, you are talking to someone and he does not appear (to you) to be listening. This makes you feel angry and hurt. You may want to say, "It appears that you are not listening to me. Is something wrong?" The answer may be, "I'm sorry. I'm trying to listen, but I have this awful headache."

Be Aware of Your Own Biases and Distortions

Often, we are not aware of our own biases when interacting with others. Assumptions about the behaviour of another person are almost made unconsciously. For example, if you have been raised in a culture that promotes eye contact when speaking, you may form a negative impression of someone who does not look you in the eye when speaking. Other cultures may define eye contact as rude. Some people are shy or withdrawn. We need to question and examine these kinds of assumptions that we make about how other people behave. What are some stereotypes that you hold? How have you been interpreting the behaviour of someone you do not like? Are you making excuses for someone you like? Being aware of your own biases will help you to correct them.

Become Other-Oriented

To really understand someone, we have to change our own focus and try to understand "where others are coming from, to get inside their head, to see things from their perspective" (Beebe et al., 1997). Developing empathy allows us to see things from the other person's perspective. Ask yourself how the other person is, what is he or she currently thinking and what things do I need to learn more about to make an accurate analysis here.

SUMMARY

In this chapter we outlined the process of perception and applied it to interpersonal perception. Attribution theory was examined as a major way of interpreting the behaviour of others as well as our own.

Now that we have covered interpersonal perception and attribution, we can see the number of barriers and problems that make perception and attribution not an accurate "science" of getting to know others. Perceptual barriers and attribution errors may give us false impressions about what another person is really like and discourage further attempts at interpersonal communication. When we come up with the conclusion that we do not like someone based on inaccurate analysis, few attempts for further communication will happen. If there is future communication, this communication will be distorted by erroneous assumptions and beliefs.

The chapter ended with a review of five strategies to assist us in becoming more accurate in our perception and attribution. By applying these strategies, our interaction with others will be based more on who the person really is rather than on an inaccurate and distorted picture of who we think the person might be or even who we would like the person to be.

JOURNAL AND DISCUSSION QUESTIONS

1. Eyewitness testimony is often very important in court cases. After reading this chapter, what do you feel about the accuracy of eyewitness testimony?

2. What are some "classic stereotypes" of police officers? Have these stereotypes changed? Once you are an officer, how can you go about changing some of the stereotypes the general public may hold about police officers?

3. What are some common examples of incidents where people may use the self-serving bias? Can you think of any examples that would pertain to law enforcement? Do you think when people use excuses, such as there must be something wrong with their speedometer, they are using the self-serving bias?

WEB SITES

www.gov.on.ca/opp/

This is the home page for the Ontario Provincial Police. From this site, access is available to the How Do We Do It manual.

www.macleans.ca

This is the site for Maclean's magazine. Each weekly issue is presented plus an editor's pick of stories from past issues.

REFERENCES

J. E. Alcock, D. W. Carment, S. W. Sadava, J. E. Collins, J. M. Green (1996). *A Textbook of Social Psychology*, brief edition. Scarborough, ON: Prentice Hall Allyn and Bacon Canada.

S. E. Asch (1946). "Forming Impressions of Personality." *Journal of Abnormal and Social Psychology*, 41, pp. 258–290.

Robert A. Baron, Bruce Earhard and Marcia Ozier (1995). *Psychology*, Canadian edition. Scarborough, ON: Allyn & Bacon Canada.

Steven A. Beebe, Susan J. Beebe, Mark V. Redmond and Carol Milstone (1997). *Interpersonal Communication: Relating to Others*, Canadian edition. Scarborough, ON: Allyn and Bacon Canada.

Steven A. Beebe, Susan J. Beebe and Mark V. Redmond (1999). *Interpersonal Communication: Relating to Others,* 2nd edition. Needham Heights, MA: Allyn & Bacon.

Robert S. Feldman (1998). *Social Psychology*, 2nd edition. Upper Saddle River, NJ: Prentice Hall.

H. H. Kelley (1950). "The warm-cold variable in first impressions of persons." *Journal of Personality*, 18, pp. 431–439.

H. H. Kelley (1972). "Causal schemata and the attribution process," in E. E. Jones, D. E. Kanouse, H. H. Kelley, R. R. Nisbett, S. Valins and B. Weiner (Eds), *Attribution: Perceiving the Causes of Behavior*. Morristown, NJ: General Learning Press.

Ronald P. Philipchalk (1995). *Invitation to Social Psychology*. United States: Harcourt Brace & Company.

B. Weiner (1974). *Achievement Motivation and Attribution Theory*. Morristown, NJ: General Learning Press.

B. Weiner (1980). "A cognitive (attribution)-emotion-action model of motivated behavior: An analysis of judgements of help giving." *Journal of Personality and Social Psychology*, 39, pp. 186–200.

Julia Wood, Ron Sept and Jane Duncan (1998). *Everyday Encounters: An Introduction to Interpersonal Communication*, expanded first Canadian edition. Scarborough, ON: ITP Nelson.

NONVERBAL COMMUNICATION

LEARNING OUTCOMES

After studying this chapter you should be able to:

1. Define and explain the five functions of nonverbal communication.
2. List and explain the six types of nonverbal communication.
3. Explain four strategies to improve your interpretation of nonverbal communication.
4. Define listening.
5. Discuss five major barriers to effective listening.
6. Explain six strategies to improve listening.

Pierre has been trying for hours to get information from an agency for an important term paper. He has been re-routed, told that he has the wrong person, been through several voice mails, and then the person he was supposed to talk to is away on sick leave. He is frustrated and angry and a little worried. This information is vital to the paper, and, as usual, he has waited until the last minute to do the work. Just as he gets up from his desk, the telephone rings. Hoping it may be someone from the agency, he realizes that it is Sara, his girlfriend.

Sara: *Hi, Pierre! When are you coming over? Remember, we were supposed to get together for pizza? I'm starved! It's almost 7:00. What on earth is keeping you?*

Pierre: *I'm too busy for pizza!! There you go again, thinking of you, you, you. You're just one more person making more demands on me. Go get your own pizza and don't bother me right now.*

Sara: *Well, if that's how you feel about it. Maybe I shouldn't bother you ever again!* (Hangs up the phone and is near tears)

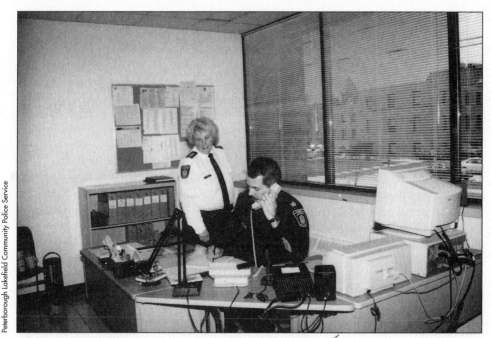

Peterborough Lakefield Community Police Service

Even on the phone, officers must be aware of nonverbal communication.

After the telephone call Sara approaches her roommate, Nadia, and tells Nadia what just happened.

Sara: *I can't believe Pierre! Everything has been fine between us and then he tells me not to bother him and all that I think about is myself. It was his idea to go out for pizza tonight, not mine. He said he would be over around 6:00 and it's after 7:00! I'm not the selfish one; he is! Boy, then I got really mad and said I didn't want to see him again.*

Nadia: *Well, I never liked him much anyway. You can do a lot better than that immature twirp!*

Sara: *He's not a twirp! I love him! I can't believe I got so mad, and I can't believe you would say that! As a friend you're not very supportive! Have you taken a good look at Doug? He's not much to write home about either!*

If you read this, you are probably "reading between the lines" as you know more about the current situation than Sara does. Pierre is frustrated, angry and maybe disappointed in himself for procrastinating on this important project. Unfortunately, Sara "timed" her call wrong, and a quick and hurtful conflict ensued. Her roommate was not much help either. Instead of being supportive, Nadia uses the opportunity to launch into her own opinion of Pierre. When we "read between the lines" we are paying attention to nonverbal cues and behaviours in an attempt to understand what is going on. Interpersonal communication is much more than words. If you recall from the first chapter, interpersonal communication is the way in which we manage our relationships through shared meanings and ideas. Interpersonal communication involves a level of intimacy and self-disclosure, and we do this through simultaneous interaction with another. These meanings and ideas can be communicated verbally, but we communicate with much more than words. We use gestures, facial and body expressions, tone of voice, loudness of voice, punctuation and voice pitch.

For future workers in law enforcement, paying attention to these nonverbal behaviours is critical to effective actions and reactions to potentially dangerous situations. How do you know if a suspect is about to lose control or is about to attempt to flee from custody? Paying attention to such cues will assist you in averting danger and keeping your suspect in custody. As well, when interviewing people, examining and checking out nonverbal behaviours will be of great benefit to assess whether the individual is telling the truth, is nervous, frightened or in some other emotional state. Similarly, we also have to pay close attention to our own nonverbal behaviours and what these behaviours may be communicating to others. If you stand with your legs spread, hand on your holster, directly in front of a suspect, the suspect may react to your "aggressive" posture.

In this chapter we will explore **nonverbal communication**, which is behaviour that communicates to others and is not written or verbal. First, we will discuss the ways in which we use nonverbal communication, then we will explore the types of nonverbal communication, the problems with relying on nonverbal communication and, finally, how to improve both the sending and receiving of nonverbal signals. To end this chapter we will examine listening. Although effective listening relies on both learning nonverbal and verbal skills, we will begin to focus on listening in this chapter and then re-visit listening in Chapter 5.

FUNCTIONS OF NONVERBAL COMMUNICATION

Most of us have heard the phrase "a picture is worth a thousand words." This statement highlights the power of nonverbal communication. Through nonverbal cues and signals, we communicate our emotions, agreement or disagreement, comfort level, level of intimacy and many other things about who we are and what we believe or do not believe in our relationships. Some of these functions may be done consciously as the practised speaker who uses his or her hands to add drama to a speech. On the other hand, we may accidentally betray nervousness in an important job interview by wringing our hands or by nervously fidgeting, and we may be unaware of these behaviours. A hug from a friend or loved one when we are upset or sad says and does much more for us than when that person simply says that everything will be fine.

Nonverbal Communication Can Replace Verbal Communication

Nonverbal communication can *replace* verbal communication (Malandro and Barker, 1983). An example might be nodding your head to indicate "yes" or "I agree with what you are saying." We can use signals at a loud party to indicate that we would like to leave. In some circumstances, an officer may not be able to speak directly to his or her partner and may use agreed-upon signals to indicate things are all clear or that a crisis may be developing. By hanging up the phone, Sara was clearly communicating a message and no words were needed!

Nonverbal Communication Can Emphasize Verbal Communication

To frown, talk loudly and emphasize your words may indicate a depth of anger that simple words alone could not illustrate to the listener. You can probably guess that both Pierre and Sara began to raise the volume of their voices when they began to argue. This is an example of how nonverbal communication can *emphasize* verbal communication (Malandro and Barker, 1983). We can also use physical touch to emphasize our verbal communication. When we are glad to see a friend, we may verbally express our happiness and hug the other person, hold his or her hand or pat him or her on the shoulder. Most police officers know that a person who is very angry, is yelling and is drunk requires intervention immediately to deter a physical confrontation.

Nonverbal Communication Can Contradict Verbal Communication

Nonverbal communication can also *contradict* verbal communication (Malandro and Barker, 1983). You may say to someone that you have time to talk, but if you take "sneak peaks" at your watch, you are indicating that you really do not have nor want to take the time to talk. A friend says to you that nothing is wrong, and yet you pick up numerous signals that say otherwise!

Nonverbal Communication Can Regulate Verbal Communication

Have you ever had the experience of talking to someone and you both start talking at once? Often what has happened is that you failed to notice or to use nonverbal regulators. Nonverbal communication *regulates* interpersonal communication by subtle signals (Malandro and Barker, 1983). These signals include averting our eyes when we are speaking and we do not want to be interrupted, and resuming eye contact to signal that it is now the other person's turn to talk. We are often not even conscious of these signals as we interact with others.

Nonverbal Communication Can Establish Relational-Level Meanings

Nonverbal communication also establishes *relational levels* with others. A **relational level of meaning** defines our identity and relationships with other people. Through nonverbal communication, three relationship-level meanings are established (Mehrabian, 1981).

One relational level meaning is *responsiveness*, or interest. Through nonverbal cues such as eye contact, body posture, spacing and facial expressions, we can express our level of interest in another. If you walk into a restaurant and observe tables of patrons, chances are you will be able to distinguish who is interested in whom and who is just plain bored with a lunch or dinner partner. When we are interested in another person, we maintain eye contact, may lean forward and may actually reflect or mirror his or her facial expressions. This author has had instances while lecturing to notice interested students actually "mouthing" words while I speak! When Pierre began to indicate that he did not have time for Sara, she started to assume that this indicated a lack of responsiveness or interest towards her.

Related to responsiveness is the relational-level meaning of *liking*. Liking refers to the positive or negative feelings that we have about another. How can you tell if someone likes you? We indicate feelings by smiling, by closing physical distance between us and by using other cultural indicators of liking. Because of gender differences, women, more than men, are more likely to use nonverbal cues to indicate liking. Women, more than men, tend to sit closer to others and to use more eye contact (Montgomery, 1988).

The third relational-level meaning aspect is *power*. We use nonverbal behaviours to communicate dominance. Men, more than women, are more concerned in asserting dominance and control. Men use more space, use greater volume when speaking and use more forceful gestures to assert dominance (Hall, 1987). Often, male officers may have more difficulty with an angry male suspect than a female officer would as the male suspect may not be as likely to try to assert dominance with a female officer. Many males have been

SKILLS PRACTICE:

Gender Differences in Communication

According to a recent publication on interpersonal communication, men and women are socialized into different communication cultures (Wood et al., 1998). When children are very young, their play is segregated, and girls and boys learn very early to favour different games (Maltz and Borker, 1982). Girls tend to prefer games that rely on cooperation, sensitivity and negotiation, such as "house" and "school." Male games tend to require less negotiation and talking as the rules are clearer, such as in baseball and soccer, and these games are often more competitive. It appears that this early socialization stays with us. Research suggests that there are distinct differences in how the two genders communicate as adults, especially if raised in a family with traditional gender roles (Aries, 1987; Beck, 1988; Tannen, 1990). Here are just a few of the differences between the gender cultures.

Women use talk cooperatively to include others, to show interest and to respond to others' needs. Men use talk more competitively to assert themselves, to show knowledge, to gain "the upper hand" and to maintain attention on themselves. Women's talk tends to focus more on feelings, personal ideas and to discuss problems and maintain relationships. On the other hand, men use talk to accomplish goals such as solving a problem, giving advice or establishing their position on an issue or idea. Women are more likely to share personal feelings and secrets, whereas men prefer less intimate topics.

These differences also appear in nonverbal behaviours and communication. Women tend to use more touching and require less personal space during a conversation with friends. Women also use more supportive verbal and nonverbal indicators of listening, such as utterances like "um-hmm" "uh-huh" and head nodding. Women also tend to use more eye contact (Montgomery, 1988; Roger and Nesshoever, 1987; Tannen, 1990). Often, women may assume men are not listening because they are less likely to ask personal questions, less likely to make comments and do not use utterances (Tannen, 1990). While we are not going to discuss the potential for conflict because of these different communication cultures, we need to be aware as people and as professionals that there are differences in how we communicate due to gender differences.

raised in a culture with an assumption that females are less powerful and thus do not have to assert such dominance in an encounter with a female officer. To explore gender differences in communication, read the box below on gender differences.

TYPES OF NONVERBAL COMMUNICATION

Many nonverbal behaviours are classified as nonverbal communication. We may use several types of communication at once in interpersonal communication, or we may rely on one mode or method of communication. According to Albert Mehrabian (1972), in the verbal communication of a message, only seven percent of the meaning of a message is verbal content. This means that 93 percent of what we communicate to others is through nonverbal channels. Nonverbal behaviours account for 55 percent of our meaning. Nonverbal behaviours include facial expressions, movement and gestures, territory and space, touch and personal appearance. Vocal cues, referred to as **paralanguage**, which include voice volume, tone, pitch and intensity, make up the remaining 38 percent of communication.

In this section, we will examine the types of nonverbal communication. While we are dividing these types into discrete categories, be aware that usually these cues occur simultaneously. For example, an officer may feel that a suspect is lying because of lack of eye contact, stammering his or her replies, fidgeting and continuously rubbing his or her arms. A second note of caution should also be discussed briefly. Much of the content below is based on North American studies that did not include cultural differences. Not all of these rules and examples will apply to all cultures.

Paralanguage

Paralanguage includes communication that is vocal but does not include words. Voice volume (from whispering to shouting), tone, murmurs, gasps, sighs, rhythm, pitch, inflection, accents, sentence complexity and how we pronounce words are all paralanguage. When we ask a question, we use inflection at the end of the sentence. Tactical communication relies on using a loud volume and inflection that indicates an order for compliance. Voices can also communicate many feelings. One comedian, George Carlin, says the word "dude" in many different ways to indicate a number of feelings from anger to surprise. Sarcasm is usually picked up due to the use of paralanguage. For instance, to say "Ya, I really want to go" has just the opposite meaning when said with sarcasm.

In the opening scenario, much of the phone conflict was evident by reading the paralanguage into the script. You can surmise Pierre's tone of voice when he tells Sara "you, you, you." As police officers, practise speaking in a professional voice that sounds firm and confident. Correct use of grammar and appropriate vocabulary is also important. To appear frightened or unsure of what to do will undermine your credibility in the situation and could be potentially dangerous.

Facial Expressions and Eye Behaviours

If the face makes up a major part (55 percent) of our communication when we speak to others, it deserves special consideration and in-depth analysis. Your face can assume a vast number of expressions, and much research has been devoted to the expression of emotion. According to research, the face can engage in 46 unique actions using the forehead, eyebrows, eyelids, nose and mouth (Ekman and Friesen, 1978). It appears, however, that facial emotional expressions can be categorized into six broad categories. These six emotions are: anger, fear, sadness, disgust, happiness and surprise (Ekman, 1992). Obviously, we express more than these six emotions as emotions occur in many combinations and occur at varying levels of intensity. For instance, if someone cuts you off while driving, you can be slightly annoyed or perhaps you suffer from "road rage" and erupt into a stream of loud curses to vent your extreme anger. You can be happy and surprised at the same time if someone throws you a surprise birthday party. While there is some evidence that these six themes of expression are universal, we need to be cautious when interpreting emotional expression (Carroll and Russell, 1996). A smile may not always indicate happiness, but can indicate other emotions depending upon the situation. Some people smile when they are embarrassed or when they get "caught" engaging in an illegal activity. We may smile because the social situation indicates that this is the appropriate behaviour, like clapping and smiling at the end of a play even if you did not enjoy the production!

Eyes have been described by ancient poets as the "windows of the soul," and in some respects this may be true. Eye behaviours, especially eye contact, provide a great deal of information about how another person feels, his or her perceptions and expectations (Nolen, 1995). Whether we choose to look at someone or not, how long we spend maintaining eye contact and how expressive our "eye area" is has a great impact on interaction and our relationship with that person. If Sara had been talking to Pierre in person, she may have seen signs of strain around his eyes, seen worry in his facial expression and may not have been as hasty in her own assumptions and behaviour. And what nonverbal cues did her roommate pick up that she chose that moment to give her opinion of Pierre?

Eye contact has four functions, according to one text on interpersonal communication (Beebe et al., 1997). First, eye contact serves a *cognitive* function. Through eye contact, you can gain an understanding of the other person's thought processes. When we are trying to remember a name or a place, we will glance slightly upwards to the right or left.

The second function of eye contact is to *monitor* the behaviour and reactions of others. Did Nadia see anger (narrowing of the eyes, frown) and feel this was the appropriate time to try to persuade Sara to break up with Pierre? When we are interacting with another person, we try to decide whether he or she is receptive to our message. By seeing anger, Nadia mistakenly thought that Sara would be receptive to her message.

Third, eye contact functions as a *regulator* in communication. We use eye contact to signal when we wish to speak and to signal when we are done speaking. Eye contact also regulates other interactions and behaviour such as taking turns and whether or not we want to participate in an activity. When a magician looks for a volunteer in an audience, those who do not want to be called on avert their eyes and may also use posture to indicate, "Please, leave me alone."

As part of the regulative function, we can also learn what behaviour may occur next by observing the eyes and the direction in which they look. Before your roommate scoops the last cookie in the bag, he or she first looks at the bag prior to reaching for it. Many officers have noted that when a suspect is about to flee, the suspect first glances towards the direction he or she is going to attempt to run. A suspect may fleetingly glance at a place where weapons or other illegal goods may be hidden. And when lying, a suspect may break eye contact more often or not look at the officer at all. For more information on lying, see the Law and Justice feature below.

The fourth function of eye contact and the area around the eyes is an *expressive* function. The eyes and the area around the eyes are very versatile and can express a number of emotions. Eyes blink, cry, open wide, close, squint and are an integral part of expressing the ways we feel and the intensity of that feeling. We express interest in what another person is saying by increasing eye contact, and we decrease eye contact if we are not interested. When trying to talk about something that is difficult or embarrassing, we may decrease eye contact (Knapp, 1978).

LAW AND JUSTICE PERSPECTIVE:

How Can You Tell When a Suspect Is Lying?

How can you tell when you are being lied to by another person? Can you tell when someone is consciously deceiving you? Is it easier to identify lying when it is someone you know or if the liar is a stranger? As an officer, people will lie to you to avoid "trouble," to avoid "turning in a friend" or to get someone else into "trouble" rather than themselves. Are lie detectors a valid means of determining whether someone is lying or not? Much research has been devoted to trying to identify deliberate deception and the accuracy of lie detector tests

Here are some *external* cues from research that may indicate lying:

- Basic discrepancies between various nonverbal channels. For example, a liar may manage facial expressions, but his or her body language may betray nervousness or tell a different story (Baron et al., 1998).

- A presence of variations in paralanguage, such as a rise in voice pitch, lack of verbal fluency (Zuckerman et al., 1991).

- More sentence repairs (Stiff et al., 1989). A liar may start a sentence, interrupt it and then start all over again.

- An unusually low level or high level of eye contact (Kleinke, 1986).

- Averting eyes before answering a question. This is often interpreted as an effort to "hide" something (Burgoon et al., 1989).

- Exaggerated facial expressions (Baron et al., 1998).

- Nervous mannerisms, such as excessive self-touching and fidgeting. Touching, scratching and rubbing suggest emotional arousal that may be caused by lying to the officer (Baron et al., 1998).

- Short and recurrent pauses that may signal that the liar has to be continually thinking about what he or she needs to say next (Anolli and Ciceri, 1997).

Internal responses that indicate deception are measured with polygraphs or lie detectors. Polygraphs record physiological reactions that occur during questioning. Results of research into the accuracy of polygraphs are mixed. While many professionals believe that polygraphs are accurate, some research has indicated otherwise (Baron et al., 1998). Under questioning, nervousness or embarrassment may also cause arousal similar to the arousal when lying. Also, people can intentionally change their level of physiological arousal (Zajonc and McIntosh, 1992). Accomplished con-artists and other criminals may also be able to control their physiological responses similar to the subjects in research. However, polygraph testing can be one method to detect lying and should not be ruled out as a method in crime investigation. In fact, one research report has pointed out that reviews of the reliability of polygraphs in Introductory Psychology texts may be negatively biased (Devitt et al., 1997). Because of this question of reliability and ongoing debate, the results of polygraphs are not admissible in Canadian courts since a Supreme Court ruling in 1987.

So how can you tell when someone is lying? Police veterans often rely on the external indicators of lying and use these indicators to increase questioning efforts. Also, it may be that experience and using "gut-level" feelings may help in the quest to find out the truth behind a crime.

Body Language: Posture, Gestures and Movement

Think back to a time when you were really happy. Maybe it was the telephone call that landed you a job you really wanted. What did you do after you hung up the phone? Some people literally jump for joy! Your **body language** reflected your mood and feelings at that moment in time. Your body language can also indicate how you feel about yourself. People who walk and stand erect, hold their heads up and do not slouch appear calm and self-assured. On the other hand, people who shuffle along, slouch over and keep their heads down appear to be unsure of themselves. As with eye contact, body posture may indicate whether or not we wish to be involved in interaction. Students who do not want to participate in a discussion often slouch over, look down and avoid looking at the teacher. We also use posture to let others know whether or not we wish to interact. We may sit slightly forward and smile to invite interaction. Flirting signals our sexual or romantic interest to a prospective partner and involves postures and other nonverbal behaviours, such as females swaying their hips and men swaying their pelvises (Rodgers, 1999). Specific postures and body movements may also be interpreted as threatening. Standing with legs apart, hands on hips, physically closing distance, suddenly standing from a sitting position, making fists and clenching teeth are all possible signals of a physical threat. Officers will watch for these indicators and also pay close attention to any sudden moves that are unusual.

Gestures are used to emphasize or replace verbal communication and are culturally determined. In North America, "thumbs-up" means "great" or "way to go." Making an "o" with your thumb and forefinger means "okay." Nodding your head up and down means "yes." Holding your middle finger up is a gesture of aggressive contempt. To illustrate the cultural determination of gestures, the North American gesture for okay means a big zero in Germany and a part of female or male anatomy in Russia (Axtell, 1989).

Touch

Touch is the earliest sense to develop and is the primary way that babies learn about their world. Touch can communicate many emotions and feelings that we have about another person. Touch can express affection, sexual interest, caring, dominance, aggression and power. Due to gender differences discussed earlier, women tend to use touching to express affection, liking and caring. Women often hug other women, and young girls can be seen holding hands more readily in primary grades than boys.

Some people are more "touching" than others. If you have been raised in a family where there was lots of touching, such as hugging, arm holding and kissing, you may be comfortable doing the same. However, some people were raised in families that were more restrained, which may lead to discomfort as adults with overt displays of affection. Cultural rules for touching may also lead to differences with the types of and comfort levels with touching. In some cultures, it is acceptable for male friends to greet each other with hugs and kissing the cheek. This is something most male college students in Canada would not do when greeting a friend at the campus library! While North Americans use handshakes to greet each other, some cultures do not like to shake hands right away particularly with strangers, such as in some Asian cultures. East Asians also do not engage in interpersonal touching and, in particular, frown upon cross-sex touching in public (McDaniel and Anderson, 1998). We will re-visit different cultural rules in Chapter 7.

The Things Around Us: Artifacts, Time and Appearance

Artifacts are the personal objects that we select to display to announce who we are and to personalize our environments. Clothing is one of the most personal displays that we use to state things about ourselves to others. If you are an uniformed officer, the public will see and react to you based on your uniform. This reaction will be positive, negative or neutral depending upon the perception of the police at that time. Since you represent the whole police service, your unit commander will insist that your uniform be clean, pressed and presentable at all times. Also, your uniformed presence is a signal of authority, and such presence is the first level of use of force.

Artifacts also help to personalize and claim our space. Often personal areas are jammed with objects that are important to us and reflect our values, ideas and beliefs. If an individual values home and family, pictures of family members and pets may be displayed. Religious individuals often decorate their homes and offices with religious symbols. One officer has his home office decorated with the "mug shots" of perpetrators he has personally helped to place "behind bars." A doctor has her office decorated with pictures of all the babies she has delivered over several years. In residence, students decorate their rooms with objects that remind them of home, current musical groups and other items that are important to them to personalize an often drab room. The next time you are in an office of a teacher or other professional, see what artifacts are present and try to determine what this says about the person.

Also surrounding us other than space is time. **Chronemics** refers to how we perceive and use time. We use time to define identities, define interaction and even to define status (Henley, 1977). In the fast-paced Western society, time appears to be valued and therefore so is speed. We often talk about the fast pace of life and look for ways to manage this pace. We want faster computers, faster highways, faster food and so on. Being used to this fast pace and high value placed on time and speed can be frustrating for Westerners who visit other cultures that do not place this value on time and speed.

The Space Around Us

All of us carry around an invisible bubble that is called our personal space. **Proxemics** is the study of spatial communication and was pioneered by Edward T. Hall (1963). Often, we are not aware of our invisible bubble until someone gets too close or does not get close enough. In fact, many of our sayings use space to demonstrate feelings. "Get out of my face," "too close for comfort" and "get off my back" are just a few of the statements that we use when people are overstepping their boundaries in a relationship. When people whom we do not know get too close, we feel uncomfortable, and we will attempt to increase the distance to feel comfortable. According to Hall, there are four interpersonal distances or circles that correspond to types of relationships: intimate, personal, social and public (see Figure 4-1).

- **Intimate Distance.** Intimate distance ranges from actual touching to 18 inches. This distance is for close and intimate relationships where touching is important. When strangers cross over into intimate distance, we feel threatened or very uncomfortable. For instance, in a crowded elevator we do not look at each other and focus our eyes ahead on the floor numbers. To deliberately intimidate, we can invade this space. Often apprehension involves invading this space, and tempers can flare at this stage. Police officers are often required to invade this space such as when handcuffing or subduing a person.

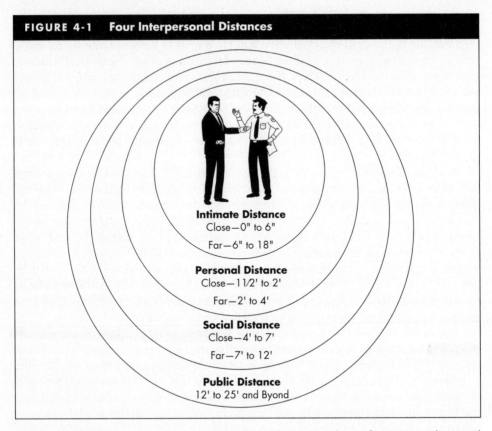

FIGURE 4-1   Four Interpersonal Distances

Intimate Distance
Close—0" to 6"

Far—6" to 18"

Personal Distance
Close—1 1/2' to 2'

Far—2' to 4'

Social Distance
Close—4' to 7'

Far—7' to 12'

Public Distance
12' to 25' and Byond

Source: Adapted from Andrew J. Dubrin & Terri Geerinck *Human Relations for Career and Personal Success*, Prentice Hall Canada Career & Technology, p. 131. Reprinted with permission of Prentice Hall Canada Inc.

- **Personal Distance.** Within personal distance, your comfort zone is from 18 inches to a far range of four feet. Many of our friendly relations stay in this zone. At 18 inches, you can still touch a person, such as shaking hands and patting backs, but the zone is less intimate. The area is still small enough for you to reach the person, and this is where the limits of physical control can be exerted. If you think someone may try to run, stay within this limit to maintain physical control without getting into the intimate area.

- **Social Distance.** Ranging from four to 12 feet, social distance is the distance where we conduct impersonal business and have less personal interaction. Conducting business across a desk is usually in this zone, and many office areas are designed to maintain this distance.

- **Public Distance.** Public distance ranges from 12 to 25 feet and beyond and is limited only when the speaker can no longer be heard. If someone is behaving in a bizarre manner, you will choose this as your safe distance since this is the distance from which you can more readily flee from a situation. Stage productions, lectures and speeches are given using this distance.

These distances are general distances and are not always followed in interaction. For example, some cultures are more comfortable with closer contact. Also, as it was stated earlier, females are more comfortable with touching and sit and stand closer together.

SKILLS FOR INTERPRETING NONVERBAL COMMUNICATION

Now that we have explored the types of nonverbal communication, the question remains how to interpret nonverbal communication accurately. By now you are probably realizing the complexity of nonverbal communication. Because there are so many types of nonverbal communication that are used simultaneously, "reading" these messages can be difficult. Nonverbal messages, because they are symbols, are often ambiguous and subject to interpretation based on culture, gender, age and the situation. When we look at a nonverbal signal, we interpret that signal based on how we select and organize the sensory input (remember the perceptual process). Interpreting nonverbal communication relies on improving communication in two areas: interpreting others' nonverbal messages and monitoring your own nonverbal communication. The following guidelines will assist you in developing better skills to avoid misinterpreting others' nonverbal communication and decreasing others misperceiving your nonverbal messages.

Be Aware of, and Monitor, Your Nonverbal Communication

What nonverbal "signals" are you "waving" at others around you? At times we may consciously control our movements, gestures and other nonverbal messages. However, we may

SKILLS PRACTICE:

What Messages Are You Sending to Others?

For the next two to three days, identify three settings where you will be interacting with others. Use a setting where you can take notes easily (such as a class, home watching television with your family and so on). During these three settings, you will need to focus on your nonverbal communication more than usual and make notes about your behaviour. Try to make at least one note under each of the categories. Design three different pages using the guidelines below:

Brief description of setting and others present:

List nonverbal behaviours that you engaged in using the following categories:

Posture:

Gestures:

Paralanguage (volume, tone, other sounds):

Eye contact and other eye behaviours:

Touching (present or not present, a hug or pat on the back):

Distance between you and others (personal, social and so on):

Chronemics (time):

When you have finished all three interactions, go over your results. Did you behave differently depending upon the situation? Did you notice any behaviours that you were not aware of previously? Often, students report some behaviours that surprise them, such as not being aware of the number of times they say "um" in a conversation. Were your behaviours interpreted correctly by the other individual(s)? Usually, we only notice misinterpretation if something does not go as planned in the interaction. Awareness of your own nonverbal behaviour is the first step in changing any behaviours that may be a problem in some situations. For instance, it may be fine to say "um" frequently in conversations with friends, but it may lead to a lower mark in formal class presentations.

often be unaware of what we are nonverbally saying to others. In our opening scenario, Sara's roommate took the opportunity to criticize Sara's boyfriend. She may have thought it was a correct response as she may have "read" Sara's paralanguage that indicated that she was having a change of heart about her boyfriend choice. By paying closer attention to our nonverbal messages, we may become more aware of what messages we are giving others. Take a moment to try the exercise below and see if you can answer the questions.

Seek Information to Confirm or Disconfirm Your Interpretation of Others' Nonverbal Communication

In Chapter 3 we discussed the ways we interpret others' behaviour in order to come to conclusions about their personality or dispositions. We also came to understand the types of errors we make in interpreting this information. We make similar mistakes when interpreting nonverbal messages. Often, nonverbal cues are more believable than what is actually said as we perceive that nonverbal cues are not under as much personal control. In other words, we choose what we say and may not be aware of the nonverbal aspects of the communication. Our true feelings may "leak out" and betray us if we attempt to hide them. A skilled observer may notice this *nonverbal leakage* (Beebe et al., 1997). If Sara had been more skilled, she would have realized that Pierre was upset, but she may not be the true source of his anger. Sara's response focused on herself rather than on being other-oriented.

First, to be more skilled at interpreting nonverbal messages, pay close attention to the entire body of the other person. While facial expressions and eye contact are important, also pay attention to hands, feet, posture, space and paralanguage. For example, I may say to a friend that I have time to chat, but taking peeks at my watch and increasing my distance may indicate otherwise. A person may say he or she has calmed down after a fight, but fidgeting and a tense posture may indicate that the person may not be as calm as he or she says, and you, the officer, need to remain very alert for the possibility of further altercation.

Once you have gathered your nonverbal "evidence," you need to check if these perceptions are accurate. The better you know the person, the better the chances that your perception will be more accurate. As professionals, we may only encounter the person once, and this may lead to more inaccurate perceptions. After a car accident, a person may say he or she is fine. However, you notice that he or she is still visibly shaking and rubbing his or her hands on his or her knees. At this point, you may want to re-check the statement of feeling fine. The most obvious way to check our perceptions is to ask the person in a non-threatening and non-confrontational way.

This **perception checking,** the third step in improving interpretation, is done by using "I language." Using the accident example, the officer may say, "You say that you feel fine, but I see that you are still shaking." By making such a statement the victim now has a chance to respond. The victim may say, "You're right. I know I don't have any injuries. I guess it is all just sinking in." If we go back to our opening example, Sara may have said to Pierre, "I sense you are really upset about something more than just a pizza." At this point, Pierre may have discussed his concerns, and the argument would not have escalated into a fight. With "I language," the key is that you *own* what you perceive to be happening and that you are tentatively checking this impression.

Sometimes you may be wrong, and this gives the other person an opportunity to tell you that you are wrong in a non-threatening way. If you feel someone is giving you the nonverbal message that he or she does not have time to talk, try checking it out this way: "I see you glancing at your watch, and I get the impression that you really do not have time to talk to me." You may be pleasantly surprised by the reply rather than feeling rushed or having hurt feelings. The reply may be, "I don't mean to give you that impression. I really want to talk to you, but I have a meeting in five minutes. Maybe we could meet later?" Because we do not want to appear rude or uncaring, we often reply in socially acceptable ways rather than in a totally honest way. When given the opportunity, many of us would prefer to be honest! Therefore, this last and final step in interpreting or checking out nonverbal communication is to then use the corrected information to continue the interaction with the other person.

Interpret Nonverbal Communication in the Right Context

In Chapter 1 we discussed how that interpersonal communication is conveyed through a medium within a situation or context. Where we are can greatly affect our nonverbal communication and change the meaning of the nonverbal communication. If someone sits beside you in a crowded bus, it does not mean the person finds you attractive and wants to get to know you. Imagine how differently you would feel if you were the only person on the bus and a stranger sat next to you! We all react to the situations that we find ourselves in. Some situations call for more formal behaviour, such as a dinner in a very expensive restaurant with your future in-laws.

Contexts may also include cultural, gender-related and specific group norms of behaviour. If someone does not look at us while we are talking, it may not signify boredom if the person is a female from Tibet. If you are male, many women from Eastern cultures will not look at you when you are speaking and may not even talk unless you make a direct request for a response. Some individuals will not talk to police because of what the police were like in their country of origin. As an officer, you need to be aware that cultural views of policing do differ, and not all police services have the goals of "to protect and serve" in their mandate.

Remember Individual Differences When Interpreting Nonverbal Communication

I have a back condition that can cause pain when I stand for long periods of time. To prevent the pain from starting, I stand with my arms folded across my chest. I have often been accused of being "stand-offish," defensive, uncomfortable or displeased when I do this. If people would take the time to check this out rather than merely accusing me, they would understand why I stand in this position. People are different and may have individual nonverbal habits that do not necessarily mean what we would traditionally think they mean. For instance, shy people are often perceived as "snobby" because they are quiet and do not engage in many conversations. Someone who is shaking may not be nervous but may have a physical condition such as Parkinson's disease that causes this symptom. Before coming to conclusions that may be wrong, use perception checking to more fully understand why the person is nonverbally communicating in a specific way.

LISTENING

While listening is both nonverbal and verbal, in this chapter we will explore listening since much of listening is nonverbal. We have just explored perception checking that relies on paying attention to nonverbal communication and then soliciting feedback on the accuracy of our perceptions. To listen effectively to someone is a skill that takes practice and the development of effective listening skills. Effective listening requires both skill in understanding nonverbal communication and then demonstrating that you have heard the other person. First, we will define listening and then examine the barriers to effective listening. Finally, we will end by discussing ways to improve listening skills.

Listening Defined

When we are listening to someone, we are doing much more than simply **hearing** what he or she has to say. Hearing is the physiological process of sound waves entering the ear and hitting the eardrums. **Listening** is an active process whereby the listener tries to understand exactly what the other person is saying and feeling. In **active listening**, we give feedback to the speaker that demonstrates that we truly understand what he or she is trying to tell us. Active listening involves reflecting back to the listener the content and the feelings of the message (Devito, 1996). In some texts, active listening is also termed reflective listening. However, when we listen we may not always have to engage in active listening as we listen for a variety of reasons. We may listen for enjoyment, such as going to a concert or listening to a favourite CD. Another goal of listening is to gain knowledge and information, as officers do when questioning witnesses to a crime. Active listening is more likely to take place in closer interpersonal relationships or in professional settings that involve counselling. A police officer may use active listening when interviewing a victim of violent crime or abuse, but often officers more fully trained in counselling skills will interview these types of clients. However, to be effective communicators in our personal and career lives, active listening is an essential skill. In this section, we will first discuss the barriers to effective listening. Next, we will explore strategies to improve our listening skills.

Barriers to Effective Listening

We are often not very good at listening to others. How many times have you misunderstood others or been misunderstood? If you are like most of us, you have probably lost count. While not all of the barriers are covered, below are some of the main reasons why we fail to listen properly to others.

- **The message: too many or too complex.** At times we may be bombarded by too many messages at the same time. It can be difficult to pay attention to one message with so much else also trying to get our attention. Also, a message may be too complicated for us to understand. For instance, if you are shopping for a computer and know very little about computers, such terms as "bytes" and "ram" are meaningless to you in the sales pitch. You may find yourself not listening to the salesperson and may even become frustrated and interrupt the speech with your own questions. This ties in with the next barrier.

- **Emotions and other internal states.** It is hard to listen when you are angry, frustrated, bored or nervous, to name just a few emotions that can hinder our listening capability. If you become angry at the salesperson in the above example, you may launch in with your own questions such as, "Will it be fast on the Internet?" or "Can you put it in regular words?" When we are arguing we have difficulty taking turns and may start interrupting or may start internally formulating our own reply. Also, when we are angry we may become defensive. If the computer salesperson tells us that we should know these terms as most intelligent people do, we may assume this person thinks we are stupid. We may also be thinking about other things rather than focusing on the speaker. You put on a favourite television program but start thinking about an essay you need to complete. You suddenly realize you have missed the first 20 minutes of the program! Other internal states, such as hunger, illness, tiredness or stress, also interfere with listening effectively.

- **Prejudgments.** Sometimes we assume that we already know what the other person is talking about and feel we do not have to bother listening (Wood et al., 1998). If we believe that someone has nothing important to say, we do not make an effort to listen. You may have heard negative reports about a professor, so instead of listening in class you do other homework or sit and daydream. Having preconceived ideas about another person interferes with listening and devalues who he or she is as an individual.

- **Pseudo-listening. Pseudo-listening.** is a type of listening that creates a barrier as the listener is pretending to listen (Wood et al., 1998). The individual who is pretending to listen often gets caught, and the speaker may feel hurt or rejected.

- **Monopolizing.** Continually focusing communication on ourselves, or **monopolizing,** creates a barrier to effective listening (Wood et al., 1998). Monopolizers re-route the conversation back to themselves by interrupting or having a story similar to the speaker's story. Interrupting does not always mean a person is monopolizing a conversation unless the goal of the continual interrupting is to re-focus the conversation on himself or herself.

Skills for Effective Listening

Being aware of the many barriers to effective listening is the first step in improving our listening skills. Rather than pseudo-listening, I can say, "I am really too tired to go over the vacation plans tonight. Could we talk about it first thing in the morning?" While you may not want to use all of the skills below, these skills will help you to become a better listener. Always keep in mind the goal that you have when listening to another person. This will help you choose the right skills.

- **Listen as if you have to write a summary of what you just heard.** If you listen as if you have to write down what you are hearing accurately, it will increase your attention to what is being said. Such listening will decrease pseudo-listening and increase your efforts to listen.

- **Use verbal and nonverbal feedback to demonstrate that you are listening.** When someone is telling us something that we find interesting, we can demonstrate this interest with cues that let the person know that we are interested and that what he or she is telling us is important. Verbally, we may say, "Wow," "I don't believe it" or "That must have been awful," and so on. Nonverbally, leaning slightly forward towards the speaker, head nods or shakes and paralanguage such as "Uh-hmm" all indicate that we are listening.

- **Seek clarification and ask questions when necessary.** As with nonverbal communication that we may not understand, ask questions when you are confused or unsure about what the other person is saying. Another way to seek clarification is to repeat back to the listener what he or she just said. For example, if you are interviewing a victim whose home has been broken into and entered, you may say, "So you are saying that you saw three men running from the house when you pulled into your driveway, or was it after you got out of the car?" Often, when people are very emotional, words can come out in a rush, and you may have to help the person go over the incident several times to get the facts in order.

- **Demonstrate understanding by using empathy.** We can also demonstrate that we are listening by giving feedback about how the person is feeling. In the above example, the officer may help the victim by simply stating, "I know that you must be feeling very upset right now, so let's try to get everything straight so that we can get these guys." When we use empathy, we are trying to demonstrate that we understand the other person's perspective, which is a cornerstone of effective interpersonal communication.

- **Be aware of differences in listening styles.** Not all people listen the same way. Previously, we discussed some cultural and gender differences in nonverbal communication. These same differences also apply when listening. Women are more responsive when listening, such as nodding their heads and using more facial expressions than men (Tannen, 1990). When men do not engage in these behaviours, women may make the incorrect assumption that men are not listening. Similarly, in some cultures interrupting may signal that they are listening, such as in the African Canadian community (Wood et al., 1998). When we develop an understanding of differences in listening styles, we may be able to adapt our styles accordingly if the situation warrants a change. For example, you make a friend at college who is African Canadian and spend a weekend with his large family. After awhile, you may find it comfortable to adapt to their listening style or at least learn to feel better when you get interrupted repeatedly at the dinner table with expressions like "Keep on talking" or "Way to go."

- **Use active listening if appropriate.** Active listening relies on **paraphrasing,** expressing understanding and asking questions (Devito, 1996). Paraphrasing is expressing what the speaker has just said in different words. Often when people are upset, we want to launch into advice about how they should manage the situation. Instead, paraphrasing reflects back to the speaker what we understand to be his or her thoughts and feelings. These paraphrases are worded tentatively so that the speaker can correct if necessary. When we express understanding, we reflect back the feeling content of the message as well. For example, your friend has just had her home broken into and vandalized and has called you because she is very distraught about the incident. After she tells you about it briefly, you say, "It sounds like you are very angry about being vandalized like this." The speaker now has a chance to clarify and elaborate. The reply may be, "I'm more than angry. I feel violated. The vandalism wasn't necessary. Why didn't they just take any stuff they wanted and leave?" The third step of active listening is to ask questions to make sure that you understand the person's thoughts and feelings and to get additional information. The next reply may be, "So it's not just the vandalism that is upsetting you, it's the feeling of violation?" Active listening gives the speaker the opportunity to express his or her thoughts and feelings and may help him or her clarify things in his or her own mind. Not all situations require active listening, but it is a good skill to have when others are upset or need to talk through an issue. If you decide to use active listening, remember that it takes time, energy and effort. In many situations as a front line officer, active listening would not be appropriate. But you may branch out into other areas of enforcement, such as victims services and crisis intervention, or you may work in a community with few other support services, and you may be the only officer on the scene. Try the activity below to enhance your active listening skills.

SKILLS PRACTICE:

Active Listening

Below are three situations. With a partner, take turns as listener and speaker for each situation. This is an opportunity for the speaker to practise acting skills while the listener practises active listening skills. Try to incorporate at least two active listening responses to each situation.

1. A friend in his last semester of Police Education is failing an essential course in the program.

   I can't fail this course. If I fail, I can't do my placement. My parents will be absolutely furious with me!

2. Your best friend has just broken up with a long-time lover (Sam can be male or female).

   Out of the blue!! No warning, no discussion, just a phone call. I had no idea that Sam was so unhappy.

3. A friend has been fired from his part-time job.

   Alan is such an idiot. He calls himself a manager. I didn't do anything to deserve this. I really need the money from this job. My rent is due and I don't have enough to cover it without a full pay this week.

When you are finished, discuss with each other what was easy and what was difficult when using active listening. What situations are appropriate to use active listening? What do you see as situations where active listening would be inappropriate?

SUMMARY

In this chapter we have explored nonverbal communication. First, we examined the six functions of nonverbal communication. Nonverbal communication can replace, emphasize and contradict verbal communication. It also regulates interpersonal communication. The sixth function is one of establishing relational-level meanings of interest or responsiveness, liking and power or dominance. These functions are accomplished through six categories or types of nonverbal communication and include paralanguage, facial expressions and eye behaviour, body language, touch, the things around us and how we use space. Paralanguage is any vocal expression that is not written or verbal communication. The face and eyes have significant impact in understanding how others feel in any situation. After an understanding of the functions of nonverbal communication, we moved on to ways to improve our skills in interpreting nonverbal communication. First, we need to be aware of and monitor our own nonverbal communication. Second, rather than making assumptions, we should seek information to confirm or not confirm our assumptions. Third, we should interpret nonverbal communication in the right context and pay attention to the situation in which the behaviour occurs. Last, we need to remember that individual differences can change the meaning of nonverbal communication.

Although not a strictly nonverbal area, listening was covered at the end of the chapter. Listening was defined as an active process of trying to understand what a person is saying. We listen for many reasons, ranging from pleasure to seeking critical information. Several barriers interfere with our ability to listen effectively. The message may be too complex, or we may be overloaded by too much information. Other barriers are more internal and include emotions and internal states, prejudgments, pseudo-listening and monopolizing. To be a more effective listener, several techniques for improvement were presented. These techniques included listening as if you have to write a summary of the content, using verbal and nonverbal feedback to demonstrate listening, seeking clarification when necessary, using empathy, being aware of listening style differences and using active listening in the appropriate situation.

JOURNAL AND DISCUSSION QUESTIONS

1. With new studies in the use of physiological measures to detect deception, do you think that results of such testing should be admissible in court? There has been new research in vocal stress and some new research on polygraphs. Examine some new research and draw your own conclusions.

2. What problems have you experienced in communicating with the opposite gender or with other cultures? What did you do about it?

3. According to many researchers, we spend at least half of our waking time engaged in listening. If this is true and you are not a good listener, it means that you are a poor communicator 50 percent of the time. Why do you find listening so hard? What are some strategies that you are going to employ to try to improve your skill?

WEB SITES

www.members.aol.com/nonverbal2/diction1.htm

From a to z, this is a complete dictionary of nonverbal terms and phrases.

www.zzyx.ucsc.edu/~archer

This is a site devoted to nonverbal communication and includes a series of pictures where you can try to "read" the nonverbal communication.

REFERENCES

Luigi Anolli and Rita Ciceri (1997). "The voice of deception: Vocal strategies of naive and able liars," *Journal of Nonverbal Behaviour, 21* (4), pp. 259–284.

E. Aries (1987). "Gender and communication," in P.Shaver (Ed.), *Sex and Gender*, pp. 149–176. Newbury Park, CA: Sage.

Roger E. Axtell (1989). *Do's and Taboos of Hosting International Visitors.* New York: John Wiley and Sons.

Robert A. Baron, Bruce Earhard and Marcia Ozier (1998). *Psychology,* 2nd Canadian edition. Scarborough, ON: Allyn and Bacon Canada.

Aaron Beck (1988). *Love is Never Enough.* New York: Harper and Row.

Steven Beebe, Susan J. Beebe, Mark V. Redmond and Carol Milstone (1997). *Interpersonal Communication: Relating to Others.* Scarborough, ON: Allyn and Bacon Canada.

J. K. Burgoon, D. B. Buller and W. G. Woodall (1989). *Nonverbal Communication: The Unspoken Dialogue.* New York: Harper and Row, p. 324.

J. M. Carroll and J. A. Russell (1996). "Do facial expressions signal specific emotions? Judging emotions from the face in context," *Journal of Personality and Social Psychology, 70,* pp. 205–218.

Joseph A. Devito (1996). *Messages: Building Interpersonal Communication Skills*, 3rd edition. New York: Harper Collins.

Mary K. Devitt, Charles R. Honts and Lynelle Vondergreest (1997). "Truth or just bias: The treatment of the psychophysiological detection of deception in introductory psychology textbooks," *The Journal of Credibility Assessment and Witness Psychology*, 1(1), pp. 9–32.

P. Ekman and W. V. Friesen (1978). "Facial action coding system (FACS): A technique for the measurement of facial action," *Journal of Personality and Social Psychology*, 39, pp. 1125–1134.

P. Ekman (1992). "Facial expression of emotion: New findings, new question," *Psychological Science, 3,* pp. 34–38.

E.T. Hall(1963). "Proxemics: A study of man's spatial relationships," in *Man's Image in Medicine and Anthropology.* New York: International Universities Press.

J. A. Hall (1987). "On explaining gender differences: The case of nonverbal communication," in P. Shaver and C. Hendricks (Eds.), *Sex and Gender,* pp. 177–200. Newbury Park, CA: Mayfield.

N. M. Henley (1977). *Body Politics: Power, Sex and Nonverbal Communication.* Englewood Cliffs, NJ: Prentice-Hall.

C. L. Kleinke (1986). "Gaze and eye contact: A research review," *Psychological Bulletin*, 100, pp. 78–100.

M. Knapp (1978). Nonverbal Communication in Human Interaction. New York: Holt, Rinehart and Winston.

L. A. Malandro and L. L. Barker (1983). *Nonverbal Communication.* Reading, MA: Addison Wesley.

D. N. Maltz and R. Barker (1982). "A Cultural approach to male-female miscommunication," in J. J. Gumpertz (Ed.), *Language and Social Identity*, p.p. 196–216. Cambridge: Cambridge University Press.

Ed McDaniel and Peter A. Andersen (1998). "International patterns of tactile communication: A field study," *Journal of Nonverbal Behaviour, 22* (1), pp. 59–75.

Albert Mehrabian (1972). *Nonverbal Communication.* Chicago: Aldine-Atherton, p. 108.

Albert Mehrabian (1976). *Public Places, Private Spaces.* New York: Basic Books.

Albert Mehrabian (1981). *Silent Messages: Implicit Communication of Emotions and Attitudes*, 2nd edition. Belmont, CA: Wadsworth.

B. M. Montgomery (1988). "Quality communication in personal relationships," in S. W. Duck (Ed.), *Handbook of Personal Relationships* (pp. 343–366). New York: John Wiley.

William E. Nolen (1995). "Reading people" (nonverbal communication in internal auditing), *Internal Auditor*, 52 *(4)*, p. 48.

Joann Ellison Rodgers (Jan/Feb, 1999). "Flirting Fascination," *Psychology Today.*

D. Roger and W. Nesshoever (1987). "Individual differences in conversational strategies: A further study," *British Journal of Social Psychology, 26*, pp. 247–255.

J. B. Stiff, G. R. Miller, C. Sleight and P. Mongeau (1989). "Explanations for visual cue primacy in judgments of honesty and deceit," *Journal of Personality and Social Psychology*, 56, pp. 555–564.

D. Tannen (1990). *You Just Don't Understand: Women and Men in Conversation.* New York: Morrow.

Julia Wood, Ron Sept and Jane Duncan (1998). *Everyday Encounters: An Introduction to Interpersonal Communication.* Scarborough, ON: ITP Nelson.

R. B. Zajonc and D. N. McIntosh.(1992). "Emotions research: Some promising questions and some questionable promises," *Psychological Science*, 3, pp. 70–74.

M. Zuckerman, R. F. Simons and P. Como (1981). "Verbal and nonverbal communication of deception," in L. Berkowitz (Ed.), *Advances in Experimental Psychology*, volume 14, pp. 1–59. New York: Academic Press.

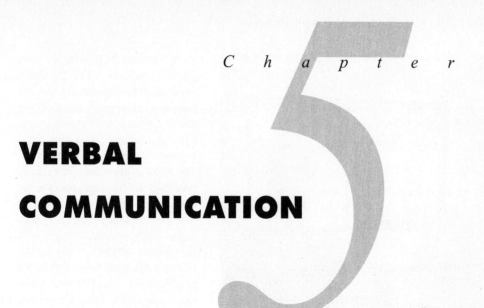

C h a p t e r

VERBAL COMMUNICATION

LEARNING OUTCOMES

After studying this chapter you should be able to

1. Describe four major characteristics of verbal communication.
2. Identify barriers to effective verbal communication.
3. Explain and differentiate between the two types of communication climate.
4. Use several of the 10 strategies to improve interpersonal communication with others.

The scenario: Two officers have been called to the home of a woman who has stated that she cannot get her drunk boyfriend to leave. As soon as the woman lets the officer in the door, her boyfriend begins with a tirade of insults. Both officers notice that the man is extremely drunk and that the woman appears frightened as well as drunk. The man is standing behind his girlfriend and is weaving. When the boyfriend speaks, his words are slurred. When they enter, one officer increases the space between the boyfriend and the woman.

Boyfriend: *Here we go again! Don't you pigs have anything better to do? There must be some real crime out there somewhere.*

Officer One: *Your girlfriend has made a call that you refuse to leave her home. I think she would feel better if you left now.*

Boyfriend: *I haven't finished my drink yet. I'll go when I'm good and ready, not when YOU say so. Maybe I'll have to show the both of you who runs this place!*

Officer Two: *Sir, we're not looking for a fight here. I just think your girlfriend has had enough for one night.*

Peterborough Lakefield Community Police Service

This officer must choose her words carefully. She displays interest by leaning forward.

If you can recall Chapter one, you will remember that the communication process has three components: the sender, the receiver and the situation or environment where the interaction is taking place between the sender and the receiver. The sender encodes a message, transmits the message, and the receiver then decodes the information. The message is sent using both verbal and nonverbal channels with face-to-face interaction having the richest sources of information. As an officer, the words that you choose when interacting with a citizen sets the climate for how that citizen will respond (McKinnon, 1993). When we use words to interact, we also use nonverbal channels to communicate how we feel as well as to express content. The actual words only comprise seven percent of the message; the balance is paralanguage and nonverbal behaviours (Mehrabian, 1972). The public react to police officers based on the verbal and nonverbal messages they receive from the officer. Uniformed officers wearing a badge and a gun are already conveying messages of authority and control to the public. With this in mind, officers must carefully choose how they will interact with the public. An understanding of verbal communication as well as nonverbal communication, which was discussed in the previous chapter, become essential to perform your professional duties effectively.

This chapter will examine the verbal communication process. Although the topic of verbal communication is emphasized in this chapter, both verbal and nonverbal communication will need to be addressed for a full understanding of this final chapter on the communication process. First, we will examine words and what they mean. We will then move on to barriers in verbal communication. Next, we will explore three types of communication climate where interaction takes place. Last, strategies to improve verbal communication will be presented to assist you in improving your verbal skills.

WORDS AND THEIR MEANING: CHARACTERISTICS OF WORDS

What are words? In our opening scene the youth labels the officer as a pig. Is this positive, negative, or does it have no meaning at all? Words have meaning because we give them meaning. For example, think about the word "gay." Fifty years ago if someone were to say he was "gay," chances are he would be expressing his happiness. "Gay" has a very different meaning now. Let's take some time and examine some of the characteristics and abilities of words.

Words Are Arbitrary

Words are **symbols** that represent thoughts, concepts or objects. In isolation they have no meaning or real connection with what they idealize or represent (Wood et al., 1998). For example, when new things are created, we design words to symbolize what they are. The new computer technology has created a whole new vocabulary for us to master with such words as "Internet," "surfing" and "downloading." While many of these words are not new, new meanings have been created for them.

Because words are arbitrary, they may not mean the same thing to everyone. If a male refers to a female as a real "dish," one female may be offended while another may not be offended. To one female it may mean she is attractive while the other female may take it as sexually offensive. Often misunderstandings occur because the same word may have different meanings for different people. Have you ever asked a question and received an unexpected answer? This may have been a result of having different meanings for the words in the question.

We Give Meaning to Words

One text (Wood et al., 1998) on interpersonal communication refers to words as being **ambiguous**. In other words, their meanings are not clear cut as in our above example of "gay." In our opening scene the word "pig" has a different meaning for the man than for others who may not have been exposed to the meaning behind this when referring to a police officer. Within groups and cultures, words are given meaning. For instance, in North America with its emphasis on sexual equality, many terms have been changed to no longer refer to occupations using gender specific words. See the box below for some of these newer ways of referring to occupations.

Since words may have different meanings to different groups and even between individuals, many conflicts arise because of the difference in interpretations. If a teacher tells

CANADIAN PERSPECTIVE:

"Politically Correct" Communication

In the past, many occupations were labelled with titles that included gender. However, as we have seen in recent years, most occupations are not specifically for men or women. Men and women can perform a vast number of jobs equally with no sex differences in performance. Here are just a few of these changes:

Instead of:	Use:
waiter, waitress	server
policeman, policewoman	police officer, constable
chairman, chairwoman	chair, chairperson
cleaning woman	cleaner
fireman	fire fighter
mankind	humankind, humans, humanity

you that he or she expects "regular" attendance in a course, this may have different meanings for students in the course. The teacher may mean that there is an expectation for you to attend *every* class. On the other hand, you may decide that regular means to attend *frequently but not every class.* If the teacher mentions at the end of the course that you have demonstrated poor attendance, you may be angry because you feel that you have attended *regularly.*

Words differ in their level of **abstraction** (Beebe et al., 1997). Words are not concrete but rather are representations of ideas, people, objects or events. For example, "law enforcement personnel" is more abstract than "police officer." And "Constable John Smith" with a specific badge number from a specific service is less abstract than "police officer." "My buddy John who is a police officer" is even less abstract. As we will see in the section on improving our verbal skills, reducing the abstraction of our communication reduces the potential for misunderstandings.

Words Have Two Levels of Meaning

Think of the word "dentist." Although most of us know that a dentist is a person who looks after our teeth, the meaning does not stop here. For many of us the word "dentist" also conjures up a host of feelings. Some of us quake at the mere thought of "dentist," likely some residual feelings of unpleasant memories from our past. Words can have both a **denotative** or literal level of meaning as well as a **connotative** level of meaning. The denotative meaning is the one that you find in the dictionary and is shared by a large culture. The connotative meaning is the subjective and personal level of meaning of the word. The job of the dentist is at the denotative level of meaning. How you feel about the dentist is at the connotative level of meaning. For many of us, the words "police officer" are a symbol of safety and integrity, but for some they mean brutality and prejudice.

Words Can Have Power

If you have ever listened to a great speaker, you have little doubt that words can inspire others to change or to behave in certain ways. Words can hurt and words can heal. How we label words can affect how we react to that label. Many labels are symbols that reflect our values and attitudes. Some of these labels take away others' individuality and group people into broad categories. The statement "All cops are pigs" takes away the individual differences among officers and groups them into a negative category. The broad use of such generalizations and stereotyping can lead to misunderstandings and prejudice. Think of other labels that stereotype others into categories that may have negative or biased meanings. Below, in the Canadian Perspective box, are some excerpts from an article about "Canucks." Calling young people "punks," elderly people, "old geezers" and people who have broken the law, "perps," is using labels that have the characteristics of **loaded language** (Wood et al., 1998). This kind of language slants perceptions and dismisses individual differences.

We also generalize when we talk about others' behaviours. Such statements as "You are always late" may be exaggerated and not reflective of true behaviour. You probably have had a similar kind of experience, and if you are like most of us, you may have reacted to this generalization with anger. Using this kind of "You-language" coupled with such a generalization of behaviour may lead to conflict.

CANADIAN PERSPECTIVE:

Canuck or Not Canuck?

A recent newspaper article discussed the use of the word "Canuck" to describe Canadians. According to the article, a writer for a campus newspaper had used the word Canucks when referring to the large number of Canadians moving into American entertainment. The newspaper, *The Statesman*, is the paper at Indiana State University. Because of this incident and others not reported, the writer was fired although re-hired later after the editor received letters from Canadians saying that they were not offended by the use of the term. Merv Hendricks, the university's director of student publications, had complained that the term was a derogatory label for French Canadians (*Peterborough Examiner*).

There appears to have been some confusion at the university as to what the term "Canuck" means and whether or not it is offensive or politically incorrect.

As mentioned in the article, the Vancouver Canucks is one of our hockey teams. The term Canuck has been around for at least a century. Johnny Canuck was a cartoon character that appeared in papers in the 1860s. During World War II, he became a cartoon hero in comic books, protecting Canadians from the Nazi threat (Phillips, 1994). If you are looking for Canadian content on the Internet, many sites have Canuck in the address or Canuck in the title. There is even a Canuck site of the day! So is the label of Canuck offensive? It would appear that Canadians themselves use this term to describe much about their own country and the people that inhabit this nation. What do you think?

Sources: "Canuck" no slur, editor rehired. *Peterborough Examiner*, Sunday February 28, 1999. Reprinted with permission from the Associated Press.

Andrew Phillips (1994) Fear and hope at home: Social changes caused by WWII, *Macleans*, June 6.

BARRIERS TO EFFECTIVE VERBAL COMMUNICATION

Although we have briefly touched upon several problems with verbal communication in the previous part of the chapter, it will benefit us to go over several barriers in more detail here. The barriers that were touched upon before will be given a cursory examination. When interpersonal communication breaks down, the problem often can be traced directly to how the two parties were speaking to each other and what they were saying (or not saying). Here we will identify seven barriers to effective verbal communication.

Same Words, Different Meanings

The same word can have different meanings. If you were not familiar with the current meaning of "pig" when referring to a police officer or "old man" when referring to a parent, some of the true meanings in the conversation may have been misunderstood.

Imprecision with Words

Many of the signs or bulletins that we see are humorous because the content is unclear and so is the meaning. This one was spotted at a highway service centre: *Cheap Food. Get Gas*

Here. Because people assign meanings to words, others do not always share our meanings or understand what those meanings are. Many professions use **jargon** or abbreviations to refer to the specialized terms in the occupation. In law enforcement, we use such words as perps, juvies, snitches, B and E, tact team and so on to refer to particular people and procedures and to abbreviate common language in the field. While it may be fine to use such jargon in your professional circle, it may be misunderstood by others.

People who are more intimate also develop their own system of words, as do subgroups and cultures (Beebe et al., 1997). This system of words is referred to as a **restricted code.** In families, aspects of toiletry, hygiene and lovemaking may all have restricted codes. Students at a college may also have restricted codes in the group that they socialize with regularly. Rather than saying, "Let's skip class and go to the pub" one group member may say to the other member, "Let's get down to some serious studying," thereby signaling that it may be time for a pub visit.

Making Generalizations and Using Extremes

Previously, generalizing was mentioned as a potential problem in verbal communication. Such statements as "All women are poor drivers" and "All cops are pigs" deny individual differences. Such generalizations are untrue. There are poor women drivers, and there are excellent women drivers. There are officers who behave in less than exemplary ways, and there are officers that go above and beyond the call of duty.

Often when we generalize, we also engage in describing events, people or objects using extremes. This generalizing by using extremes is referred to as **polarization**. When we use polarized language, we fail to communicate individual or subtle differences. When we polarize our perceptions and verbally describe these inaccuracies, we are on the path to conflict. Such statements as "You're either for me or against me," "You either love me or you don't" and "You're always lying to me" illustrate this type of polarized communication.

Biased and Loaded Language

The words that we choose can alter the perceptions of others. Earlier we discussed loaded language and stereotyping. An example of loaded language would be the sexist language that is used to describe occupations (refer to earlier box). Referring to a position with a male gender term negates that women can or do perform the same job. When we use language to refer to other cultures, the same is true. Loaded language can also include emotional appeals and can use language to conjure up pictures in order to make a point or to change another's perception. As a political candidate dedicated to ending homelessness, I might make some statements about the "greedy rich," "the isolated and sobbing children of the streets" and "uncaring bureaucrats" rather than give statistics, review current practice and other less emotional facts. Many articles in newspapers and magazines also use biased or loaded language to get your attention. Advertising also uses such language to try to convince you to buy the product.

Culture Makes a Difference

"Although all humans use symbols, we use them in different ways" (Wood et al., 1998, p. 109). Cultures and groups different from your own may use symbols differently from your culture or group. These shared **norms,** or shared expectations of how to behave, may not be understood by non-members of that particular culture or group. Canadians from Italy use more gestures and talk more loudly than Canadians of Anglo-Saxon descent. To those of Anglo-Saxon descent, these discussions may appear to be angry discussions. Recently, at a Greek community event, an individual not aware of Greek traditions and customs thought it comical to see men dancing together holding hands in a line. In Chapter four we examined some of these differences in communication patterns of male and female gender cultures. Failure to understand and to respect cultural and group differences can create significant barriers for effective interpersonal communication.

Rigid Thinking Leads to Static Evaluation

Failure to see and adapt to change can pose a significant problem in the world of interpersonal communication. **Static evaluation** is a tendency to retain evaluations without changing them over time (Devito, 1996). It is like taking a snapshot of someone and then viewing that picture over time without incorporating the changes that take place as the person grows and changes. Realizing that time and people are not static will help you avoid the pitfalls of making a "one-shot" evaluation. For example, if you meet someone at college and become friends and then meet years later after losing touch, this person is not that college friend. There have been many changes as a result of many life experiences. You cannot assume that this person still likes the same music, holds the same political views and so on. You might say, "The last time we talked, you were still voting Conservative. Whom do you support now?" Such statements allow the other person to voice his or her changes since you last communicated.

Voicing Inferences as Facts

"She is wearing blue pants" is a statement of fact. You can see the pants and the colour of the pants. However, saying she is nervous is an inference that you make by observing what you perceive as indicators of nervousness. **Inferences** are guesses, opinions or ideas that you have about a person, object or event. They are not reality. Treating inferences as if they are reality can create barriers to communication. The person may not be nervous. She may be chilled or have a physical condition that includes shaking or other physical signs that can be misunderstood for nervousness. Police officers must interview witnesses carefully to uncover facts rather than accept inferences. Learning effective techniques to separate facts from inferences is essential to accurately interview witnesses to a crime.

COMMUNICATION CLIMATES: DEFENSIVE VERSUS SUPPORTIVE

Interpersonal communication takes place within a climate that is created by the persons involved in the exchange. You have most likely had the experience of feeling defensive when talking to someone. The other person "puts you on guard," and you may feel attacked, unimportant, inferior and hurt. On the other hand, you have had experiences in which you found it easy to talk, and you felt supported, encouraged and valued as a person in your own right. The first experience was a defensive climate where **disconfirming responses** to you were made (Beebe et al., 1997). In this defensive climate, statements were made that attempted to devalue you. You may have responded similarly, resulting in a climate that is not conducive to honest interpersonal communication. The second climate, the supportive one, was one where **confirming responses** to you were made (Beebe et al., 1997). In a climate where confirming responses to each other are made, people value themselves and others. In our opening scene, the man immediately makes the climate a defensive one by using derogatory terms and remarks. What are the differences between a supportive and defensive climate? One researcher, Jack Gibb, has identified six types of communication that foster one climate or the other. We will examine each one very briefly (adapted from Wood, 1998, pp. 193–198).

Evaluation versus Description

By being called names or assuming that we are similar to another person, we feel that we are being evaluated. When others evaluate us, they often use sentences that begin with or use "you." For example, "Don't you pigs…" from the opening scene immediately evaluates the officers in unfair and negative terms. On the other hand, using descriptions from observations fosters a more supportive climate. If I describe what I see without passing any judgment, I can keep the climate supportive. Using statements that begin with "I" is less offensive and does not lead to such a defensive climate. For example, "I feel hurt when you don't call when you are going to be late" is much less defensive than saying, "You never call when you're going to be late." Describing behaviour rather than evaluating it will lead to a more supportive exchange. "You" versus "I" language will be discussed further in the next section as a method to improve communication.

Certainty versus Provisionalism

The language of certainty allows things to be only one way without room for other ideas or opinions. Have you ever tried to argue with someone whose mind is already made up? Banging your head against a wall may be less painful! On the other hand, stating your ideas as if they are not carved in stone keeps a discussion open. If you keep your discussion and your mind open, beware that you run the risk of being changed! By stating your ideas in a provisional manner, the climate is more supportive and open. For example, I might say, "The way I tend to view communication courses is that they are essential for learning good communication skills." By using provisional statements, I am stating that there are other views, other ideas and other ways to approach problems. Such statements leave room for further discussion and other opinions.

Strategy versus Spontaneity

When we think others are trying to manipulate us or are not being honest with us, we become defensive. If others appear to be "planning" what they are saying, we become suspicious of their motives. For instance, if I start off my conversation to you, "Remember when I helped you with that essay you were having so much trouble with?" you may start to wonder what I am leading up to with this start to our conversation. On the other hand, spontaneous communication is just that; it feels open, honest and unrehearsed.

Control versus Problem Orientation

When we attempt to control others, we do so by using communication that asserts our solutions or ideas are the only acceptable ones. When we attempt to control another this way, we are demonstrating that we are more superior, have more power, have more rights, have more intelligence and more abilities than the other person. We may try to control others by pointing out what it is that we control and what they do not. For example, "I'm the one paying the bills here. So we are going to buy the stereo that I want and not the one you want."

Opposite to control is to use communication that is problem-oriented to maintain a supportive climate. When we problem solve, we attempt to find a solution that is satisfactory to everyone involved with the issue. For example, "Why don't we take a look at both stereos and draw up a list of their respective features and choose based on that?" Regardless of who is paying for the stereo, making joint decisions as co-members of a household demonstrates respect and fosters a supportive climate in the second example. We can view differences as opportunities to reach mutually satisfactory solutions.

Neutrality versus Empathy

According to Gibb (1970), when people react to us in a neutral or detached way, we become defensive with this lack of demonstration of caring or concern. To foster a more supportive climate, using empathy demonstrates concern for the other person's thoughts and feelings. Empathy demonstrates acceptance of the other person even if his or her opinion is contrary to your own.

Superiority versus Equality

When people act as if they are better than we are, communication is adversely affected. Similar to the control orientation earlier, a person fostering a defensive climate asserts his or her superiority in a number of ways, such as trying to demonstrate superior knowledge, intelligence and power. If a teacher states, "What do you know? You're only a student," he or she is trying to demonstrate that he or she possesses superior knowledge. What are the chances of you having a second discussion with this teacher?

When people treat us like equals, it creates a climate of support and mutual respect. If the teacher were to say instead, "That is a very interesting observation. You have taken some time to think this issue through," he or she is demonstrating that your thoughts are valued and deserving of attention. We feel more comfortable to self-disclose in this more relaxed and supportive climate.

IMPROVING COMMUNICATION: LISTENING AND RESPONDING

Creating a supportive climate is really a major step in developing a ground for effective interpersonal communication. When we communicate with others, we are engaged in two processes that are intricately connected. We listen and then respond to what we assume or perceive we have heard. The other person is engaged in the same process. We pay attention to nonverbal communication, verbal content and to our own thought processes and ideas. The rest of this chapter will be devoted to developing better communication skills. Many of these skills rely on both verbal and nonverbal abilities. Remember, it is not only what you say that matters but how you say it. Also, when studying these skills, realize that you would not use all of these skills for all situations. Depending upon the level of intimacy you wish to achieve, the purpose of the interaction and the outcomes that you desire, you will vary the skills that you use for each encounter.

Create a Supportive Climate

We have just finished discussing the differences between supportive and defensive climates. So how can you create a supportive climate? Now that you know the differences between the two climates, you can actively work on ensuring that you create the supportive climate. Recall that a supportive climate includes *descriptive communication, provisionalism, spontaneity, a problem-orientation, empathy* and *equality.* Use the suggestions in the section on climate as the base and then use the following suggestions to keep building the base for effective interpersonal communication.

Use "I" Language and Active Listening

We have briefly touched on "I" versus "You" language as a method of perception checking when interpreting nonverbal messages and as part of active listening. When you use I-language, you are demonstrating that you are the owner of the statement and that your perception is open to re-interpretation. Often, we accuse others of making us feel certain ways. If I say, "You make me angry when you don't call when you are going to be late," that statement assumes that it is you who is making me feel angry. It is your fault that I am angry. You-language creates defensiveness. The climate changes when I demonstrate that these are my feelings towards your behaviour. Instead, if I say, "I feel angry when you are late and don't call to let me know," the level of defensiveness decreases. Instead of saying, "You never give me a chance to pick out the new family car," say, "I would like an opportunity to help pick out the new car." We can use I-language to demonstrate how we feel about another's behaviour in a non-threatening way and to demonstrate our needs in positive terms.

We can also use I-language to check our accuracy when interpreting another's behaviour. This is the skill of active listening. Many of the barriers above can be avoided by using I-language to check the accuracy of our interpretation of another's behaviours, feelings and/or words. If your roommate comes in, slams the door, throws down his or her books, sees you and immediately says, "Well, I'm glad you're relaxed enough to be enjoying a sandwich even though you haven't done the dishes as usual," your first reaction may be to defend yourself. But if you use I-language instead, you may find out the true cause of the anger. "I get the feeling that something is really bugging you" may be a better way to find out what is the real cause for the anger. After all, the door had been slammed before you were spotted eating with dirty dishes in the background.

By using I-language, we can also check the depth and accuracy of our perception of a feeling. What if your roommate slams the door, throws down his or her books, sits and turns the

TV on. When you say "Are you alright?" and the reply is "I'm just fine," you know that things are not "alright." Use I-language to open up a dialogue: "You say that you are fine, but I still get the feeling that something is making you really angry." Be prepared, the floodgates may open and you may get an earful. Only use I-language if you really want to open the lines of communication. With people that we care about, and even in a professional capacity, our goal may be to talk and find out more about, the other person. Below is an exercise to help you improve your ability to use I-language. Students often feel uncomfortable with this skill and state that it feels phony. New skills often feel funny or strange at first, and remember that it is not in every situation that you will want to use I-language. In many settings, it would be inappropriate to use this skill. For instance, you would not use I-language when interrogating a hostile perpetrator.

Tie in your active listening skills as you use I-language. Remember that active listening includes paraphrasing, expressing understanding and asking questions (Devito, 1996). Review active listening in Chapter 4, pp. 62 to 63 and use them to further your ability to communicate effectively.

SKILLS PRACTICE:

I-Language

Below are three scenes. For each one, reply using I-language. Practice with a partner. The first one is completed as a demonstration using two different replies. In order to become familiar with I-language, use sentences that begin with "I sense ..," "I get the feeling ..," "I feel ...," "I hear ...," "I would like ...." As you get more skilled, you will be able to use I-language in more unique and individual ways. You do not have to solve the problem, just use one reply.

1. You are home for a holiday, and your parents are delighted to see you since you have not been home for almost a year. You are very tired and are looking forward to a good rest. As soon as you walk in the door, your mother says, "Oh, we're so thrilled you're home! I have organized a family party, and we'll go visit your aunt and uncle for a couple of days, and your dad needs some help with some painting."

    REPLY 1: *I'm really glad to be home too, Mom! I sense, however, that you have a real schedule lined up for me, and I am really exhausted and looking forward to resting.*

    REPLY 2: *I get the feeling that you have a real calendar of events lined up for me. I'm glad to be home, but I'm looking forward to some serious relaxing.*

2. You and your partner have agreed to put money away every month and not to spend any major amount unless agreed upon by both of you. You are trying to save for a down payment on a house. Your partner walks in after work and says, "I can't believe my good luck!! I just bought that new stereo system that I have wanted for so long! It was on sale—only $600.00!!"

3. At your part-time server job, your co-worker feels that you put in very little effort and do not help enough with the cleaning up before closing on this particular night. On your last shift, this co-worker did very little, and you see this as payback time. The co-worker says angrily, "You're a useless good-for-nothing!! I just did all the work and you did nothing! You never help out!"

Be Other-Oriented

In earlier chapters we briefly discussed being other-oriented as a skill for improving inter-personal communication. Rather than being self-focused in a conversation, we need to be able to focus on the other person's thoughts, needs and feelings. We demonstrate other-orienta-tion by decentring, which is being attentive and interested in the other person. There are several specific ways to do this (Devito, 1996; Wood et al., 1998):

- Display nonverbally and with paralanguage that you are listening. Use eye contact and other nonverbal cues that you are paying attention and listening. We enjoy talking to people who tell us nonverbally that what we are saying is important. Smile, use facial expressions and orient your body toward the speaker. Use paralanguage indicators such as "Hm-mm" and "Oh" to indicate listening as well.

- Ask the other person questions. Ask for suggestions, opinions and ask questions for clar-ification. For example, such questions as "How do you feel about that?" and "What would be your ideas to help?" and also "What did you think about him reacting like that?" all encourage continued conversation from the speaker.

- Use **positive reinforcement** to encourage and praise statements during interaction. Positive reinforcement is rewarding a behaviour to increase the likelihood that the behaviour will be repeated. Some people have difficulty talking, may be anxious about the topic or may be shy or insecure. Using positive reinforcement such as "I appreciate your input" or "That's an interesting idea" encourages the speaker to par-ticipate further. Teachers of young children often positively reinforce a wrong an-swer to encourage the children to keep trying. You do not have to indicate that the person is right; your goal is to encourage a continued dialogue. An officer may use this technique with a victim who may be reluctant or afraid to speak. Even encouraging a small amount of talk may allow the officer to offer a supportive environment.

- Express your agreement if the situation is appropriate. You may make comments such as "You're right, that was a hard time for you" or "That's true." When people feel that what they are saying is acceptable to you, it encourages continued interaction.

Use Empathy

Using empathy is part of developing a strong ability to become other-oriented and deserves to be discussed briefly on its own. When we empathize, we understand the feelings of oth-ers and can predict how they might feel in a specific situation (Beebe et al., 1997). A friend once stated that she poured her heart out to her partner after a particularly disturbing event at work. Her partner replied with a noncommital "hmm-mm." It was then that she realized he had the TV on without the sound and was watching a hockey game! When people react with neutrality, they are dismissing our feelings. On the other hand, empathy demonstrates that we care enough to take the time to listen and to try to understand another point of view.

Demonstrate Respect

If you heard a police officer use the term "white trash" to describe a client, what yould you think? Although the officer may not have meant anything negative with the use of such a term, this term did not demonstrate respect or acceptance. Also, using such a term may have demonstrated a feeling of superiority. Asserting superiority over others also does not demonstrate acceptance or respect.

To demonstrate respect means to be non-judgmental in your interaction with another person. You may disagree with prostitution, but this does not preclude you from treating a suspected prostitute with respect. You may not personally believe in some of the values, beliefs or orientations of others, but this does not limit your capability to demonstrate respect and acceptance of others.

Many citizens will respect your authority as officers and sincerely believe and trust in the judicial system. This respect will place certain demands upon you when you are on patrol, interviewing witnesses, victims and suspects and when testifying in court. The Law and Justice box discusses some tips to help you present yourself in court to maintain the respect of others.

LAW AND JUSTICE PERSPECTIVE:

Presenting Yourself in Court

Part of an officer's duty is testifying in court. The courtroom can be an uncomfortable and adversarial environment. Whether called by the defense or by the Crown, testifying in court can be stressful and unpleasant. How an officer presents himself or herself can make lasting impressions on the judge, the jury, other witnesses, lawyers, Crown attorneys and other onlookers in the courtroom. Captain David W. McRoberts (1996), a division commander and an author in many law enforcement publications, offers a few guidelines for an officer to be an "effective law enforcement witness."

- **Integrity.** Don't lie. Often the testimony of an officer is given more weight and believed to be more credible than other witnesses. Lying puts you at risk and reflects negatively upon the whole law enforcement field.

- **Understanding.** Understand your role as a witness for the defense or as a witness for the Crown. Also, understand that you will feel a certain amount of fear or nervousness when testifying due to the rules of the courtroom. When you walk into the room, walk to the witness stand assertively, as you will be the focus of attention.

- **Be prepared.** Be as prepared as possible for courtroom testimonies.

- **Appearance.** There are two separate issues regarding appearance. One is clothing. If in uniform, it should be clean and pressed. If out of uniform, the attire should be conservative. Second, as part of the total package, the officer should have a well-kept and groomed appearance.

- **Demeanour.** Project self-confidence and positive self-esteem when you walk and with your posture. To appear unsure, arrogant or indifferent will destroy the effectiveness of the testimony.

- **Delivery.** Speak clearly, avoid non-words and phrases such as "ya," "um" and "well, uh." Speak loud enough to be heard and concentrate on a "smooth delivery." Stick to the facts and do not give additional information after you have given the appropriate answer.

A good performance in court by an officer will have positive effects. It will reflect upon the officer, the effectiveness of the court system and upon the police force itself. As you read back over this list, notice that the tips include nonverbal and verbal communication skills.

Source: Captain David W. McRoberts. (1996). Courtroom demeanor and testimony. In Ed Nowicki (Ed.). *Total Survival,* pp. 249–259. Powers Lake, WI: Performance Dimensions Publishing. Reprinted with the permission of the author and the publisher.

Don't Interrupt

How many times have you started to say something only to be interrupted? Sometimes, the interruption is legitimate such as a phone call or your two-year-old has to go to the bathroom. Often, the interruptions are unnecessary. When you interrupt someone, you may be giving the impression that what you have to say is more important than what he or she is currently saying. Rather than interrupting, practise listening carefully and then talking when it is your turn to speak.

Be Honest and Assert Yourself When Necessary

Many of us have difficulty being open and honest with others. This can occur for any number of reasons. We might be afraid we are going to hurt someone's feelings. Maybe it is easier to give in rather than to open ourselves up for a potential conflict. We may feel this person has power over us, and we are genuinely afraid to engage in any confrontation at all. Whatever the reasons, being assertive can be difficult. And yet in intimate and close relations, such lack of honesty may eventually erode the relationship. Even in professional relations, we need to be assertive and tell it like it is.

If we cannot assert ourselves, some of us become **non-assertive**. Non-assertive people let things happen to them without making their feelings known. They give in to another person's requests. Some of us can also become **aggressive.** Aggressive people are overbearing and push for what they want without concern for the feelings of others. There often will be times when, as an officer, you may need to be aggressive and use force. The skill is to be able to choose the correct skill to match the situation. Chapter 6 discusses use of force in more detail. Responding to others using assertiveness is a technique that not only assists you in everyday communication but is also an essential skill for conflict management.

Assertive people communicate in a direct and straightforward manner (Dubrin and Geerinck, 1998). Let's look at an example: A fellow student continually borrows your notes. Twice, the notes were not returned when there were tests pending. You have decided that you will not let this student have your notes again. It is the night before a major test, and you are studying in the library when this student approaches you. "Oh, thank goodness you're here! I need your notes right away. I missed the last two classes. I need them right now!"

Non-assertive response: *Oh, okay. Here you go.*

Aggressive response: *Forget it! Quit whining and complaining. You're an idiot and you are not touching any of my notes again.*

Assertive response: *I will not be able to lend you my notes. I also need them to study for the test.*

To assert yourself in a conversation, maintain a straight posture, keep your body well balanced and use gestures that support your key words. Choose words that express your feelings and needs and that do not insult the other person. For example, if a classmate asks you out, you can say no in an assertive manner that should not hurt the feelings of that person. You can say, "Thank you for the invitation, but I would prefer not to go out with you." This is better than being non-assertive by going when you don't want to or by making up some sort of excuse of being busy that evening, which only leaves you open to being asked again. Telling the person to "get lost" is aggressive and hurtful. Being open and assertive in your communication will help you to keep honesty in your relations with others and to have your needs met in a fair and non-manipulative way. Try the box below to improve your skills in assertiveness.

SKILLS PRACTICE:

Assertive Responses

Below are several statements. For each one, practise an assertive reply. You may want to practise with a partner who can help verify whether your responses are assertive, non-assertive or aggressive. Tip: Remember that an assertive response makes your needs known without demeaning or belittling the other person.

1. You are at a shopping mall and are just about to leave to go and pick up your friend from work. Just as you approach the exit, a person who is obviously taking surveys approaches you: "Hi, my name is Jenny and we are doing a consumer survey. It will only take a few minutes. If you would just come and sit over here, we can get started right away."

2. You are just about to approach your boss to book next Saturday off. You have worked every Saturday for three months, and your partner is counting on you to attend a wedding next weekend for a very close friend. When your boss sees you, the boss says: "Great, there you are. I was just on my way to find you. We have a really big shipment coming in at the end of next week. You'll need to put in a few extra hours over and above your usual weekend time."

3. Your partner is really excited and has asked you to join him or her at a concert for one of his or her favourite groups. You really hate this group and would prefer to have a quiet evening. You do not mind if he or she goes to the concert. He or she says: "I'm so excited about this concert! I can't believe I actually got the tickets!"

Use Self-Disclosure Appropriately

We have many different relationships in our lives. Some of them are close and intimate while others are temporary and are encountered in our professional lives. In Chapter 1 we examined the continuum of self-disclosure or intimacy. In some relationships, we disclose more than in other relationships because of the difference in level of intimacy. When communicating with others, especially in professional settings and relationships, we need to be aware of what we are telling the other person. For example, a victim of a violent crime does not need to hear about how you have apprehended such perpetrators in the past. Instead, concentrate on reassuring that all will be done to apprehend this suspect while you interview for necessary details.

Be Accurate and Communicate Clearly

Some people reply to a question incoherently with stammers and the like. Others use language that we cannot understand, such as jargon or complex vocabulary. When you talk to someone, speak clearly and be as accurate as possible with your choice of words, especially during a professional task. On the other hand, if you are the listener and do not understand the speaker, do not hesitate to ask for clarification. Teachers will peruse the room to gauge student understanding. If there is a sea of confused looks, the teacher will backtrack and repeat the content in a different way or ask if clarification is required. We should do the same when we talk to others; if you feel you are losing your audience, ask if the message has been understood.

Make Allowances for Cultural, Gender and Individual Differences

In Chapter 4 we discussed a number of cultural differences that affect nonverbal communication. These same differences also have an impact on a verbal exchange. East Asians do not touch as often; this does not mean they are cold and aloof. Many other Asian cultures do not engage in high levels of contact; this does not mean that they are not interested in the speaker. Women more than men may engage in touching. Refer back to Chapter 4 to review some of these conclusions, and more differences will be highlighted in Chapter 7 on diversity.

Also, people are individuals. We grew up in different families and have unique personalities. When people are strangers to us, we can misinterpret their behaviour and what they say to us. Some people are shy and have a difficult time initiating and maintaining conversations (Hendersen and Zimbardo, 1996). Some people grew up in families where there was lots of touching, hugging and other verbal and nonverbal gestures of affection, whereas some people grew up in more reserved family atmospheres. As we meet people and get to know them in our personal and professional lives, we have to remember that these individual differences do lead to different reactions and ways of interacting in conversations. Therefore, before you become defensive, or when you become confused, take time to check out your perceptions using active listening, clarification of questions or other questions to increase your own understanding of the situation.

If you feel overwhelmed with the number of suggestions mentioned, remember that the purpose is to assist you in becoming a more effective communicator. Try adding a couple of skills to your current strategies until you feel comfortable with using the new strategies. Add a couple more and so on. No one is a "perfect" communicator, but we can all become "better" communicators.

SUMMARY

In this chapter we explored verbal communication. First, we examined the characteristics of words. As symbols, words are arbitrary, ambiguous and abstract. Words have two levels of meaning: a literal level and a subjective level. Words can also have power.

Next, we reviewed seven barriers that interfere with effective verbal communication. Seven barriers were identified: words can have different meanings, words can be imprecise, making generalizations and using extremes, biased and loaded language, cultural differences, rigid thinking and treating inferences as if they were facts.

Two communication climates were identified. The supportive climate allows for open and honest communication, whereas the defensive climate operates to destroy or impede true attempts at open and honest communication. Ways to maintain a more supportive climate were discussed. Establishing a supportive climate was the first of 10 strategies that were discussed to improve our ability to communicate more effectively with others. As well as establishing a supportive climate, using I-language and active listening, being other-oriented, using empathy, demonstrating respect, not interrupting, being honest and assertive, self-disclosing appropriately, being accurate and communicating clearly and allowing for cultural and individual differences were all presented as strategies.

JOURNAL AND DISCUSSION QUESTIONS

1. What do you see as essential interpersonal skills for a police officer? Why? Which of the skills do you find the most difficult to practice? Why? Which ones are easiest for you? Why?

2. Research on shyness indicates that shyness is widespread in North America? Why can shyness be a problem in our society?

3. Identify a conversation that you have had recently that did not turn out the way you would have liked. Perhaps, a conflict started or you did not get the points across as you had intended. What were the main causes of the problems in the conversation? What might you have done differently to avoid the problems?

4. Many of your calls and dealings with the public as an officer will involve communicating with individuals who have been drinking. What do you view as essential skills for these types of contacts?

WEB SITES

www.shyness.com

This site has a large amount of research and information on shyness and social phobia.

www.open.gov.uk/home_off/prghome.html

A police site that contains information and some research on a variety of topics in social science.

www.oape.org

This is the site of the Ontario Association of Police Educators.

www.cpc.gc/links_e.html

Use this site to link up with many law and justice agencies as well as various police agencies.

REFERENCES

Steven A. Beebe, Susan J. Beebe, Mark V. Redmond and Carol Milstone (1997). *Interpersonal Communication: Relating to Others.* Scarborough, ON: Allyn and Bacon Canada.

Joseph A. Devito (1996). *Messages: Building Interpersonal Skills.* New York: Harper Collins College Publishers.

Andrew J. Dubrin and Terri Geerinck (1998). *Human Relations for Career and Personal Success,* Canadian edition. Scarborough, ON: Prentice Hall Canada.

Lynne Hendersen and Philip Zimbardo (1996). Shyness, *Encyclopedia of Mental Health,* On-line. www.shyness.com/encyclopedia.html

Murlene "Mac" McKinnon (1993). Looking Glass Cops, in Ed Nowicki (Ed.), *Total Survival,* pp. 239–248, Powers Lake, WI: Performance Dimensions Publishing.

David W. McRoberts (1993). Courtroom Demeanor and Testimony, in Ed Nowicki (Ed.), *Total Survival,* pp. 249-259, Powers Lake, WI: Performance Dimensions Publishing.

Albert Mehrabian (1972). *Nonverbal Communication.* Reading, MA: Addison-Wesley, p. 108.

Andrew Phillips (1994). Fear and hope at home: Social changes caused by WW II, *Maclean's,* June 6.

Julia Wood, Ron Sept, and Jane Duncan (1998). *Everyday Encounters: An Introduction to Interpersonal Communication.* Scarborough, ON: ITP Nelson.

CONFLICT MANAGEMENT SKILLS

LEARNING OUTCOMES

After studying this chapter you should be able to:

1. Define conflict.
2. Outline the major causes of conflict.
3. Differentiate among five conflict management styles.
4. Explain effective strategies for managing conflict.
5. Compare effective strategies with ineffective methods of conflict management.
6. Define and identify the four stages of a crisis.
7. Explain strategies to prevent a crisis.
8. Explain strategies to manage a crisis.
9. Discuss use of force by police officers.

Situation #1: An officer has been dispatched to deal with a person who is creating a disturbance outside a small office building. When the officer arrives, he sees the person talking incoherently to himself. He is wearing dirty clothes, is unshaven and is acting like he is drunk. The officer thinks to himself, "Another nut out on the loose." The officer gets out of his car and approaches the man.

Officer: *Hey there, how are you doing?*

Male: *Huh! You talking to me, officer?*

Officer: *Yes, I am sir. Are you having any difficulty? You seem to be having a problem.*

Good conflict resolution skills can lead to positive outcomes.

Male: *I'm not having any problems. I am exercising my rights as a free man. I have every right to be on this street and I can protest! That's legal too! These bums kicked me out of my apartment! And I'm doing something about it! I'm protesting!*

Officer: *You don't have any rights to behave this way! So move on down the street and attend to whatever other things you need to do.*

Male: *What other things? They took away my home! They don't care and you don't care either! You're just another guy out to hassle me!*

Officer: *Calm down!*

Male: *Don't you go telling me to calm down!!*

Officer: *You really need to take a few breaths here buddy!*

Situation 2: An officer and her male partner have been called to a home where a loud party is taking place. It is just after 3:00 a.m. on a Tuesday night. After repeated and loud knocking, the door is finally answered. The individual stares at the officers, and it is obvious he is quite drunk. There are several voices in the background, blaring music and a couple of voices are at the level of shouting.

Female officer: *Excuse me, sir. We have had a report of a loud party here. We are going to have to ask that you please turn down the music and noise level.*

Male: *Oh, I'm sorry that it got so loud. I guess no one can have a good time in this neighbourhood. Probably, Ms. Busybody across the street is all upset. She's just dying to be part of the action, but I can't stand the ____! Why don't you come in and join us? Just leave that guy out here. We're low on girls and you look real curvy.*

Female officer: *Sir, I am not coming in. I am requesting that you turn the music down immediately.*

Male: *Or what? Going to bring that baboon in with you and start smashing heads? Hey fella, are you deaf or what? Got nothing to say?*

Male officer: *If you do not comply with the request, I'm afraid we will have to come in and assist you in ending this party.*

Male: *Try it!* (Attempts to fight male officer)

After reading these two situations, can you identify what went wrong in each case or did nothing go wrong? Both situations involve officers being called to handle disturbances, and both situations involved conflict. Conflict is a part of life. But for many of us, conflict and managing conflict are also part of our professional lives. The very nature of police duties "requires police officers to participate in confrontational situations" (Dantzker and Mitchell, 1998, p. 199). In police work how you manage conflict can be the difference between life and death in some situations. Police officers are more likely to find themselves in confrontations and in confrontations involving the use of force than other professionals or citizens

(Dantzker and Mitchell, 1998). A common conflict situation for police officers is dealing with individuals who have been drinking or who are under the influence of other drugs. At other times, conflict with the public, co-workers, members of other agencies and other law enforcement personnel can just be inconvenient and just another daily hassle. In this chapter we will take a closer look at conflict. We will look at what conflict is, the causes of conflict, the types of conflict and how people manage conflict. We often do not manage conflict well, so we want to devote much of this chapter to improving your conflict management skills. Next, we will examine crisis and crisis management. Situations can escalate very quickly into a crisis, or you may step into one already in full swing. Learning some crisis intervention techniques will end this section on crisis management. Last, we will take a very brief look at the use of force guidelines for police officers.

DEFINING CONFLICT: GOOD OR BAD?

Both opening situations illustrate a conflict. **Conflict** is a condition that occurs when two sets of demands, goals or motives are incompatible (Dubrin and Geerinck, 1997). In both situations the police officers are interfering with the motives and goals of the two males. One male wishes to continue his party, and the other male wishes to continue his "protest." When people experience such differences, antagonistic or hostile relations may begin between the two parties.

Conflict cannot be avoided. Even when we try to ignore the signs of an impending conflict, eventually we have to face it. Often we avoid conflict because we are fearful of the many negative consequences that accompany a poorly managed conflict. Prolonged conflict can lead to stress and impair your emotional and physical well being (Dubrin and Geerinck, 1997). In conflict, we may ignore the needs of family, our profession and society (Dubrin and Geerinck, 1997). Embroiled in conflict at work, an employee may be short-tempered at home and take out his or her professional frustrations out on those at home. Unresolved or poorly resolved conflicts can lead to further problems in a relationship. An employee can make costly mistakes on the job by not paying attention and by letting his or her mind wander. An extreme negative consequence is violence at home or on the job. We have read about incidents where disgruntled employees engage in violence or sabotage at the workplace.

Another reason we may hesitate to engage in conflict is the type of family we grew up in and how conflict was managed in the home. Families that do not voice differences or that do so in inappropriate ways make us uncomfortable to manage conflict when we are older. However, we need to realize that conflict can have many positive consequences. When faced with conflict, we may come up with novel solutions and ideas, and new talents and abilities may emerge. People can become closer as managing conflict may lead to heightened understanding of others. Managed properly, conflict may be an opportunity for you to achieve personal and/or professional goals. As future police officers, learning how to manage conflict with members of the public is an essential professional skill. Therefore, it is in your best interest to learn good conflict management skills.

CAUSES OF CONFLICT

While conflicts seem to be very individual, we can actually divide the causes of conflict into six major types. Often when we think about conflict, we think about people having heated arguments. In reality, whatever the cause, conflict can be overt or covert. **Overt conflicts** are conflicts that are openly discussed. **Covert conflicts** are hidden. When a covert conflict occurs, people may hide their feelings and express them indirectly in a variety of ways. People may play "games" or deliberately hurt the feelings of another person when they feel angry or hurt. You may have had an experience when someone does not come out and tell you what the problem is directly but expresses his or her discontent in more indirect ways, such as picking fights about unimportant or inconsequential things. Although we do not have time to deal with all of the ways that covert conflict occurs, be aware that they can and do happen. Eric Berne (1964) wrote a classic book on interpersonal games entitled *The Games People Play*. To learn more about these games you may want to read this book. The following are some of the major causes of conflict.

Competition for Limited Resources

When there is only so much to go around and everyone wants at least part of something, conflict is bound to occur as people compete for those resources. Think of three children fighting over the last two chocolate chip cookies, adults in a business setting trying to allocate limited funding to a wide range of corporate needs or of police management trying to allocate too few officers over a wide area. Differences of opinion about allocation of limited resources may result in conflict.

Differences Between Personalities and Cultures

Personality and cultural differences may also be a potential source of conflict. For instance, one police manager may be a strong supporter of crime prevention and therefore wants to assign more officers to prevention posts than another police manager does. This difference in beliefs may create conflict. In Canada, there have been many conflicts that have their roots in cultural differences and values. These conflicts become larger when entire groups adopt one attitude or belief over another. At times, these personal differences may result in a **personality clash** (Dubrin and Geerinck, 1997). A personality clash is an antagonistic relationship between two people due to differences in characteristics and attributes, preferences, interests, values and personal styles. It may be difficult for two people to work together with such an antagonistic relationship between them.

One good example of the possibility of conflict due to a personality clash in policing is the type of policing style an officer may adopt. Although based largely on American research, there are different styles of policing, and these styles have fundamental differences (Greenberg and Ruback, 1982; Walsh, 1977). For instance, Greenberg and Ruback (1982) have identified four different styles: *crime fighter, social servant, law enforcer* and *watchman*. The *crime fighter* is focused on capturing the perpetrator and does so in an authoritarian and aggressive manner. The *social servant* identifies that the major part of his or her job is to help others. The *law enforcer* enforces all the laws rather than focusing on the more aggressive pursuits of the crime fighter. The *watchman* does no more than what is required and often displays an uncaring attitude. The crime fighter may not agree with much of what the social servant feels and may even be critical of the helping attitude. On the other hand, the social servant may disagree with the aggressiveness of the crime fighter. These different styles may be the "seeds" of future conflict.

Different Priorities and Goals

In our opening situations there are definitely differences between the priorities and the goals of both the officers and the citizens. The priorities and goals of the officers are to uphold the law and maintain public peace. Both males are interfering with these goals and priorities as they have different priorities and goals. We may often share the goals but may place them in different order of priority. A father may want his son to find a job immediately after finishing college. The son may also share this goal but not the immediacy. The son does not see finding a job as a priority and another goal of having some fun may be higher on the "priority list."

Role Conflict

Role conflict occurs when we experience two competing demands or expectations. These demands or expectations can cause internal conflict but may also create conflict between two people. On the one hand, your partner wants you to earn good money so you take as much overtime as you can get. Then your partner starts to complain that you are not home enough. So what can you do? As an officer, do you really want to arrest the man in the first situation? He is "disturbing the peace," but you may also feel sorry for him. As is often the case, you have to use discretion as to what you are going to do. This may create internal role conflict that may manifest itself in conflict with your partner or superior officer.

The Building of Stone Walls

Richard J. Mayer (1990) referred to the slow and steady growth of a conflict as the building of a stone wall. Some conflicts begin with something minor, a *pinch*, that is not managed immediately or as it should be. The individual who receives the pinch starts to unconsciously gather evidence to support his or her viewpoint. In policing, this pinch could be an arrest that an individual does not feel the officer conducted properly. However, much of this information is distorted because of the perception of the person. These incidents build up to become a *wall* that becomes difficult to overcome. The person who has been pinched may not be able to overcome this barrier and have open and honest communication with the *pincher*. Another example to illustrate the long-term effects is a police officer being praised for how she handled a situation when it was really the partner who handled the situation well. The police officer does not mention that it is the partner who deserves the credit. This becomes the minor incident, or pinch. The officer who has been pinched now starts to notice other evidence that this person is not honest. Before long, these two officers begin to argue, and it becomes more and more difficult for them to work together. If the officer had approached the officer at the beginning, the rest of the situation would not have developed into an ongoing "war."

CONFLICT MANAGEMENT STYLES

Regardless of the cause of a conflict, we often manage conflict by relying on a particular style. A discussion of these five styles, or orientations, will help you to better understand the nature of conflict and the different ways that people handle a conflict. Kenneth Thomas (1976) identified these styles as competitive, accommodative, compromising or sharing, collaborative and avoidance. Each style is based on how concerned you are about satisfying your own needs and achieving your own goals and how concerned you are about the other person's needs and goals. In other words, the styles vary in how concerned you are about yourself versus how concerned you are for the other. Refer to Figure 6-1 where the five styles are plotted in a graph.

- **Competition.** Competition is based on the idea of **win-lose**. One party has his or her needs and goals met while the other party loses. There is very little concern about the other person's thoughts or feelings. People who rely on competition can be aggressive and argumentative.

- **Accommodation.** When using accommodation, you are more concerned with satisfying the other's concerns rather than with taking care of your own needs and goals. This person puts the other person's needs ahead of his or her own and can be called self-sacrificing or generous. For instance, if you go along with a friend who wants to go bowling even though you preferred going to a movie, you are accommodating your friend's needs.

- **Compromising.** When you compromise or share, both parties get at least part of what he or she wanted. You state that you will go bowling tonight if next week your friend accompanies you to a movie.

- **Collaboration.** Collaboration is based on the idea of **win-win** where both parties can get what they want. When you use a win-win strategy, you are genuinely concerned with satisfying both your needs and the needs of the other party. You discuss that the reason your friend does not want to see a movie is because he or she would prefer to do something more active than sitting. You state that while you don't mind being active, bowling doesn't exactly thrill you because you are not very good at it. After some discussion you both decide to go golfing. One party has his or her needs met and you get to do an activity that you are skilled at.

- **Avoidance.** People who rely on avoidance can be both uncooperative and unassertive (do not voice their needs). This type of person may physically or mentally withdraw from the conflict and has little concern for his or her needs or the needs of the other person. This person may adopt a "who cares" attitude. For example, you propose bowling and the reply is "Ya, whatever." You press further for a commitment to a plan, and the reply "I don't care" is next. This type of conflict is **lose-lose** as neither person gains anything from such a conflict.

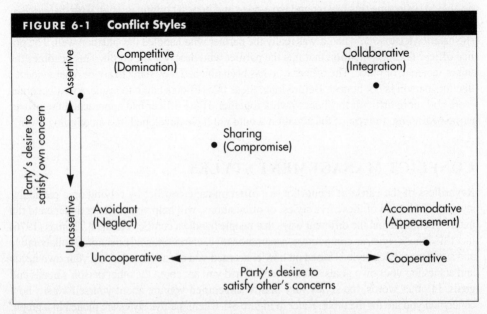

FIGURE 6-1   Conflict Styles

Source: Kenneth W. Thomas, "Organizational Conflict," in Steven Kerr, Ed., *Organizational Behaviour* (Columbus, Ohio: Grid Publishing, 1979), p. 156.

All of these styles or orientations are neither correct nor incorrect. Any style may be correct if it matches how important the goal is to you (satisfying your own concerns) and how important it is that you also satisfy the goals and concerns of the other person. For example, if the relationship and the individual goals of each party are very important, collaboration is the right strategy to choose. If your goals are not that important but those of the other person are, you might choose to use accommodation. For example, if you don't care what you do as long as you get out for an evening, you can go along with your friend's choice of activity. We could re-label the X-axis "Importance of the Relationship" to assist you in your choice of strategy. In reality, we often do not make a conscious choice of style, and many of us rely on a preferred style that may not always be appropriate. One essential conflict management strategy therefore is to choose a style that suits both the conflict and the relationship.

CONFLICT MANAGEMENT STRATEGIES

In this section we will review effective methods of conflict management from a variety of texts and articles (Beebe et al., 1997; Devito, 1995; Devito, 1996; Dubrin and Geerinck, 1997; Tannen, 1998; Wood et al., 1998). For several methods we will compare the effective method with some of the more inappropriate ways that are often the opposite of the recommended method. As you become involved with a conflict, you may choose one or several strategies to help you. It should be noted that not all conflicts can be "managed" or solved. If they could be, there would be fewer divorces! At times, you and the other party may have to realize that some issues may never be resolved. You may have to reconcile yourself to the notion that you may have areas of disagreement in even the closest of relationships and that such differing views do not mean the end of the relationship. For example, two friends have differing opinions on the issue of abortion. Rather than continued heated debate about who is wrong or right, they may "agree to disagree" on that topic. However, "armed" with good strategies, you will be able to solve more interpersonal problems and conflicts than you would without having these strategies available.

Choose an Appropriate Conflict Management Style

When experiencing conflict with another person, you need to ask yourself a couple of questions. First, how important is this relationship to me? Second, how important is this issue or goal? If the goal and the relationship are important, then you will want to use collaboration or compromise to manage the conflict. If the issue is more important than the relationship, you may need to adopt the competitive and more aggressive style. If an individual refuses to comply with a police officer's order to stop a loud party, the officer will have to use more force to gain compliance. If the issue is not important to you and neither is the relationship, avoidance may be the most appropriate strategy. For example, if you are at the supermarket and a stranger "buds in line" in front of you, should you now engage in conflict? If you are in no hurry and your ice cream is not going to melt in the next 30 seconds, it may be better to simply avoid the situation. Accommodation is used when the relationship is more important than the issue or your goals. If a friend really wants to go to a concert of a group that you do not like, you go along to please your friend. The real key is to choose the right style to match your goals and what you want from the exchange.

Control Your Emotions

When we experience strong emotions, we also experience heightened physiological arousal (Baron et al., 1997). Anger, frustration, fear, sadness and happiness all create physiological responses. For example, when you are angry do you feel your heartbeat increase, do you turn red in the face, clench your teeth? When we are in this state, we may not be objective. Think about the discussion of road rage in Chapter 3. The old advice of "counting to 10" may be a good one when we want to manage our emotions. If you feel that your emotions are too intense for a discussion, you may want to request that you discuss this issue at another time and set a time to meet again. This will give you time to "cool down" and plan what you want to say.

If you do not give yourself time to control your emotions, you may regret the things that you say and do. Some people in the heat of debate launch into name-calling, engage in personal attacks and become overly emotional, losing all objectivity. Some people become physically violent and may lose control. Such displays may only escalate the conflict into something worse that may be hard to "back out of" later. In the second situation, the male has decided to fight, and this may lead to legal consequences for him. Police officers may have to work hard to control their body language to display a more neutral demeanour in a conflict situation with members of the public.

Use Empathy and Practise Being Other-Oriented

According to Devito (1996, p. 389), a "frequently used fight strategy is to blame someone." In a relationship, we try to find out whose fault the event is and may attribute motives to the other person. If one officer blames the other officer's style on a liberal upbringing and lack of discipline, this blaming does little to resolve the conflict. These motives and attributes are not necessarily true and may further remove the two parties from actively trying to resolve the real problem at the root of the conflict.

Instead of blaming the other person, use empathy and be other-oriented. Try to understand what the other person is really feeling, what his or her thoughts and motives could be from the other perspective. The officer may not have had a liberal and undisciplined upbringing. He or she may be an individual who deeply believes that his or her role as an officer is to help everyone regardless of circumstances. Once the other officer fully understands, he or she may not be so ready to discuss the issue further. Verbally express your empathy, "I can understand you being angry. I really should not have called you a 'bleeding-heart liberal.' It was an unkind thing to say." Empathy does not mean that you agree with the other person; it forms a basis for further understanding and further interpersonal communication.

Be Open and Honest

At times we are reluctant to engage in conflict for many reasons. We may lack assertiveness, we may be afraid we may hurt another's feelings and we may even be afraid of possible retaliation. When we are reluctant to manage a conflict, we may not be open and honest about the issues and about our feelings. Instead, we do not tell the truth. We say nothing is wrong and keep our feelings to ourselves, refuse to talk about what is troubling us, talk about irrelevant concerns or downplay the conflict. A consequence of not dealing with the conflict may be the building of stone walls, and it may become more difficult to manage the conflict as feelings become hardened and anger develops. If people do not discuss their differences, it may become harder to do so as time passes.

If the issue is important and maintaining the relationship is important (whether it is a personal or professional relationship), conflict needs to be dealt with honestly and openly. Referring to conflict management styles, collaboration should be used, or, depending upon the level of importance, compromise may be another option. Both strategies rely on expressing what you want in an open and honest manner.

Maintain Your Focus on the Present

In our first situation the male starts to discuss what has happened in the past. Have you ever had the experience in a conflict where suddenly everything that you did wrong in the past is brought up? You are late picking up your partner, but an old grievance from last summer is suddenly being discussed.

During a conflict it is important to stay in the present and discuss the current conflict. If there are other issues, now is not the time to discuss them. You may want to state something like, "I understand that last summer is still bothering you, but let's continue with what the current problem is. We can discuss last summer at another time if you wish."

Be Assertive, Not Aggressive

Many strategies rely on you being able to express yourself in an assertive way. Remember that people who are assertive state what they want in a direct way. People who are assertive can express themselves without infringing upon another person's rights. During a conflict, assertive people express their feelings, thoughts and views in a straightforward manner. See the Skills Practice box for a "crash course" on how to be assertive.

SKILLS PRACTICE:

Using Assertiveness to Manage Conflict

Many people struggle with shyness and/or the inability to be more assertive. Do you ever back down in response to someone's request even though you do not want to do it? Do you have trouble telling someone what you truly feel or think, so you just keep pretending that you feel the way he or she thinks you do? Do you have trouble expressing your view on a certain issue or idea? If you have answered "yes" to any of these questions, you may be having difficulty being assertive. Working in law enforcement requires a high degree of ability to be assertive with the public and to project an attitude of competence and authority. Below are some tips, adopted from several texts and sources, that should help you become more assertive (Beebe et al., 1997; Dubrin and Geerinck, 1997; Zimbardo, 1977; Shyne, 1982).

1. **Rehearse a Difficult Situation.** If a particular situation is one in which you need to develop your assertiveness, rehearse what you are going to say. Like an actor, memorizing your lines may help you when you get nervous in the

situation. If it is helpful, rehearse with someone who can give you feedback on your lines. For example, a student was convinced that a mark she received on a paper was much lower than necessary. She wanted to talk to the teacher about it but was afraid of "how it might look" if she questioned the grade. By rehearsing what she was going to say with the help of another teacher, she was more confident in approaching the teacher.

2. **Practise the broken record technique.** Some people do not take "no" for an answer, and it can be difficult to maintain your stand in the face of some crafty onslaughts that work on trying to make you feel guilty or that you owe someone. Using the broken record technique, you just continue to refuse and repeat your viewpoint without showing frustration or anger. For example, if someone is trying to get you to assist with homework that he or she should complete by himself or herself, you calmly state, "No, you must do it on your own." At every angle and corner, simply repeat the statement. Usually the person will stop making the request.

3. **Know your rights and know where to go if your rights have been violated.** You have rights as a person and as a citizen. For instance, if approaching your landlord has not changed problems with your apartment, you can get assistance from agencies that will be assertive for you. Read the Human Rights Act and other documents so that you know where you stand on a wide range of rights.

4. **Practise conversations with strangers.** If you are shy and find yourself stumbling over words when trying to meet people you would really like to get to know, practise with strangers where it does not matter so much if you stumble. In a long line, comment on how long you have been waiting. Such small exchanges may help you with the bigger and more important ones later.

5. **Monitor your nonverbal and verbal communication.** Part of being assertive is to look assertive. Walk with confidence with head high, shoulders back and a purposeful stride. Speak clearly, loudly enough to be heard, and do not use "ums" and "ahs." Do not end statements as if they are questions. For example, a non-assertive person states, " I, ah, think I would, ah, like, ah, a coffee?" An assertive person states, "I would like to have a coffee."

6. **Use I statements and state your feelings and goals.** Assertive people state their feelings and goals directly without violating the rights of others. They do not allow others to play games, use intimidation or other ploys to get them to go along or to do something that they personally disagree with for their own reasons. "I do not wish to go out on a date with you" is an assertive statement. If the person launches into other statements, simply repeat your position (broken record).

These are just a few strategies. Shyness can be more difficult to change and requires more time, effort and strategies than what is listed here. A shy person may want to look at the web sites at the back of this chapter for further assistance. However, we can all benefit by being more assertive when standing up for our rights and ideas. If people can practice being assertive, they are less likely to use aggressive strategies or give in to others.

Unfortunately, many people use aggression when faced with conflict, anger and frustration. Police officers often deal with angry and aggressive people. **Anger** is an emotion that includes feelings of hostility, indignation and frustration. When people become angry, they can become highly argumentative, openly hostile and/or physically aggressive. Judgment can become impaired (Dubrin and Geerinck, 1997). We will deal with the hostile and physical consequences of anger later in the section on crisis management.

Many people when they are angry engage in verbal aggression. According to Deborah Tannen (1998), North America has an argument culture. This culture has lead many of us to approach any issue in an adversarial way where there are only two sides rather than grey areas or a middle ground. The ability to argue is not necessarily negative, but people who are highly argumentative may argue unnecessarily and too forcefully (Devito, 1996). Becoming highly argumentative may lead to managing a conflict using the competitive style where the goal of winning is done at the expense of the relationship. Before getting into a heated debate, ask yourself "Is it worth it?" "How important is maintaining the relationship?" At times, it may be worth the risk if the issue is extremely important to you. For example, if you truly believe that child pornography should be illegal, you may argue strongly for your view. If you do engage in an argument, you can keep it from becoming verbal aggression by focusing only on the issue, avoiding personal attacks, taking turns and refraining from interrupting, expressing interest in the other viewpoint and allowing for **face-saving** (Infante, 1988).

Use Effective Responding and Listening Skills

During conflict we do not always pay attention to how we are saying things. We interrupt, misinterpret, make assumptions and generally do not use very good responding and listening skills. Although we have discussed some of these in prior chapters, we will briefly list the skills here:

- **Use I-language.** The feelings that you have are your feelings. Avoid statements such as "You make me so mad," "You don't understand" and "You never ...." Describe what you feel and what your perceptions are with I language. "I feel really mad when you don't call when you are going to be late."

- **Describe the conflict-producing events clearly.** When emotions are high, we are not always very coherent. Stay calm and state clearly what is on your mind. Ask for feedback if the other person looks puzzled or does not appear to understand.

- **Pay attention to nonverbal language.** During conflict, nonverbal cues are important. For example, someone may say that he or she is not angry, but nonverbally he or she may be demonstrating anger or defensiveness. Use the nonverbal language to check and maintain the communication. For example, "You tell me that you are not upset, but you keep wringing your hands. Is something still bothering you?"

- **Use effective listening skills.** When we are upset or when others are upset, we need to use effective listening skills. You may want to paraphrase what the speaker has said to verify that you have heard the message correctly.

Manage the Conflict Using a Problem-Solving Approach

One way to view a conflict is to see the conflict as a problem that requires a solution. If both parties can agree to sit down and solve the "problem," a better understanding can be reached with a mutually made and agreed-upon solution. If you can structure conflicts as problems to be solved, you are well on your way to seeking strategies to manage the issues that confront you and the other person involved with the conflict. There are many models of problem solving that can be used to assist in arriving at a solution. Most models rely on a set of defined steps. These models can be found in business texts, counselling texts and are actively used by many organizations, including police services. For example, the Ontario Provincial Police uses PARE Analysis. Because PARE Analysis is used by groups for making decisions it will be discussed in greater detail in Chapter 10. Here, we will focus on a very straightforward model that can be used for interpersonal conflict. Define the problem, analyze the problem, generate many possible solutions, select the best solution that achieves the goals of the conflicting parties, implement the solution and then finally evaluate the solution at a mutually agreed-upon date. For purposes of understanding the model, we will use an example of a policing style difference that is creating a problem for two officers who have recently been partnered. In the first two weeks of working together, twice one officer has responded to a call that should have been done by officers closer to the scene. This officer, Tara, appears to be more of a crime fighter and is very aggressive and has little patience for the social aspects of the job. On the other hand, Chan is very caring with victims and uses very little force with perpetrators. A few arguments have followed after several arrests, and Chan is becoming frustrated with Tara's behaviour. Tara has accused Chan of being "too soft" on several occasions.

1. **Define the Problem.**   Most conflicts and problems boil down to something you want more or less of. You can think of a problem as a "deviation" from where you would like to be or what you want regarding a specific issue. Chan prefers a higher focus on treating people with respect and answering a wide variety of calls. Tara is a crime fighter and wants to go after the offenders. Chan wants Tara to be less aggressive and more humane in her approach to policing. Make sure that you define the "real" problem and not just the symptoms. Lately, they have been fighting over small arrests, so they may need to spend some time talking about what is wrong and trying to understand each other. Rather than just dealing with symptoms (like a specific arrest or incident), they will need to get at the larger issue responsible for the conflict.

2. **Analyze the Problem.**   Next, analyze the problem to determine the cause of the conflict. When we analyze something, we reduce it or break it down into smaller pieces. With the other person, begin by describing the conflict-producing events in the order you feel they have happened. Describe the events in an unbiased way without evaluating the other person. Chan can describe the events that made him feel uncomfortable during the last couple of weeks, and Tara can do the same. You do not want to start an argument here. Remember that you are trying to get at the root of the conflict not start a new one! Is the conflict centred on one major issue or are there several issues? As Chan and Tara discuss the events, they discover that the conflicts they are experiencing are being generated by a basic philosophical difference in what they feel are the major goals of policing.

3. **Generate Solutions.**   For any problem there may be multiple solutions. Part of resolving a conflict using the problem-solving approach is to list as many solutions that could solve the problem. One of them could request a new partner. Both of them could request a new partner. They could continue on and do nothing. They could try to be more understanding of their differences and learn to work together effectively. Chan could

apply for a social worker position. Tara may want to try to get on a force where she could enjoy more opportunities for fighting crime, such as a tactical unit. The key at this stage is to generate solutions. Some of them may be strange, impossible or highly improbable; just keep up the momentum. You may even want to write them down.

4. **Evaluate the Solutions.** Once you have a few solutions, you need to evaluate them based on the goals of the individuals. For instance, Chan's goal is to remain a police officer so applying for social work positions would not help him with this goal. Requesting new partners is something that could be done, but how would it reflect on both officers in the future? Would they be evaluated as unable to get along with team members, or might there be other negative side effects of making this request? The two partners then decide that they will need to become more understanding of their different styles and philosophies of policing. But this is not a very concrete solution. Generate objective criteria for a solution. The more measurable, verifiable and objective the criteria, the greater the likelihood that both parties will be able to agree to the solution and implement it. They will need to refine this solution so that they both have a firm grasp of how they will behave differently with each other. Tara states that they will answer "crime-fighting calls" only when the calls are in their area. Chan states that while he will continue to be concerned with victims, he will end his conversations sooner by notifying an appropriate agency or by giving out the number of such an agency.

5. **Implement the Solution(s).** Once the solutions have been defined in clear terms, the solutions are then implemented.

6. **Set a Time to Re-evaluate the Chosen Solution(s).** It is not enough to agree to a solution. Both parties must live up to their end of the agreement. Once a solution has been agreed upon and implemented, many variables can get in the way of the intended goals. Therefore, particularly with long-term solutions, periodic checking is necessary to keep the parties focused and to examine if other problems are creeping into the solution. Chan and Tara agree to try their solutions for two weeks and set a time to discuss progress after work at that time.

CRISIS MANAGEMENT

Occasionally, a conflict can become a **crisis**. As many police officers and others in law enforcement can verify, routine calls can quickly become a state of crisis. There are several definitions of crisis. The common thread running through the definitions is that a crisis is a reaction to an event that goes beyond the individual's capability to cope with it at that time (Arnold, 1980; Golan, 1978). A crisis can be a sudden change or turn in behaviour, and often a crisis has the potential to become violent or may already be violent when officers arrive at the scene. By their very presence, officers can precipitate or escalate a situation just by showing up. The second situation escalated into physical confrontation and a state of active crisis. Could the officers have prevented this? This last section will examine the stages of a crisis, discuss preventative strategies to avoid a crisis and offer crisis intervention techniques. A very brief look at use of force will conclude the chapter.

Crises appear to go through a set of identifiable stages (see Arnold, 1980; Golan 1978). Although labelled differently depending upon the research source, there are four stages. First, there is the *hazardous event,* which may be one event or a series of events that trigger stress. Second, the impact of this event throws a person "off balance" and places him or her in a *vulnerable state.* If the problem continues, tension continues to rise, and a *precipitating factor* (sometimes called a turning point) can occur that no longer allows for the individual to use his or her current coping mechanisms. This is the third state of *active crisis.* During an active crisis, an individual may act out aggressively or turn inward and withdraw. The fourth phase is *adaption* where an individual adapts and changes to cope with the crisis.

Crisis Indicators Before a Crisis

How can you tell if a conflict or intervention is about to turn into a crisis? There are many signs that an officer needs to be aware of that will help him or her gauge if an attack or other crisis is imminent (Ouellette, 1996; McKenna, 1998). First, *the nonverbal language* of the attacker will change. The person may move into a defensive stance with the feet moving to shoulder distance apart and the strong foot moving back. The eyes may shift to an escape route or glance at a target such as the chin of the officer or the officer's gun. The person may appear more agitated, may use more gestures and may engage in more fidgeting. The person may begin to talk louder or may begin shouting. Personal space may change as he or she tries to get closer for an attack or tries to get further away for flight.

The verbal content may also change. The person may start to swear, engage in name-calling and may attempt to verbally aggravate the officer for a confrontation with such statements as "What kind of a man are you?" or "Throw down your gun and I'll show you who's the boss." They may also start to talk about weapons or acts of violence. At this point, you want to engage in **crisis prevention** to avoid a continued escalation and possible physical intervention. Below are 10 tips for preventing a crisis from the Crisis Prevention Institute (1986).

SKILLS PRACTICE:

Ten Tips for Crisis Prevention

1. **Be empathic.** Try not to be judgmental of the other person's feelings. They are real even if not based on reality and must be attended to.

2. **Clarify messages.** Listen to what is really being said. Ask reflective questions, and use both silence and restatements (paraphrasing).

3. **Respect personal space.** Stand at least one and a half to three feet from the acting out person. Encroaching on personal space tends to arouse and escalate an individual.

4. **Be aware of body position.** Standing eye to eye, toe to toe with the person sends a challenging message. Standing one length away and at an angle off to the side is less likely to escalate the individual.

5. **Permit verbal venting when possible.** Allow the individual to release as much energy as possible by venting verbally. If this cannot be allowed, state directives and reasonable limits during lulls in the venting process.

6. **Set and enforce reasonable limits.** If the individual becomes belligerent, de-

fensive or disruptive, state limits and directives clearly and concisely.

7. **Avoid overreacting.** Remain calm, rational and professional. How you the officer, or other personnel, responds will directly affect the individual.

8. **Use physical techniques as a last resort.** Use the least restrictive method of intervention possible. Employing physical techniques on an individual who is only acting out verbally can escalate the situation.

9. **Ignore challenge.** When the client challenges your position, training, etc., redirect the individual's attention to the issue at hand. Answering these questions often fuels a power struggle.

10. **Keep your nonverbal cues non-threatening.** Be aware of your body language, movement and tone of voice. The more an individual loses control, the less he listens to your actual words. More attention is paid to your nonverbal cues.

From www.crisisprevention.com, Crisis Prevention Institute Inc., © 1986. Reprinted with permission.

Crisis Intervention Strategies

Often, no matter how hard you try, a situation can escalate into a crisis. As an officer, you may enter into a crisis that is already taking place, such as a domestic incident, an incident involving impaired individuals or other violent crime scene. Other courses will go into more detail about tactics and strategies to defuse violence. Also, many different and specialized units manage the types of crises that police may encounter, such as emergency task forces, hostage rescue teams, hostage negotiation and domestic violence teams (McKenna, 1998). In this text we want to concentrate on the interpersonal components of managing a crisis that may occur during regular patrol. First, you need to quickly assess the situation. If the person is in immediate danger to himself or herself or to others, you may need to react quickly with physical use of force. You may need to immediately call for other emergency assistance such as back-up, specialized force units, Children's Aid Society or an ambulance. If no other assistance is required and the crisis is non-violent, you can apply the strategies listed here that rely on the ability to communicate effectively.

Nonverbal Skills

Be Aware of Personal Space In a crisis people may need more personal space if they are agitated or hostile. You can allow as much as six feet unless you feel the person may attempt to flee.

Use Eye Contact Appropriately The proper use of your eye contact is an important nonverbal strategy. Eye contact by the officer can convey concern, support, confidence and authority. By reducing eye contact, the power role is lessened and the helper role is increased. Maintain eye contact but break it occasionally when the other person is speaking (Ouellette, 1996). As the Law and Justice Perspective box indicates, eye contact is a powerful tool to use for assessing potential aggression.

LAW AND JUSTICE PERSPECTIVE:

Watch the Space, Eyes and Gestures

One leading trainer in law enforcement and security writes that monitoring three areas of nonverbal communication can assist officers in decreasing their chances of being assaulted. The three areas are space, gestures and eye contact. Here are just a few of his suggestions:

Space:

- Allow enough space for control but do not violate personal space.

- Approach the person's weak side. Some ways to identify the weak side include nine out of ten people are right-handed, and we gesture with our strong hand.

Eyes:

- If the person's eyes alternate between the officers' eyes, chest and hands, this may indicate that the person is sizing the officers up.

- If the person's eyes dart from side to side or up and down, this may indicate agitation and that the person feels cornered by the officers.

- If the person's eyes are glazed, empty or appear to be "looking through the officers," this may indicate the person is drugged, drunk, deranged or has other medical problems. This may mean a higher potential for aggression.

- Target glances are when a person looks at his or her target before he or she attacks. For example, a person may look at the chin of an officer before trying to hit it. According to this author, there is usually a pause of at least four-tenths of a second between the target glance and the behaviour. This gives the officer a good advantage to react.

Gestures:

- If the face turns from red (anger) to white (rage), attack is imminent.

- Hands that are open and then become clenched into fists suggest that there is a good chance of being attacked.

- If the lips are pushed forward bearing the teeth, this means anger. If the lips are tight over the teeth, this indicates possible attack.

- If the aggressor is beyond the reach of the officer, the final gesture may be the individual lowering his or her body to push off for an attack.

Source: Roland Ouellette, President, REB Training International Inc. Management of Aggressive Behaviour, in Ed Nowicki (1996). *Total Survival.* pp. 289-297. Powers Lake, WI: Performance Dimensions Publishing. Printed with permission of the author and publisher.

Web site for REB Training International is www.rebtraining.com

Use Non-threatening Body Positions Do not stand directly in front of the other person. If both the person and the officer sit, this is not aggressive and can help open the door to verbal interaction (Ouellette, 1996). Not only is the probability of aggression reduced, people who have been victimized are more approachable if you let them sit down. Sitting has a calming effect as we usually relate sitting with relaxing activities such as eating and watching television.

Monitor Other Nonverbal Behaviour What are your hands doing? Are they clenched into fists, resting on your hips? Are your arms crossed? During a crisis situation it may be easy to forget many of the nonverbal communicators and what they may appear to be saying to the other person. Gestures should be natural as if you were speaking to a friend. This does not mean that you are not wary of the individual but that you do not want to give any signs of aggression. Pay attention to your nonverbal behaviour.

Demonstrate That You Are Listening The man in our second situation may have needed time to just vent his frustration and anger. The officer telling him to calm down cut off and interrupted this venting. At times you need to listen, and listening takes time. But time spent listening is better than time spent trying to defuse a violent attack. Use the strategies from Chapter 4 to demonstrate listening. Listening is a sign that you care on a professional and personal level.

Verbal Skills

What you say is also important and will demonstrate your relationship with the person. Officers need to remain courteous, although this may be difficult if being verbally assaulted.

Use Paraphrasing of Content and/or Feelings Both of the situations may have been handled more effectively if the officers had used some paraphrasing. For example, "I know when you're having a good time, it can be hard to call it to a close" can help defuse the second situation. In the first situation, paraphrasing and reflecting feelings may have helped. "It must be really upsetting to lose your home" might have reduced the anger instead of telling him to calm down. Statements such as "calm down" rarely produce the desired effect in a crisis.

Use Direct and Simple Language During a crisis, people may not be thinking clearly. It is best to use direct, clear and simple language. Keep your sentences short. If you need to issue a directive, state it firmly and clearly. Most tactical communication follows this simple rule.

Use Verbal Instructions to Remove Onlookers If people are watching what is going on, this may add fuel to the person who has lost or who is about to lose control. If it is possible, firmly ask onlookers to remove themselves from the immediate area. In the first situation, the officer would want to ask people who have come from inside the office to go back into the building.

Use Humour if Appropriate Sometimes laughter is the "best medicine" when used wisely. Make sure, however, that the humour does not include laughing at the person in crisis. For instance, a domestic violence victim who was in a lot of pain was lying on the floor waiting for an ambulance. The officers did not want to move her as she may have had a back injury. One officer kept her company. She suddenly noticed, from her reclining position, some dirt on her ceiling and made a funny comment to the officer. This small bit of humour helped to reduce the emotional level of the incident for both her and the officer.

USE OF FORCE

Often crises do require the use of force by police officers. What starts as a conflict may lead to a crisis and, even further, require the police to use force. Police officers must constantly assess situations and identify and act upon a plan in response to the behaviours of individuals. Police are authorized to use force by the provisions of the Criminal Code of Canada (section 25(1) and section 27). However, excessive use of force can be met with criminal and civil action (Dantzker and Mitchell, 1998). In essence, police officers may use force with their discretion but only as much force as required by the situation. Using force is a method of obtaining compliance or obedience to a request made by the officer, such as lowering a weapon or getting out of a vehicle. Proper use of force may not result in any injury to either the officer or the individual.

A continuum has been developed with four types of coercion (Dantzker and Mitchell, 1998). The first level is verbal, which includes promises and threats. The second level is physical, which includes using various physical restraint techniques. The third level includes the use of non-lethal weapons such as a baton or pepper spray. The fourth level is the use of lethal weapons that would normally be firearms. Police are supposed to assess the level of force being used by the individual and then respond with only a slightly higher use of force (Stansfield, 1996). Below (Figure 6-2) is a diagram of the Province of Ontario's Use of Force Response Options for you to examine as you may be trained in the use of force if you continue to pro-

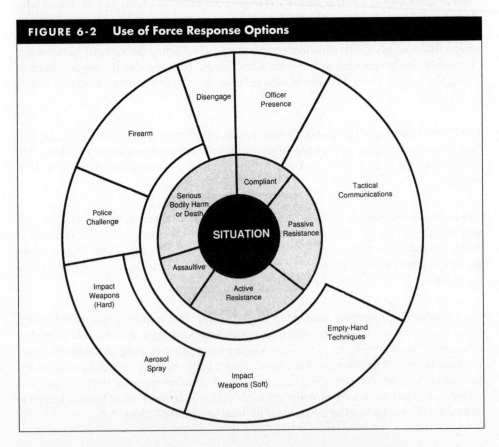

FIGURE 6-2   Use of Force Response Options

FIGURE 6-2	**Use of Force Response Options (continued)**
Profiled Behaviours	**Use of Force Response Options**
I. **Compliance** is "a cooperative and willing compliance in response to lawful police officer's request or direction."	I. **Officer Presence** includes manner of arrival (eg., foot, cruiser), number of officers at scene, etc.
II. **Passive Resistance** is "non-compliance to a lawful request or direction through verbal defiance but with little or no physical response (e.g., refusal to leave the scene, failure to follow directive, taunting officers, advising others to disregard officer's lawful requests, etc.)."	II. **Tactical Communications** includes both verbal (i.e., crisis intervention skills) and non-verbal (i.e., proxemics) behaviours (ibid., 4).
III. **Active Resistance** is an "increased scope and intensity of resistance beyond verbal defiance" that includes pushing or pulling away with intent to escape, or verbal refusal to respond to lawful commands.	III. **Empty Hand Techniques** include "soft control" (i.e., restraining techniques and joint locks) and hard strikes (i.e., punches, and elbow, leg, and knee strikes).
IV. **Assaultive** is an "active, hostile resistance exhibited whether an actual assault has occurred or is about to occur on an officer or a citizen in response to the officer's attempt to gain lawful compliance or in an unprovoked assault (e.g., kicking, punching, spitting etc.)."	IV. **Impact Weapon** when used for "soft control" include the use of batons in restraining techniques and joint locks.
V. **Serious Bodily Harm/Death** is a "behaviour likely to cause death or serious bodily harm to an officer or a citizen (e.g., choking, holding at gunpoint, brandishing an edged weapon, threatening and approaching with a weapon."	V. **Aerosol Spray** includes oleoresin capsicum, orthochlorbenzalmalononitrile, and chloroacetophenone.
	VI. **Impact Weapon** when used for hard control includes baton strikes and blocks.
	VII. **Police Challenge** includes verbal commands such as: "Police, don't move!"
	VIII. **Firearm** includes the drawing and discharging of service revolvers and pistols or the use of supplementary weapons such as shotguns and rifles.
	IX. **Disengage** includes calling for back-up and creating time and distance.

Source: Reprinted with permission from: Ronald T. Stansfield, *Issues in Policing: A Canadian Perspective* (1996). Toronto, ON: Thompson Educational Publishing, pp. 112, 113.

ceed in a career in law enforcement (or have already received this training in your current career). This model is used for training as the "proper use of force is a critical concern in contemporary law enforcement" (The Province of Ontario, 1993).

Training in Canada and in the United States emphasizes the use of the least intrusive measure of force to gain compliance. According to one defensive tactics instructor (Klugiewicz, 1996, p. 204), "Any use of force has to be based on a system of verbalization skills coupled with physical alternatives." The officer's physical presence, the words he or she says and the tone of voice are critical verbalization skills for defensive tactics. These skills must be used before, during and after the use of force. Many police services require officers to engage in specialized training to handle the challenges of dangerous situations where force may have to be used. For example, Toronto police officers in the Public Safety Unit take intensive training in several areas of crisis resolution including training in stages of crisis development, verbal interventions, appropriate use of force and officer response to crisis stages (McKenna, 1998).

SUMMARY

This chapter gave you an overview of conflict. A conflict occurs for many reasons including competition for limited resources, personality and cultural differences, different priorities and goals, role conflict and the building of stone walls. People manage conflict by adopting one of five styles: competitor, accommodator, compromiser, collaborator and avoider. The appropriate style that an individual should use is based on assessing the importance of the goal or issue and the importance of the relationship. Inappropriate use of a style occurs when the two are not assessed correctly.

There are several conflict management strategies that you can use depending upon the nature of the conflict and what you want out of the conflict. The first and most basic strategy is to choose a conflict management style that matches your goals and what you want from the exchange. When involved in a conflict you should also control your emotions, use empathy and be other-oriented, be open and honest, maintain a present focus, be assertive and use effective listening and responding skills. Managing the conflict as a problem situation may also be beneficial and may lead to a mutually agreed upon solution. The six steps of problem solving are defining the problem, analyzing the problem, generating solutions, evaluating the solutions, implementing the solution and then re-evaluating the solution at a later time.

A crisis that is a very difficult conflict situation can occur and may have to be managed by police officers. There are several indicators that a crisis may develop, including a change in nonverbal language and changes in the verbal content of the individual(s). Crisis intervention strategies include both nonverbal and verbal strategies. Last, use of force was briefly discussed as many police officers must use force in a crisis or hostile situation.

JOURNAL AND DISCUSSION QUESTIONS

1. What are the major causes of conflict in the life of a college or university student? Identify several sources of conflict.

2. Identify a current conflict that you are trying to manage. Using the problem-solving method, outline a strategy that could be used to solve this conflict.

3. What are your views on the use of force by police officers?

WEB SITES

www.crisisprevention.com
This is the site of the Crisis Prevention Institute. It offers good lists of strategies, and you can get copies of some of these strategies by sending away for free posters.

insight.mcmaster.ca/org/efc/pages/law/cc/cc.html
The Criminal Code of Canada is posted here.

www.ncjrs.org/txtfiles/ppsyc.txt
This is a paper about the excessive use of force by police officers and the factors that may contribute to the excessive use of force.

www.shyness.com
This is a site devoted to shyness and helping those with shyness or social phobia.

REFERENCES

William Arnold (1980). *Crisis Communication.* Dubuque, IO: Gorsuch Scarisbrick Publishers.

Robert A. Baron, Bruce Earhard and Marcia Ozier (1997). *Psychology,* 2nd Canadian edition. Scarborough, ON: Allyn and Bacon Canada. A summary of various theories of emotions, including the physiological indicators of emotions, can be found in Chapter 10.

Steven A. Beebe, Susan J. Beebe, Mark V. Redmond, Terri M. Geerinck, and Carol Milstone (2000, 1997). *Interpersonal Communication: Relating to Others.* Second Canadian Edition. Scarborough, ON: Allyn and Bacon Canada.

Eric Berne (1964). *Games People Play.* New York: Grove.

Mark L. Dantzker and Michael P. Mitchell (1998). *Understanding Today's Police,* Canadian edition. Scarborough, ON: Prentice Hall Canada

Joseph A. Devito (1995). *The Interpersonal Communication Book,* 7th edition. New York: Harper Collins College Publishers.

Joseph A. Devito (1996). *Messages: Building Interpersonal Skills,* 3rd edition. New York: Harper Collins College Publishers.

Andrew J. Dubrin and Terri Geerinck (1997). *Human Relations for Career and Personal Success,* Canadian edition. Scarborough, ON: Prentice Hall Canada.

Naomi Golan (1978). *Treatment in Crisis Situations.* New York: The Free Press.

M. S. Greenberg and R. B. Ruback (1982*). Social Psychology of the Criminal Justice System.* Belmont, CA: Wadsworth Publishing

Dominic Infante (1988). *Arguing Constructively.* Prospect Heights, IL: Waveland Press.

Gary T. Klugiewicz (1996). "An introduction to defensive tactics," in Ed Nowicki (Ed.), *Total Survival,* pp. 203–207. Powers Lake, WI: Performance Dimensions Publishing.

Richard J. Mayer (1990). *Conflict Management: The Courage to Confront.* Columbus, OH: Batelle Press.

Paul F. McKenna (1998). *Foundations of Policing in Canada.* Scarborough, ON: Prentice Hall Canada.

Roland Ouellette (1996). "Management of Aggressive Behaviour," in Ed Nowicki (Ed.), *Total Survival*, pp. 289–297. Powers Lake, WI: Performance Dimensions Publishing.

The Province of Ontario (1993). *Use of Force Model Training Manual.*

Kevin Shyne (1982). *Shyness: Breaking Through the Invisible Barrier to Achievement, Success,* July, pp. 14–16, 36–37, 51.

Robert Stansfield (1996). *Issues in Policing: A Canadian Perspective.* Toronto, ON: Thompson Educational Publishing.

Deborah Tannen (1998). "How to stop the war of words." "How to turn debate into dialogue." "Why it's so important to end Americans' war of words and start listening to one another." *USA Weekend.* March 1, 1998.

Kenneth Thomas (1976). "Conflict and conflict management," in Marvin D. Dunnette (Ed.), *Handbook of Industrial and Organizational Psychology*, pp. 900–902. Chicago: Rand McNally College Publishing.

J. L. Walsh (1977). "Career Styles and Police Behaviour," in D. H. Bayley (Ed.), *Police and Society* (pp. 149–176). Beverly Hills, CA: Sage Publications.

Julia Wood, Ron Sept and Jane Duncan (1998). *Everyday Encounters: An Introduction to Interpersonal Communication,* expanded first Canadian edition. Scarborough, ON: ITP Nelson.

Philip Zimbardo (1977). *Shyness: What It Is, What to Do About It.* Reading, MS: Addison Wesley.

UNDERSTANDING AND MANAGING DIVERSITY

7

LEARNING OUTCOMES

After studying this chapter you should be able to:

1. Define culture.
2. Define beliefs and values.
3. Identify five major differences among cultures.
4. Be more aware of the diversity and types of groups in Canada.
5. Identify barriers to effective intercultural communication.
6. Identify and be able to practice various strategies to reduce barriers in a diverse society.
7. Explain the challenge of diversity for policing.

Some overheard statements:

> *I can't believe that he wears that turban to work. I hear that he doesn't even cut his hair!*

> *When I went over to Lingh's house for dinner, her mother put the meal on the table all at once instead of one course at a time.*

> *Do you believe it? One of their national symbols is a cop on a horse!*

> *He got so offended because I called him by his first name when I was introduced.*

What do all the above statements have in common? If you came up with the answer that they all demonstrate cultural insensitivity, you are on the right track. There is little doubt that Canada is a diverse nation. Canada is made up of people from diverse cultures, diverse lifestyles and people with a wide range of needs and challenges. As future police officers and other law enforcement personnel, you will have little choice with whom you have contact professionally.

This newer focus in texts and teaching reflects the changing nature and diversity of this nation. As a quick exercise in realizing the nature of our diversity, try the activity below. Depending upon where you live and your own associations, your answers may differ from with others. Understanding and managing diversity will help you to be better police officers and better citizens. With the skills and increased depth of understanding after you have completed this chapter, you will be better equipped to manage the diverse relationships that you will undertake both on and off the job. The Canadian Perspective box below illustrates the powerful changes that are occurring in our population with regard to cultural diversity.

SKILLS PRACTICE:

Awareness: How Diverse Are Your Contacts?

Take a minute and think about all the people with whom you have come into contact in the last **seven** days. These contacts may be friends, family, classmates and other casual contacts such as customers, sales associates, servers and others you have interacted with in some manner. Using the following guidelines, fill in who this person was or how you came into contact with him or her. For each category, insert the name, occupation or other information that identifies your experience.

1. A person who is member of a visible minority: _____

2. A person of a different gender: _____

3. A person whose mother tongue is different from your own: _____

4. A person with a different ethnic background from your own: _____

5. A person with a sexual orientation different from your own: _____

6. A Native Canadian (if you are not Native Canadian): _____

7. A senior citizen (if you are not a senior): _____

If you have put at least one experience or person in each category, you have met people from seven different groups in one week on average!

For the first part of this chapter, we will explore cultural differences. Then we will look at other diverse populations with a very brief examination of the family, the implications of an aging population and people with disabilities and other physical and/or emotional challenges. Some of these groups are referred to as **co-cultures** or as a culture within a culture. The issue of diversity in policing will also be touched upon as an ongoing issue for many services. The chapter will conclude with several strategies to assist in communicating with people from diverse backgrounds.

UNDERSTANDING CULTURE

Culture comes in many shapes and sizes! **Culture** can be defined as a learned and shared system of knowledge, behaviour, **beliefs**, attitudes, **values** and norms. Cultures and

CANADIAN PERSPECTIVE:

The Facts and Statistics of a Culturally Diverse Population

- In 1996, 95 percent of Canada's population were Canadian citizens. The majority was born in Canada while 13 percent were naturalized citizens.

- In 1996, Europeans made up the largest share of all immigrants living in Canada and accounted for 47 percent of all immigrants. However, the proportion of new immigrants who are European has steadily been declining since 1961. Before 1961, 91 percent of new immigrants were from Europe. This proportion dropped to 20 percent between 1991 and 1996.

- Between 1991 and 1996, Asian-born persons represented 57 percent of immigrants. Most came from Hong Kong, the Philippines, China and India.

- New immigrants are settling predominantly in large urban centres. In 1996, 42 percent of immigrants settled in Toronto, 18 percent settled in Vancouver and 13 percent settled in Montreal.

Along with this diversity, the number of mother tongues or home languages are also changing. English and French are still the predominant mother languages. Here are the top 20, excluding English and French, according to Statistics Canada:

1.	Chinese	11.	Greek
2.	Italian	12.	Tamil
3.	Punjabi	13.	Cree
4.	Spanish	14.	Persian
5.	Portuguese	15	Korean
6.	Polish	16.	Ukrainian
7.	German	17.	Urdu
8.	Vietnamese	18.	Guiarati
9.	Arabic	19.	Hungarian
10.	Tagalog	20.	Hindi

Immigration statistics adapted from "Report on Demographic Situation in Canada, 1995," Catalogue No. 91-209; "Annual Demographic Statistics," Catalogue No. 91-213; and "The Daily," Catalogue No. 11-001, November 4, 1997. Languages adapted from "The Daily," Catalogue No. 11-001, December 2, 1997.

Statistics Canada information is used with permission of the Minister of Industry, as Minister is responsible for Statistics Canada. Information on the availability of the wide range of data from Statistics Canada can be obtained from Statistics Canada's Regional Offices, it World Wide Web site at http://www.statscan.ca, and its toll-free access number 1-800-263-1136.

co-cultures in many ways refer to the lifestyle or way of living of a group. This system or way of life is shared by a group of people. Beliefs are the ways in which you structure your view or understanding of reality as to what is true and what is false. For instance, you may have a religious belief that Jesus was the Son of God. Values are more enduring than beliefs and are central to who you are and can be defined as a set of central and enduring goals in life and ways of living that you feel are important, right and true. The belief in Jesus may be part of a much larger value that you have in Christianity as an important part in your life. Others may have different religious beliefs and a different religious value system. Religions are part of a cultural heritage for many people. Your cultural background and all the things that make up your culture affect and impact on how you communicate with others.

Your culture came from others around you as you grew up. Through a process of **enculturation**, culture is passed on or transmitted from one generation to another. We learn our culture through the teachings of our parents, teachers, peers, various institutions and government agencies (Devito, 1996). As we come into contact with other cultures and other cultures come into contact with us, **acculturation** occurs. Acculturation is the process in which a person's culture is modified by contact with another culture. Through contact with people from other cultures, our own beliefs, values, attitudes and ideas may change through this intercultural communication. If we look at North American culture today, there are many examples of acculturation. Many of us undergo acupuncture, take part in karate and judo, enjoy East Indian foods, eat hot dogs and watch baseball or do other things that were not initially part of our "home culture." Intercultural communication can occur among many different types of cultures and co-cultures. Communication can occur among different religions, different cultures, different races, different nations, different co-cultures and different groups within a culture. However, we need to be aware that as we communicate with others from different cultures, we are always communicating from our own cultural perspective. For example, many "Western" women criticize the wearing of hijab by Muslim women due to their "Western" views. On the other hand, Muslim women who wear hijab believe that Western women are "slaves" to their appearance and see their choice of dress as being more "liberated." Both sides are expressing their beliefs based on their cultural perspective.

DIMENSIONS OF CULTURAL DIFFERENCES

Although cultures can be very different, one researcher identified four variables that differentiate cultures. These four variables, or **cultural values,** are masculine versus feminine perspectives, avoidance of uncertainty, distribution of power and individualism versus collective achievement (Hofstede, 1980). A fifth area of difference is the dimension of high context versus low context.

Masculine versus Feminine Perspectives

Some cultures emphasize traditional male values. Other cultures emphasize more feminine perspectives. **Masculine cultures** value such things as material wealth, assertiveness, achievement and heroism. On the other hand, **feminine cultures** value relationships, caring for and nurturing others, particularly those less fortunate or unable, and the quality of life (Hofstede, 1980). The older, traditional cultures of much of Europe, Asia, the United States, Great Britain and Canada are more masculine in their cultures. However, today most of these cultures are changing as social and legal changes reflect more equality between the sexes.

Tolerance of Uncertainty versus Avoidance of Uncertainty

Some cultures are more tolerant of ambiguity and uncertainty than other cultures. Cultures that value avoiding uncertainty are more likely to have more rigid rules for behaviour and more likely to develop more elaborate codes of conduct. Cultures that are highly tolerant of uncertainty are more relaxed with rules of conduct and more permissive with the latitude of what is acceptable conduct. It has been demonstrated that people from Portugal, Germany, Russia and Japan have a low tolerance for uncertainty. People from the Scandinavian countries are more tolerant of uncertainty (Hofstede, 1980, 1991).

Concentrated versus Decentralized Power

Some cultures accept the fact that power is hierarchical and that some people should have more power than others. In such cultures, there are more bureaucracies that are based on power with those higher on the ladder having more power than those lower on the ladder. Russia,

France and China are strong on the value of concentrated power (Hofstede, 1991). Recent studies continue to indicate that this notion is reflected in a wide range of institutions, including schools and businesses (Bolman and Deal, 1992; Schmidt and Yeh, 1992). The United States, Australia and Israel value more decentralized power and tend to minimize power differences between people. People who are not used to hierarchies may have difficulty adjusting to these differences in power. Many young people in Canada who join the army or police services may have some problems doing something because they have been ordered to do it!

Individualism versus Collectivism

Individualistic cultures emphasize the individual person and give priority to personal goals over the goals of the group. Western cultures such as in the United States, Canada and Great Britain all emphasize the importance of individual goals and being responsible for yourself and for your immediate family (Hofstede, 1980). Collectivistic cultures emphasize the importance of a larger social group, and individual identity is based on the identity within a unit or group. Priority is given to group goals over personal or individual goals (Hofstede, 1980). For example, in many Western cultures if you were to ask someone, "Who are you?" the response would probably be a set of personal attributes. In a more collectivist culture, such as in Japan, the response may include whose son or daughter he or she is and some information about descendants (Lebra, 1976). Some research also indicates that African Americans tend to be more oriented towards collective interests, such as family, than European North Americans (Gaines, 1995).

High-Context Cultures versus Low-Context Cultures

People from high-context cultures rely heavily on context and nonverbal cues in their interaction with others. Cultures that are characterized as more low-context rely on verbal language to communicate messages to others. Low-context cultures use fewer nonverbal cues to send and interpret messages (Hall, 1976). To more fully understand the difference between high- and low-context, think of eating at a familiar restaurant (context) that you and your friends enjoy every Friday night after work. You are well known at this establishment by the servers. You simply have to catch the eye of a server and lift your arm and wave. At this signal, the server comes back with your favourite before-dinner beverage. This is a high-context situation. Suppose there is a new server. You wave your arm and he or she waves back with a smile. Suddenly, you are now in a low-context situation, and you will have to verbally indicate what you would like (or you may just get smiles and waves for awhile and be very thirsty). Some cultures that are more high-context may use such nonverbal cues as dress, jewellery, hairstyles and body marking to enhance messages for others within the culture. Young Amish men who are single do not have beards. Once married or at least betrothed, the young men grow beards to indicate their marital status.

THE GROUPS AND CULTURES OF CANADA

As professional law enforcement workers, your contact will be wide and varied depending upon where in Canada you work. As stated earlier, large urban centres tend to be more culturally diverse than smaller rural communities. However, this only pertains to cultural diversity in terms of nationality and ethnic or racial origins. We also need to be aware of other cultural differences and their prevalence in Canada today. Before we begin to examine the barriers that effect our communication with other cultures, let's briefly look at other cultures, co-cultures and diverse groups that make up Canada. These groups have impact on law enforcement as many of these groups are actively seeking rights or are becoming more visible on the "streets" due to funding cuts and other social and political changes in the country.

Visible Minorities and Other Cultural Groups

According to Statistics Canada (1996), 11.2 percent of the population is comprised of visible minorities. Asian-born immigrants are a continuing area of growth in Canada as are people from the Caribbean and Oriental cultures.

Native Canadians

Native Canadians make up a significant group in our country. Approximately three percent of Canadians reported that they were identified with a least one Aboriginal group (Statistics Canada, 1996). The many First Nations that have Canada as their home are making significant changes for their peoples and will continue to do so in coming years. In many ways, such as in education and jobs, Native Canadians still face prejudice and discrimination. However, Native Canadians offer a rich source of cultural diversity, and many of their practices, such as healing circles, medicines and religious practices, are being adopted by non-Native Canadians

CANADIAN PERSPECTIVE:

Wage Inequalities and Native Canadians

A recent study examined the wage gaps between Canadian workers as a whole and four main Aboriginal groups: North American Indians on reserve, North American Indians off reserve, Inuit and Metis. This study confirmed what Native Canadians have known for a long time; Aboriginal peoples earn less than Canadians as a whole. The most disadvantaged group was North American Indians living on reserves. Another interesting finding was that there is greater disparity on the distribution of wages between Aboriginals and Canadians as a whole. In other words, a high-earning, medium-earning and low-earning Aboriginal was still making less than his or her Canadian counterpart in each cat-

egory. For example, the mean annual wage of a worker in the top quintile (high earning bracket) is $63,720 for Canadian workers as a whole and $48,720 for workers of Aboriginal identity. As wages increase, this gap increases. While there may be several mitigating factors, such as educational attainment differences and age of workers (Aboriginal workers are younger), this gap is of major concern to many of those who are striving to increase equality among groups in Canada. Further research will be required to investigate this problem and solutions put in place to reduce this disparity in the future.

Source: Rachel Bernier, "The dimensions of wage inequality among Aboriginal People," Catalogue No. 11F0019MPE97109, December 1997. Statistics Canada. See p.109 for complete Statistics Canada reference.

Families Today

Families are very different today from what they looked like 40 years ago. Then, the traditional family was made up of two parents, one of each sex, and their children. Recently, however, the family make-up is changing. For example, Statistics Canada has defined a family as "a now married couple (with or without never-married sons and/or daughters of either or both spouses), a couple living common-law (again with or without never-married sons and/or daughters) or a lone parent of any marital status with at least one never-married son or daughter living in the same dwelling" (Statistics Canada, 1992). Rather than having an emphasis on traditional roles and stereotypes, the interpersonal relationships and interpersonal commitment are emphasized in the new definitions.

There is little doubt that families and how we choose to live are changing dramatically. Common-law families and lone-parent families, a family type of a lone parent of either sex with children, are also on the increase. According to a Statistic's Canada 1996 census, these types of families made up 26 percent of all families in Canada, up six percent from a decade earlier. The vast majority of lone parents are women. In 1994, one in six children under the age of 12 lived in lone-mother families (Canadian Social Trends, 1997). Also, according to the National Foundation for Family Research and Education (NFFRE) Family Health Index, common-law unions are not as stable as marriages, and approximately 70 percent of such unions end within the first five years (NFFRE, 1998). Also, according to the Family Health Index, many of us are choosing to live alone and stay single. By 1996, the number of Canadians who had never been married rose to 89 percent for the age group of 20 to 24. In 1971, this number was 56 percent (NFFRE Family Health Index, 1998).

Alternate Lifestyles

Many Canadians are adopting alternate lifestyles different from the traditions of the past. Notice that in the definition of a family the word used is "couple" and not man and woman. The definition recognizes that one family of choice is a same-sex couple who may or may not have children. While recognized in this "official" definition of family, many same-sex couples are still fighting for the rights afforded by opposite-sex couples, such as survivors' pension benefits and Canada Pension and Quebec Pension plans. In May 1996, the Canadian Human Rights Act was amended to include sexual orientation as prohibited grounds for discrimination. At the federal level, family status still does not include families with a homosexual couple.

Other alternate lifestyles that should be mentioned are communal living arrangements where a group chooses to live together in a wide variety of arrangements based on a common system of beliefs.

As these groups continue to assert their rights, such as through public awareness marches or protests, police officers may find that contact with these groups and those who disagree with these groups may continue to rise. Even such groups as anti-abortionists and those who support abortion have come into increasing contact with law enforcement personnel.

Disabilities

Another group is one consisting of members of various co-cultures with people who have various disabilities and other physical challenges. Many people with a wide variety of physical challenges have formed their own co-cultures separate from the dominant cultures. Often, agencies have been formed to assist these groups to gain rights and access to many services or jobs that had previously been denied them. Other reasons for forming their own cultures and groups has been for support, increased knowledge, sharing of problems, concerns and solutions. One such co-culture is the deaf culture that has a large and diverse group within its culture.

The Growing Senior Population

Demographic trends continue to show that the Canadian population is rapidly aging (Statistics Canada, 1996). The elderly will become a growing consumer of police services (Plotkin, 1996). The elderly tend to be more vulnerable to many crimes such as elder abuse, fraud and the misuse of their financial assets (McKenna, 1998). The elderly may also call on the police in a variety of emergencies that may not be related to crime.

Mental Illness

Reorganization and restructuring of care facilities has had an impact on individuals who have been classified as having mental illness. In large urban areas, many individuals who may be suffering from a mental illness wander the streets. As well, there are many support groups for those who are mentally ill and who continue to lobby for the rights of people who may be incapable of lobbying for themselves. Many people suffer from various mental illnesses, and this can be a cause for concern by law enforcement personnel. Depression is the most commonly diagnosed mental illness. It has been estimated by the Canadian Mental Health Association that 15 percent of the population will experience a major depression episode in their lives (CMHA, 1993). Dealing with mentally ill people can be a challenge for police officers as many officers may not understand the symptoms of various mental illnesses.

Other Co-Cultures

There would not be enough room in this book to mention all the groups, movements and societies that make up this nation. Regardless of the group, culture, reform movement or lifestyle, all individuals deserve the protection of the law. There is no doubt that there are many kinds of influences that are having impact on policing and on the delivery of policing services (McKenna, 1998). The challenge is to be able to cope with these influences and to effectively deliver policing at an individual and force level. Since the focus of this chapter is to improve interpersonal effectiveness, let's focus now on the skills required to manage in a diverse society after we examine the barriers in effective intercultural communication. While we will largely focus on major cultures, keep in mind that these strategies can also be applied with co-cultures and other groups.

BARRIERS TO EFFECTIVE INTERCULTURAL COMMUNICATION

In a multi-cultural and multi-group society, problems in communication are bound to happen as we attempt to communicate with those different from ourselves. What creates true problems is not the struggle that occurs as we attempt to understand others' messages but the barriers that we consciously or even unconsciously erect. Let's examine some of these barriers in more detail.

Stereotypes, Prejudice and Discrimination

If you can recall from Chapter 3, we discussed the formation of stereotypes. Stereotypes are formed as part of the categorization process of perception. When we **stereotype**, we place people into categories or groups based on broad generalizations and assumptions that we hold about a particular group. The problem with stereotypes is that we "lump" large groups of people into the same category often with a minimum of knowledge and experience about that particular category. For example, if you were to find out that I wear glasses and had extremely high marks during high school and now write textbooks, you may categorize me as a "brain" or a "nerd." This would be based on very little knowledge about all the other things that make up "me." Police officers, like all of us, have stereotypes also. Some of these stereotypes are ones that include criminals (Stansfield, 1996). The box below lists just a few of these stereotypes. The first part of the box includes general cultural stereotypes, and the second part includes common criminal stereotypes.

Once we have a stereotype of a person, we tend to treat them according to this stereotype, and as such our responses become biased and limited. We also tend to seek information that fits with the stereotype and ignore or dismiss information that does not fit (Philipchalk,

LAW AND JUSTICE PERSPECTIVE:

Awareness: Stereotypes

Although inaccurate, many stereotypes still persist today.

Common Cultural Stereotypes

"Jews are good with money"

"All women are soft"

"All cops are pigs"

"Arabs are sneaky"

"Oriental students are smart"

"Blacks have rhythm"

"Mentally ill people are violent"

"Gay men are effeminate"

Common Criminal Stereotypes

"All Italians are Mafia"

"Young people are troublemakers"

"Native Canadians are drunks"

"Sikhs are terrorists"

"Blacks and Jamaicans are drug dealers"

"Bikers are gang members"

"White trash cause trouble"

Source: Adapted and expanded from Robert Stansfield. (1996). *Issues in Policing: A Canadian Perspective.* Toronto, ON: Thompson Educational Publishing, p. 136.

1995). For example, once a police officer has formed the stereotype that bikers belong to gangs, will he or she treat a young man on a motorcycle differently from an older woman on a motorcycle if he or she stopped either one for a speeding violation?

If we start to treat someone differently due to this stereotyping, we have developed a prejudicial attitude and may discriminate against members of this group. **Prejudice** is an unjustifiable negative attitude toward a group and its members; **discrimination** is the resulting unjustifiable negative behaviour based on this attitude (Philipchalk, 1995). Our behaviour may include verbal expressions of dislike, avoidance of group members, actual discriminatory practices such as excluding group members from certain activities or rights, and physical attacks. At the furthest extreme is the extermination of this group, such as Hitler attempted during World War II (Allport, 1958).

The problem with stereotyping, prejudice and discrimination is that these processes deny the individuality of people. Once denied individuality, people may actually begin to behave and react according to these stereotypes. If the police hold true that the "typical criminal" is a young, black or native, urban male, then police no longer have to evaluate each individual upon individual characteristics and evidence (Stansfield, 1996). In the United States this typical criminal stereotype exists if we omit the "native" component (Stansfield, 1996). While police officers may hold these stereotypes, the public becomes aware of them. Therefore, when dealing with members of these groups, the members themselves become very aware of how they may be perceived by the police officers or by other members of society.

Let's take a look at a real example of this effect. An officer spotted a car driving excessively slowly around 3:00 a. m. on the outskirts of a city. She pulled the vehicle over. When she approached the vehicle, the window opened and a black Canadian started to yell at her that the only reason she pulled them over was because they were black. However, in reality, it was a dark night with no street lights, the vehicle's windows were tinted and she could only make out that there were two people visible to her from her vantage point behind the vehicle. What had alerted her was the slow driving, which may indicate that the driver may be impaired. Her suspicions were confirmed; the driver was impaired, and there was also a quantity of drugs and a weapon. It was not the race of the driver that alerted the officer but the manner in which the vehicle was being driven.

When we judge others based on stereotypes and then treat them in negative ways or treat them as a result of our perception of the group membership, we are building barriers to honest and open communication. To treat me like a "nerd" denies that I am a unique person, and being a "nerd" is only part of who I am. When police officers use their powers of discretion, they must be aware of the dangers of stereotyping, prejudice and discrimination.

Ethnocentrism

When you belong to a certain culture or group, you usually prefer the way things are done within that group. For example, many people celebrate a holiday on December 25 that involves a figure called Santa Claus who brings toys, presents that are exchanged among friends and family, a tree covered in decorations, a meal complete with a bird that is cooked and stuffed and the singing of special songs. If you are part of this culture (or maybe even if you are not), you know that this is called "Christmas." Other cultures also celebrate at this time of year, but it does not involve giving gifts. I have heard people say that children should receive gifts anyway or that it is not fair that these children should suffer. This type of thinking demonstrates **ethnocentrism**. Ethnocentrism is a belief or conviction that your own cultural traditions, beliefs, ideas and convictions are somehow superior or better than those of others. When we state that others' ideas and beliefs about how to celebrate a holiday are erroneous, we are making the assumption that our way is better, more just, more fair or simply right. This means that their way is worse, unjust, unfair or wrong. If you want to erect a communication barrier, voicing ethnocentric views such as this is one good way to do it!

Verbal and Nonverbal Communication Barriers—Different Words, Gestures and Symbols

In Chapter 5 we discussed a number of problems with words. Words can have different meanings. This may be especially true when they are translated into another language. In Roger Axtell's book, *Do's and Taboos of Hosting International Visitors* (1989), he presents a number of examples of advertising "gone bad" because of mistranslated advertisements. Here are just two examples:

- Pepsi's slogan "Come alive with Pepsi" translated to "Pepsi brings your ancestors back from the grave" in the Taiwanese market.
- Parker Pen's famous "Jotter" ballpoint pen translated into something like the "jockstrap" pen in some languages and so could not be advertised as a "Jotter" in some cultures.

Gestures also vary depending upon culture. In you recall from Chapter 4, what is an appropriate gesture in one culture may have an inappropriate meaning in another culture. Giving the "thumbs up" sign in much of North America means "way to go" or "great." In other cultures it translates to "up yours." Just imagine a situation where as a police officer, a foreign visitor asks for directions in almost non-existent English. You basically sign the direction using gestures and pointing. He smiles and gives a nod of thanks and you feel good after helping someone. As the foreigner walks away in the right direction, he turns around and you give him the "thumbs up" gesture. Imagine your feelings when he screams back at you, gives you the same gesture (or one you do not understand) and storms on down the street!

Other symbols of what is important or cherished by one culture may also be misunderstood by another culture. Remember that symbols represent objects, concepts and thoughts, as was discussed in Chapter 5. Christians value the symbol of the cross and display or wear crosses as symbols of their beliefs. The Star of David is an important religious symbol to those of the Jewish faith. The turban and the "kirpan" (a kind of dagger that is a religious symbol) worn by Sikhs are important to their faith (Singh, 1990). In recent years the wearing of turbans by Sikh members of the Royal Canadian Mounted Police was a cause for some heated discussions (and perhaps still is) in the Canadian government, the RCMP and in other interest groups.

Different Norms and Codes of Conduct

Norms are guidelines (usually unwritten) that govern the behaviour of members within a specific group. It should come as no surprise to you that different groups have norms that may be similar or different from other groups. Also, what is permissible conduct in one group may be frowned upon and even punished in another group. Below is some information about business and social etiquette in China. For each "rule" identify how your cultural group would do this activity.

SKILLS PRACTICE:

Business and Social Etiquette in China

Here are a few rules from China:

1. When greeting a Chinese person, use his or her family name only. The Chinese family name comes first. For example, a male Ling Pan Fu would be addressed as Mr. Ling.
   Your group

   _____

2. The Chinese way of greeting is a nod or slight bow.
   Your group

   _____

3. At a dinner, always leave something on your plate.
   Your group

   _____

4. Never wrap a gift in plain black and white paper as these are the colours of mourning.
   Your group

   _____

5. Deny a compliment graciously.
   Your group

   _____

Source: Adapted from Sunun Setboonsarng, Greater China and SE Asia Trade Development Officer. *Business and Social Etiquette in China.* Oregon Economic Development Department, 1999. Visit the web site at www.econ.state.or.us/intl/travel/etchina.htm

At times we may also make the mistake that others are similar to us and then become confused when they act differently. We may unknowingly insult others from a different culture, or they may unknowingly insult us. If you are from a culture that highly values time, such as Austrians, Swiss or English, you may feel anger when your new Italian acquaintance arrives 30 minutes late for a party. Since most Italians do not adhere to rigid time schedules for social events, you have just experienced a clash of different cultural norms.

IMPROVING INTERCULTURAL COMMUNICATION AND FOSTERING UNDERSTANDING

Depending upon where you choose to work, your contact with various cultures and groups will vary. If you work in larger urban centres, the cultural and ethnic diversity will be more pronounced than in more rural settings. However, all settings will have a large diversity of groups. It is in your best personal and professional interest, then, to learn skills that will help you in this nation of diversity.

Actively Seek Knowledge and Information

Often ignorance of different groups and their codes of conduct or other characteristics may be at the root of many communication problems and barriers. We all have our views of the world and how it works, but we must remember that this view was taught to us within the confines of our mother culture. In order to understand other groups, you need to prepare yourself by gaining knowledge and information.

When the controversy raged over the Sikh RCMP officers wearing their turbans, many people had little idea about the significance of the turban. A little research would have answered the religious significance of the turban and why it was and is important for Sikh men to wear it. There are a number of sources for you to use to find information. There are books about different countries, travel brochures, art, geography books and maps, and the Internet. The previous box about China was accessed via the Internet. Before we launch into criticism or express our own ethnocentric views, we should take the time to research the differences. Such knowledge will often lead to better understanding.

Be Other-Oriented and Use Empathy

When you meet or deal with an individual from a different background, try to put yourself in his or her place. Listen and respond actively using the skills from Chapters 4 and 5. The person may have trouble with your language, and you may have trouble with his or her language. Your nonverbal communication may be more important than words as you may have to rely on gesturing and pointing. Just be careful of how you gesture! The key is to try to understand the person and his or her point of view. Understanding and empathy do not necessarily mean agreement, but understanding and empathy will create the groundwork for mutual respect.

Do Not Be Afraid to Ask Questions

Sometimes we are afraid to ask questions. We engage in some negative self-talk and say things to ourselves such as "I don't want to appear stupid," "This will be too embarrassing" or "What if I offend him/her?" If you have travelled, you may have found yourself in the uncomfortable position of not knowing what to do next. So you try to watch and copy (like using chopsticks for the first time) and end up feeling foolish. Most people are rarely offended by you asking questions. For instance, "I'm not sure how I am supposed to do this, could you show me?" is rarely cause for alarm by the other party. In fact, many people are pleased and complimented by your desire to learn their traditions or way of doing things. Once at my college, the Native students were performing a pow wow. One of the students was in my course and was not offended by my asking about pow wows, a ceremony that I had no knowledge about previously.

Develop Tolerance

In this context, tolerance does not mean that you stoically put up with something whether you like it or not, such as tolerating lectures for a course you dislike. In this context, **tolerance** means being aware of and acknowledging that cultural differences do exist. This kind of tolerance is based on empathy and knowledge that will allow you to cope with cultural and group differences. If your son or daughter comes home from a new friend's house and exclaims that Sam lives with two moms, you can use this opportunity to explain about same-sex couples (depending upon the age of your son and daughter) in a positive and enlightened manner. This kind of tolerance depends upon your flexibility and your willingness to understand how others are different.

Avoid Making Negative Judgments

"Here we go again, back to welfare alley for another domestic" is a statement that is negative and prejudiced. First, the assumption is that because the call is in a higher-than-average low-income area, the call must be coming from someone on welfare. Second, this statement also indicates how the person feels about this area for calls. Could this attitude then lead to different treatment by the officer when at the scene? It is possible and probable.

There is evidence that attitudes can influence behaviour. For example, according to the **theory of reasoned action**, strong norms about how you are expected to behave and strong beliefs that a certain outcome will occur will influence your behaviour (Ajzen and Fishbein, 1980). In other words, your attitude about the behaviour and your norms about complying with the behaviour will lead you to behave in a specific way. For example, if I believe in the platform of the Conservative Party and all my friends know and expect me to vote Conservative, chances are my friends can predict my behaviour. I will most likely vote Conservative.

A good example of negative attitudes and negative judgment followed by negative treatment is a case study in Robert Stansfield's book, *Issues in Policing: A Canadian Perspective* (1996). The woman in the case was Kitty Nowdluk-Reynolds, an Inuk woman. She had been viciously raped and beaten. Based on her description, the attacker was arrested and charged with aggravated sexual assault. She continued with plans to move to Surrey, B. C., and a month later was served with a subpoena to testify at the trial. She was not informed of how to get travel assistance. In August 1990, she was arrested and was to be transported to testify at the trial. She was handcuffed, stripped, de-loused, fingerprinted, photographed and put in a cell. Basically, she was imprisoned for five days, was denied her right to counsel and was not even allowed basic personal hygiene. At the trial she was even transported in the same van as her attacker! She was poor, Native Canadian and unaware of the intricacies of the law. Would she have received different treatment if she had been "white," rich and had a lawyer for a husband?

Of course not all attitudes lead to a specific behaviour, for a number of reasons. The behaviour may be illegal, you may not have the skills, and often good intentions do not materialize for a whole host of factors and mitigating circumstances (Alcock et al., 1998). The real point is that having negative attitudes and making negative judgments will influence how we think about and perhaps how we treat or mistreat others. Negative judgments make huge communication barriers as we saw in the earlier case study. For instance, why did no one inform her of her rights? Why was she not told about how her expenses would be covered when she testified?

How can we avoid making negative judgments? First, remind yourself that you may be suffering from a bout of "ethnocentrism." Your ways and ideas are not better, just different. Second, ask yourself, "Am I thinking about this person in a stereotypical way?" As a police officer, you may have much in common with other officers, but you are also very different from other officers. Last, acknowledge differences as challenges not barriers. A challenge is something that we can "take on" and accomplish rather than a barrier that has to be overcome, broken or made to disappear.

A FINAL NOTE: DIVERSITY IN POLICING

Our look at diversity is not complete until we examine diversity and policing. Let's look at the make-up of the police in Canada. As of June 15, 1998, there were 54,722 police officers. Women accounted for nearly one in every eight officers, or 12 percent of the total, their highest proportion to date. There were 48,036 male officers, down 1.2 percent from 1997. Manitoba had the highest number of police officers per capita, and Newfoundland had the lowest number per capita (Statistics Canada, 1999).

SKILLS PRACTICE:

A Plan for Learning

Identify a culture, race or group that you have had very little experience with and limited knowledge about. Develop a plan that will help you learn the following things about this culture:

1. How do they greet friends and strangers?

2. What are some special holidays and celebrations?

3. What is the structure of the family?

4. What are the foods they typically eat and how do they organize their meals?

5. Are there significant religious practices or rites of passage in this culture?

While these are only a few questions, you may want to add a few of your own. Where can you get this information? Try the library, travel agencies, personal interviews of members of this culture, phone associations, or try the Internet. You may be surprised by what you learn, and you will have developed at least one skill (knowledge) to help you with diversity!

While the country is becoming more diverse, this trend is lagging in the ranks of police officers. For example, women make up over 50 percent of the Canadian population whereas only 12 percent of police officers are women (Statistics Canada, 1999). According to the 1996 census, 11.2 percent of the Canadian population was made up of visible minorities. An additional three percent of the population is made up of people who identified themselves as belonging to at least one aboriginal group. As stated earlier, the large urban centres have higher concentrations of some of these minority groups. When people and groups feel underrepresented by professional service organizations such as police, it may make it more difficult for the organization to do its job effectively.

"During the past few years, relationships between the police and some groups representing visible minorities have been somewhat strained" (Linden, 1989, p. 117). If the Canadian immigration trends continue and the Canadian birth rate does not significantly increase, there is a definite need for the police to continue to make efforts to improve relationships with ethnic and cultural groups (Linden, 1989). These changes in the racial and ethnic population structure have five major implications for the police (Linden, 1989):

1. The effects of racism when combined with social and economic deprivation may lead some groups to increased involvement in crime.

2. There will be an increasing number of immigrants who do not speak English or French and who will need police services.

3. Some immigrant groups bring their own crime patterns with them.

4. The increasing presence of visible minorities may lead to an increase in racial tensions. Racism is still alive in Canada as in other countries. Some minority groups already have longstanding conflicts that may spill over in areas where both groups are present.

5. In many parts of Canada, there is already tension between minority groups and the police. A great deal of work will be required to ease these already existing tensions.

In response to these demographic changes, two major areas of change need to be implemented in police services. First, it is becoming apparent and more important that the police officers require training in diversity. "Members must be familiar with the customs and values of various ethnic and visible minority groups within our society" (Working Group Response to Linden, 1989, p. 134). This training should ideally include officers already on forces, new recruits and the inclusion of diversity training in police programs.

Second, recruitment practices must change. Police organizations have been making efforts across the country to ensure "that their policies, programs and practices bring forward a better cross-section of candidates for careers in policing" (McKenna, 1998, p. 84). However, as the Law and Justice box below indicates, the promises of increasing diversity are not always enough.

LAW AND JUSTICE PERSPECTIVE:

Minority Police Officers in Toronto

According to a recent article from *The Toronto Star*, the Toronto police service is going to become more active in its recruitment of visible minority officers. According to force statistics, of the 4,905 officers, only 10 percent are members of racial minorities. And when you examine frontline troops, only 8.7 percent are from racial minorities and 87 percent of these troops are male. This is in stark contrast to statistics from a diversity survey that indicates 42 percent of those residing in Toronto are members of visible minorities. By 2001, it has been estimated that racial minorities will be the majority (or even earlier than this estimate according to another later report).

For years the force has promised that it would increase the diversity of its force. Now it is making good its promise. The good news is that the force hopes to hire 306 people this year, and the recruitment team is working hard to ensure that more Blacks, Chinese, Koreans, Aboriginals and Vietnamese will apply to be on the force. Women are also on the list for increasing the diversity of the force. And while not all in the force may be happy with the changes for various reasons, the push is on to diversify the Toronto Police Force.

Source: John Duncanson. "Mostly white, mostly male: Why police are reaching out again," *The Toronto Star*, March 6, 1999. Excerpted from an article originally appearing in *The Toronto Star*, March 1999. Reprinted with permission- The Toronto Star Syndicate.

It should be noted that it is not only police forces that will need to increase their diversity. It is a common problem in other agencies and in other areas of public service as well. Agencies that equip their employees with skills to communicate with diverse populations and that make concerted efforts to reflect the diversity of their service area with that of the population will be ready for the next millennium.

SUMMARY

In this chapter we have explored diversity in Canada. We defined and looked at what a culture is and how culture is transmitted to others through acculturation and enculturation.

Cultures differ along five dimensions that include masculine versus feminine perspectives, tolerance of uncertainty, concentrated versus decentralized power and high-context versus low-context cultures. We also briefly examined some of the diverse groups in Canada, including visible minorities and other cultural groups, family styles, Aboriginals, alternate lifestyles and various other groups that are having an impact in Canada.

A significant barrier to effective intercultural communication includes stereotyping, prejudice and discrimination. Often stereotypes and prejudicial attitudes lead to discrimination that can take a number of forms ranging in severity from negative feelings about a group to actual elimination of the group members. Other barriers include ethnocentrism, different verbal and nonverbal communication and use of symbols, and different norms and codes of conduct.

To improve our ability to span and conquer these barriers, there are a variety of strategies that you may use to increase your intercultural competence. Actively seek knowledge and information about others different from you, use empathy and be other-oriented, don't be afraid to ask questions and develop tolerance. The sixth important strategy is to avoid negative judgments as such judgments may lead to unfairly treating the person you are judging.

Last, we looked at the issue of diversity in policing. Two strategies are important for police services and police personnel today. First, police officers need to be trained in understanding and managing diversity. Second, police services need to mirror the diversity of the population that they serve.

JOURNAL AND DISCUSSION QUESTIONS

1. What do you see as the main reasons for intolerance and prejudice?

2. Have you been a victim of prejudice or discrimination? How did it feel? What was your reaction?

3. Many people are against the active recruitment of visible minorities and women in many professions, including policing. Should hiring be based solely on group membership, or should the best person be hired regardless of race, ethnic origin or gender? Support your opinion.

WEB SITES

www.cs.cmu.edu

This is the site of Canadiana, The Canadian Resource Page with links to a variety of Canadian sites including government, entertainment and so on.

www.gmag.ca/magic/mhome.html

This is the Magic Assembling showcase where you can take a tour and explore the "multicultural complexity of Metro Toronto." There are also articles about different cultures and cultural traditions.

www.cmha.ca

This is the site for the Canadian Mental Health Association. From this site, you can access information on mental health and mental illnesses.

www.seb.apc/~ara

From Toronto, this is an anti-racist site for Anti-Racist Action Toronto.

www.infoability/resource/culture.html

This is a large Canadian site with resources on society and culture. These resources are listed under various categories such as race relations, gender relations and language services.

REFERENCES

I. Ajzen and M. Fishbein (1980). *Understanding Attitudes and Predicting Social Behaviour.* Englewood Cliffs, NJ: Prentice-Hall.

J. E. Alcock, D. W. Carment and S. W. Sadava (1998). *A Textbook of Social Psychology.* Scarborough, ON: Prentice Hall Allyn and Bacon Canada.

Gordon W. Allport (1958). *The Nature of Prejudice.* New York: Doubleday.

Roger E. Axtell (1989). *Do's and Taboos of Hosting International Visitors.* New York: John Wiley and Sons, p. 118.

Lee. G. Bolman and Terrence E. Deal (1992). "Leading and managing: Effects of context, culture and gender," *Educational Administration Quarterly, 28,* 314–329.

C. M. H. A. (Canadian Mental Health Association) (1993). "Understanding Depression." Vancouver.

Canadian Social Trends (1997). Canadian children in the 1990s: Selected findings of the national longitudinal survey of children and youth. "Canadian Social Trends," Spring 1997.

Joseph A. DeVito (1996). *Messages: Building Interpersonal Skills,* 3rd Edition. New York: HarperCollins College Publishers.

S. Gaines Jr. (1995). Relationships among members cultural minorities, in J. T. Wood and S. W. Duck (Eds.), *Understanding Relationship Processes, 6: Off the Beaten Track: Understudied Relationships* (pp. 51–88). Thousand Oaks, CA: Sage.

Geert Hofstede (1980). *Culture's Consequences: International Differences in Work-Related Values.* Beverly Hills, CA: Sage.

Geert Hofstede (1991). *Cultures and Organizations.* London: McGraw Hill.

T. S. Libra (1976). *Japanese Patterns of Behavior.* Honolulu: University of Hawaii Press.

Rick Linden (1989). "Demographic change and the future of policing," in Donald J. Loree (ed.) *Future Issues in Policing: Symposium Proceedings,* pp. 111–127. Ottawa, ON: The Canadian Police College.

Paul F. McKenna (1998). *Foundations of Policing in Canada.* Scarborough, ON: Prentice Hall.

The National Foundation for Family Research and Education. Family Health Index. November 1998. www.nffre.com

Ronald P. Philipchalk (1995). *Invitation to Social Psychology.* Orlando, FL: Harcourt Brace and Company.

Martha R. Plotkin (1996). Improving the police response to domestic elder abuse victims, *Aging, 367,* 28–33.

Stuart Schmidt and Ryh-Song Yeh (1992). The structure of leader influence: A cross-national comparison. *Journal of Cross-Cultural Psychology, 23,* 251–264.

Pashaura Singh (1990). Sikh traditions in Ontario. *Polyphony, 12,* pp. 130–136.

Robert Stansfield (1996). *Issues in Policing: A Canadian Perspective*. Toronto, ON: Thompson Educational Publishing.

Statistics Canada (1992). *Families, Number, Type, and Structure.* Catalogue No. 93-312, Ottawa:13

Statistics Canada (1996). 1996 census data. *The Daily.* Tuesday, January 13, 1998, Ottawa.

Statistics Canada (1999). Police personnel and expenditures 1997 and 1998. *The Daily,* February 9, 1999, Ottawa.

Working Group Response to Rick Linden's paper. Demographic and economic disparity: The community challenge, in: Donald J. Loree (Ed.), *Future Issues in Policing: Symposium Proceedings.* pp. 129–136. Ottawa, ON: The Canadian Police College.

P a r t

II

THE DYNAMICS OF GROUPS AND TEAMS

INTRODUCTION TO WORK GROUPS AND TEAMS

LEARNING OUTCOMES

After studying this chapter you should be able to:

1. Define groups and teams and note differences between them.
2. Explain how groups and teams meet members' personal and professional needs.
3. List the types of teams and groups.
4. Explain the stages of group development according to Tuckman's model.
5. List the common characteristics of groups and teams.
6. Discuss conformity, compliance and obedience as related to groups and behaviour within teams.
7. Identify the characteristics of an effective group and differentiate an effective group from an ineffective group.
8. Identify skills required for effective performance in teams and groups.

This chapter is the introductory chapter to the second part of this text. An understanding of groups and teams is critical to your future success in the field of law enforcement. The "old days" of crime fighting are gone, and the development of a new form of policing is unfolding in response to the changes of a modern nation (Stansfield, 1996). The new trends in community policing, as well as other trends such as increases in private policing, all require candidates to be able to work well with others in teams that can perform at a high capacity (McKenna, 1998). Team-based organizations are the "wave" of the future in Canada and in other countries (Harrison et al., 1994). Similar to other businesses and agencies, policing has undergone, and continues to undergo, many transformations. Being able to work in teams and groups is essential to your career and personal success.

A canine unit is a specialized team.

Throughout life, you belong to a number of groups. Some of these groups, such as your college class, your ethnic or cultural group, are very large. Other groups such as your immediate family, a small circle of friends or a study or work group are smaller. In this chapter we will define teams and groups and why we want and need to be part of groups and teams. Then we will explore the common types of work groups and teams as well as the characteristics of groups and teams. The advantages and disadvantages of working in groups and the barriers to effective team and group work will then be discussed. Last, strategies to improve your ability and skill to work on teams and groups will be provided.

Before moving on to the rest of this chapter and the next chapters, try the quiz below to assess your current level of skills, knowledge and abilities in relation to groups and teams.

WHAT ARE GROUPS AND TEAMS?

People often use "group" and "team" interchangeably as if they are one and the same. You talk about the group that you have to work with and that the group has no team spirit. The next day you refer to the same group as your work team. However, while we do this we need to realize that the two terms are different. First, let's examine groups and then switch our focus to teams.

As you walk down any street downtown on a busy afternoon, you will see large numbers of people. Some of these people are obviously together; they may be holding hands, chatting with one another or sitting at the same cafe table. You can also identify people who are alone even though they may be walking side by side. These people are not part of any group although they may be engaged in similar activities such as standing in line at the bank machine, looking through the same outdoor sales rack or watching a downtown player perform a song. A

SKILLS PRACTICE:

Group and Team Skills

This is a little quiz for you to try. The answers can be found in this chapter and Chapters 9 through 12. For each of the following, answer True if your response is true or mostly true, and False if your response is false or mostly false.

1. Team is another word for group.

2. Teams always have one leader.

3. Heterogeneous teams have members with diverse backgrounds and characteristics.

4. Competition between team members fosters supportive team climate.

5. One method to reduce social loafing is to evaluate individual member progress.

6. People who behave inappropriately on a team should be automatically expelled.

7. Creative thinking is also referred to as lateral thinking.

8. Groupthink tends to occur in highly cohesive groups.

9. Group polarization is the making of risky decisions by a group.

10. Leadership and management are not the same.

11. There has been some research that supports the notion that leaders do have some unique qualities.

12. Leaders are usually low self-monitors.

13. There is a natural tendency for people to want to keep things the same.

14. Coercion is the method for overcoming resistance to change in a police organization.

15. According to force-field analysis, transition is the easiest part of the change process.

Scoring: Give yourself one point if you answered true for questions: 3, 5, 7, 8, 10, 11 and 13.

Give yourself one point if you answered false for questions: 1, 2, 4, 6, 9, 12, 14 and 15.

Results: 0-5   Your knowledge about skills and abilities of groups and teams requires some hard work ahead.

6-10   You have a moderate level of skills and abilities in group and team dynamics. Pay special attention to the areas that you answered incorrectly.

11-15   You are highly skilled in the area of group and team dynamics. Practice your skills so that they match your knowledge level.

After you have finished this part of the book, try this quiz again!

---

group is different from this collection. A **group** consists of "two or more people who are aware of each other, who both influence and are influenced by one another, who are engaged in an ongoing and relatively stable relationship, who share common goals and who view themselves as belonging to the group" (Alcock et al., 1998).

Let's examine each component of the definition so that we are clear as to what a group really is. First, a group consists of at least two people. Some researchers actually define a small group as being comprised of three or more people (Engleberg and Wynn, 1997).

Being aware of each other and being influenced by each other means that group members have interdependence. The members depend upon each other and therefore must communicate and interact. As we are well aware, this interaction will involve both verbal and nonverbal communication. Through communication, meanings and relationships are developed that establish a group context. For example, some groups develop special language or codes that only those within the group understand. In the group, members establish what is considered to be appropriate and inappropriate behaviours. For instance, you may have a group of friends who get together regularly for a meal. Is being late for the meal okay, or is it met with frowns of disapproval and a few sarcastic remarks?

Groups also share common goals. A **goal** is the purpose, circumstance, event, condition or the object that the group strives for in its interaction. Some goals may be informal, such as friendship. Some goals may be more formal, such as raising a certain amount of money for a specific charity.

Last, people consider themselves to be part of the group. Group membership is deemed as important and necessary for the individual. If the group loses its importance for a member, the individual may opt out of the group or engage in other behaviours that may go against group rules or norms. You may have belonged to a group of friends in high school, but physical distance and new interests may diminish the importance of this group for you. On the other hand, some of these members may still live in your hometown, and membership continues to be an important part of their lives.

You most likely belong to several groups. Your family is a group, the friends that you do things with, study groups, sports groups, volunteer groups, are all groups according to the definition. You may belong to a group at work. Some groups can be very large, such as ethnic and cultural groups, while other groups are small and may consist of you and one other person. In Chapter 2 we discussed self-concept. Part of who you are and how you feel about who you are (self-esteem) may be strongly attached to the groups that you identify with over time. Groups are an important part of our lives both on and off the job. As the focus of this text is on work skills, the balance of this chapter will focus on groups and teams in the workplace.

So the question now is how do groups differ from teams? A team starts out as a group, but reaches a new level of quality. Special feelings are created among members, and teams create their own processes and take leadership for its own development and performance (Kinlaw, 1991). A team is a special kind of group that is usually brought together for a special task and has some special characteristics (Lumsden and Lumsden, 1997):

- **A team is a diverse group of people.** In order to achieve its goal(s), a team is made up of people with specific abilities and resources. A group is often made up of a more casual alliance. For instance, a professional sports team usually draws from a wide arena of players with very different talents required for diverse positions on the team.

- **Members share leadership responsibility.** Because of the diversity of talents and abilities, each member must assume leadership as required for the task. For example, on a murder investigation team, one person may be more knowledgeable about one area of the crime scene than the others. At this point, this member gives direction to the other less knowledgeable members.

- **A team creates an identity.** More than an ordinary group, teams develop specific self-images. This image creates cohesiveness and helps to motivate the team. Players begin to see themselves as a "Blue Jay" or "Canadien."

- **Team efforts are interconnected.** A team continuously weaves and interconnects individual team member efforts to develop a tighter energy and higher focus than most groups have. Each team member's efforts become an integral part of the team effort.

- **Members work to achieve a mutually defined goal.** Like groups, teams also have goals. However, team goals involve more intensive communication to develop a consensus as to what the goals are and how they should be achieved.

- **The team works within the context of other groups and systems.** "A team affects, and is affected by, the context, situation, the environment and the system within which it works" (Lumsden and Lumsden, 1997, p. 15). While groups are affected the same way, the relationships within these systems are more likely to be more critical to team functioning.

When these factors are put together, a **team** can be defined as "a diverse group of people who share leadership responsibility for creating a group identity in an interconnected effort to achieve a mutually defined goal within the context of other groups and systems" (Lumsden and Lumsden, 1997, p. 15). In general then, teams are often more tightly knit and cohesive, more focused on mutually defined goals, have more diverse members' backgrounds and are usually formed for a specific purpose. Within police work, there are many highly specialized and trained teams such as special weapons and tactical teams, body recovery teams, forensic teams and so on. These teams are usually made up of highly trained personnel, may have complementary and diverse talents and have specialized goals.

WHY DO WE BELONG TO GROUPS AND TEAMS?

If you examine all the groups that you belong to currently, you can probably list several reasons why you belong to these groups. Being with others socially and professionally meets a number of needs. Using the exercise below, list some of the groups you belong to and identify why you belong to these groups.

SKILLS PRACTICE:

Awarenesss: My Group Memberships

According to several researchers, as we will see below, group memberships fulfill various needs. These groups or teams can be any groups or teams that you currently belong to as well as a group or team you would like to belong to in the future, such as a police tactical unit and so on. Beside the name of the team or group, explain the purpose of this group, such as for studying, and list the reasons why you belong to this group. In other words, what purpose(s) does membership serve for you personally. Refer back to your answers as you read the research and theories of membership after this exercise.

	Purpose of Group	Reasons You Belong
Team or Group #1:		
Team or Group #2:		
Team or Group #3		
Team or Group #4		

Several different theories can be applied to the reasons why we interact with others and interact with others in groups. While we cannot cover all the theories here, we will concentrate on two theories: Maslow's theory that you have seen before and the work of David I. McClelland.

In Chapter 2 we reviewed Maslow's theory. Interacting and communicating with others assists us in meeting needs that include basic physiological needs as well as higher order needs of self-esteem. Maslow called it belongingness and self-actualization. You may wish to quickly review this theory in Chapter 2. In terms of group membership, you need people and need to join groups to help you satisfy basic needs, but you also join groups to help you reach your full potential. Many of you may want to join the police service to satisfy basic needs, but you may have higher order needs such as helping others and protecting those who cannot protect themselves.

David I. McClelland and his associates have done considerable research on what is now termed **McClelland's acquired needs theory** (in Schermerhorn et al., 1994). These three needs are acquired or learned over time through life experiences. The **need for achievement (nAch)** is the need and desire to do something very well, to do something better or more efficiently, to solve problems and to master complex skills or tasks. The **need or affiliation (nAff)** is the desire to have and maintain warm and friendly relations with others. The **need for power (nPower)** is the desire to control and have influence over others and over their behaviour, the desire to be responsible for others. People vary in the strength and magnitude of these needs. Some people may have a low need for affiliation and are content with just a few close friends and enjoy personal solitude and happily work in jobs where there is little contact with others. Others have a high need for affiliation and are continually surrounded by others and like to work in large groups. Most of us fall somewhere between the extremes of each of the three needs. When you review your list, you will probably notice that your answers may have reflected some of these needs. For example, if you have a group of friends that you study with, this group may meet both affiliation and achievement needs (if the group actually studies). Groups and teams in the workplace may help fulfill all of these needs. As a group leader, your need for power may be met as you guide the group towards goal completion. Warm and friendly relations within the group may satisfy your need for affiliation. A group that strives for excellence may meet needs for achievement.

However, a word of caution should also be noted. As we will see later, groups in which members have diverse needs or very different needs can come into conflict. For example, a group of low achievers or people who are content doing just the minimum required to get by can become a source of frustration for the group member with a high need for achievement. Two group members with a high need for power may jostle with each other as they both try to assume group leadership. A group with members all of whom have a high need for affiliation may accomplish little if social needs get in the way of business goals.

TYPES OF GROUPS AND TEAMS IN THE WORKPLACE

There are several types of teams and groups both in and out of the work place, and many different books and articles give them different names or titles. You belong to several different groups right now, and your future in law enforcement will lead you to working on several different teams and with several different groups. Some of these teams and groups will be within your own service. Other groups may include membership across services, and others may be comprised of both police and other personnel. Here we will briefly review some (but not all) of the types of groups and teams that may be found in the workplace. While there are many different types of groups that you belong to outside of work and school, such as primary groups of friends and families, we will concentrate our efforts on the work environment. Several different sources have been used and adapted for this list (Harrison et al., 1994; Lumsden and Lumsden, 1997).

- **Staff groups.** A *staff group* consists of people who work together and meet periodically to discuss and share information such as new policies and procedures, review of previous recommendations and so on. These may be routine (and sometimes boring) meetings that may or may not have a formal agenda. A small business may hold weekly staff meetings to discuss new products, customer complaints and to air any other grievances with the owner or with each other.

- **Ad hoc groups.** *Ad hoc groups* are usually formed to discuss a special issue of concern for those effected by the issue. For example, a group of concerned citizens may get together to discuss the proposal for a site for a new garbage dump in their rural area.

- **Task forces.** As the name implies, *task forces* are set up to work on a specific task, which is often a problem or issue that concerns a larger number of people and various groups. A task force may be set up in a community to examine current youth crime rates and to propose possible solutions. This task force may have representation from several agencies including police, city representatives, school board members and other concerned agencies.

- **Work unit teams.** *Work unit teams* are very similar to traditional workplace organization. The major difference is that there is a much sharper definition of the team's responsibilities and objectives (Harrison et al., 1994). The team is still very traditional in that the team still meets with a superior to review its performance and to solve performance problems.

- **Self-managed teams.** *Self-managed teams* operate similarly to work unit teams, but the responsibility for performance and review of performance rests with the team. The team is responsible for all aspects of its performance. Leadership within the team may vary according to required tasks, or leadership may be done on a rotating basis. To be a truly self-managed team, the team must manage all tasks required for its performance. Much recent research has been devoted to analyzing self-managed teams to determine who make good team members on such a team and under what conditions such a team is most useful (Kichuk and Wiesner, 1998). Self-managed teams may be specialized units that manage special projects or areas within an organization.

- **Project teams.** Similar to a task force in some respects, *a project team* comes together to accomplish a specific goal or task from beginning to end. A project team, like a task force, is usually made up of people with varied backgrounds required for task completion. Unlike a task force, project teams usually occur exclusively within a specific organization. Although task forces can be within an organization, task forces may also exist in the greater community. A task force also usually recommends a course of action, unlike a project team that completes the project. For example, one recommendation of a task force is to have youth more involved in community projects or community efforts. A project team may actually set up the various projects and oversee the initial running of these projects.

- **Specialized Units and Teams** Although not found in other texts, specialized units are part of police services. These units are responsible for specialized areas in policing that require extra or different training from routine patrol work. In some services, a routine officer may also be a member of a specialized unit. Read the Law and Justice Perspective box below for one such specialized team.

LAW AND JUSTICE PERSPECTIVE:

Crisis Intervention Teams

When mentally ill people are in crisis, often it is the police who are the first on the scene. It is important that the first person on the scene has the skills to calm and control the situation rather than someone who may unintentionally make the scene worse and potentially more dangerous. Calls where individuals are out of control or suffering from some sort of mental illness can quickly become a tragic incident. In order to more effectively monitor such calls, the Memphis Police Department has put into place Crisis Intervention Teams (CIT). Officers are trained in techniques to manage disturbed behaviours and then dispatched to calls relating to "mental disturbance."

These officers are not a specialized unit as such but regular patrol officers. These officers continue to handle regular service calls in their assigned areas but also respond to "mental disturbance" calls throughout the jurisdiction. Because these officers are already working and out in the community, the response time is reduced more than in jurisdictions where specialty units may have to be dispatched from further and more remote areas.

There are several advantages of this type of team training. First, it is cost effective, and the mental health training is done by local community members. It is cheaper to train a selected group than an entire service. Also CIT training prevents the occurrence of tragic incidents and reduces the number and severity of injuries to officers and citizens. Third, CIT training saves time as the trained officers can liaise quickly with mental health facilities and reduces the number of arrests of mentally ill people. As more officers are being trained, the team is growing larger. This is truly an example of community policing at its best with a unique partnership of police, mental health providers and advocates.

Source: Donald G. Turnbaugh. Crisis intervention teams: Curing police problems with the mentally ill. *Police Chief*, February 1999, pp. 52-54. Reprinted with the permission of The International Association of Chiefs of Police, Alexandria, VA.

THE ADVANTAGES AND DISADVANTAGES OF GROUP/TEAM WORK

Often when it is explained to a group of students that part of a course grade will rely on team or group work, large moans can be heard throughout the lecture hall. Why is there this flurry of negativity that teachers often hear to such proclamations for team spirit and group effort? Try the box below and assess your best and worst groups! Here we will examine some of the advantages and disadvantages of working in teams and groups.

SKILLS PRACTICE:

Best and Worst Group Assessment

Think about groups that you have been a member of in the past. In particular, think about groups that were formed in order to get something done, such as a school or work project. Of these groups, think of the best group and then think of the worst group and fill in the information below. If possible, try to use headings such as Member Relations or Getting Along. While only four blanks have been provided, feel free to write as many reasons as you can think of.

My Best Group:

The reasons why I liked this group:

1.

2.

3.

4.

My Worst Group:

The reasons why I disliked this group:

1.

2.

3.

4.

When you are finished, read the advantages and disadvantages of group/team work below. Do they match the ones that you have also chosen?

Advantages of Group/Team Work

If there were not significant advantages to working in teams and groups, such work would not be growing in popularity and, as we saw in Chapter 1, listed as an essential skill for today's workers. Let's briefly review some of the advantages that occur in a team or group that is working effectively.

- **Group Performance.** The old saying of "two heads are better than one" may be true when it comes to work groups or teams. Team or group members can bring to the task a wide array of talents, abilities and knowledge that can enhance performance. This is particularly true when the task is complex and when the answers are unclear. With more perspectives and expertise, groups perform better and make better decisions (McClernon, 1991). Also, jobs can be delegated within a group according to member preference or expertise. By delegating, the group may finish a task sooner, and individuals can choose to do the tasks they prefer to do to assist in goal completion. It is important that teams and groups be used for appropriate goals that are better completed by a group than by an individual.

- **Cohesiveness.** Although more likely to occur on teams, highly cohesive group members tend to like and have high positive regard for each other. **Cohesiveness** refers to the desire for the group or team to stay together and is demonstrated by feelings of harmony and solidarity (Alcock et al., 1998). In a highly cohesive group, members are attracted to, and want to be part of, the group or team. Thus, effective groups and teams may also meet our social needs even within a professional setting.

- **Learning.** In effective groups and teams, a great amount of learning can be accomplished in a short amount of time. "By sharing knowledge, stimulating critical thinking, challenging assumptions and even raising standards of achievement," learning can be enhanced for group members (Engleberg and Wynn, 1997, p. 11). In a group, people can learn from each other and can learn effective team skills.

Disadvantages of Team/Group Work

On the flip side, there are many potential negative outcomes of working in groups or teams. How many of us have sat in meetings feeling that the entire meeting was a waste of valuable time? How many times have you said to yourself, "I could have made that decision on my own in half the time"? Of course, we all know the saying that a camel was the invention of a group that was trying to invent a horse. There are many pitfalls to team and group work. Most of these result from having groups or teams work on the wrong goals, having a team make a decision that is better made by an individual or, when there are other group problems, making it difficult for group or team members to interact (Engleberg and Wynn, 1997).

- **Time.** Groups and teams take time to make complex decisions and to come up with answers to difficult questions. Without allowing for time, groups or teams that are hurried or have rigid time constraints may not be capable of making good decisions.

- **Energy and Other Resources.** If organizations cannot provide the resources, including training, required for group and team efforts, the process will waste the time and energy of the participants. While often fulfilling, working on teams and in groups can be draining, and company support is a requirement for successful outcomes.

- **Conflict.** When we work with others, the potential for conflict exists. Some people may not have effective conflict management skills or may cope with a conflict by using avoidance or becoming more aggressive. Mismanaged conflict may be one reason why you now do not like being part of a team or group effort.

- **Personality Clashes and Personal Differences.** When people come together from a diversity of backgrounds, interests and viewpoints, they will not always share our ideas and views on a topic. While such differences may not lead to conflict, these differences can lead to dislike of other team members. Some people are not confident in their own abilities and may go along with others rather than share their own thoughts. Other group members may be quiet. Later in this chapter we will look at roles in the group and review some negative roles that group members may adopt in a group or team setting.

HOW TEAMS AND GROUPS DEVELOP

Teams and groups do not "just happen." Teams, in particular, go through a series of developmental stages that can be identified. There are several theories of group development, including the stages of group development by Tuckman (1965) and the four phases of decision-making groups by Fisher (1970). For our purposes, we will examine the four stages of the Tuckman model, which includes the stages of forming, storming, norming and performing. A fifth stage, adjourning, has been added to these four stages (Laiken, 1994).

The *forming stage* usually occurs when the group or team is new or there are a number of new members. Members are cautious and uncomfortable as they attempt to determine personal relationships and define their tasks. Little work is accomplished. Once the group or team has some idea about goals and responsibilities, the *storming stage* begins. During this stage, members may argue, become more emotional, and conflicts and differences of opinions emerge during team meetings. Important issues and ideas are tabled, and emotions may run high. The *norming stage* can be identified as conflicts are resolved and the group develops approaches for goal completion.

The *performing stage* is entered when the group now focuses its energy on tasks to attain goals. Decisions are reached, problems solved, and the group is now a fully functioning team.

A final stage can be added to this model, which is the *stage of adjourning*. Some teams, such as task forces and ad hoc committees, may be disbanded once the task has been completed or the goal has been reached. During adjournment, group members may experience several different and mixed emotions. They may be sad that the group is now about to be disbanded and may actually experience emotions similar to the grieving process. There may also be relief that the work is now completed and members can focus their energy elsewhere. Members may also feel proud of their accomplishments (Laiken, 1994).

COMMON CHARACTERISTICS OF GROUPS AND TEAMS

All teams and groups share some common characteristics in varying degrees. For example, a sports team adheres to a formal structure with clearly defined roles and responsibilities within a larger system of teams, leagues and so on. Other groups such as friendship groups may have less formal structure with less clearly defined member roles and responsibilities. Professional teams such as tactical units are more formal, although the personal relationships may be less formalized. Let's examine some of the common characteristics of groups and teams. These characteristics include the presence of norms to govern members' behaviour, structure, degree of cohesiveness, roles and status and patterns of communication.

Norms

Norms are shared beliefs about what behaviours are acceptable or unacceptable for members within a specific group or team. Some norms may be **explicit,** which include ones that are stated verbally, or may actually be written down. For example, a team may have a manual of policies and procedures that clearly states how team members file complaints or how team members are to interact in a meeting. Some business teams have their norms of how they are to behave posted on the wall on their meeting rooms.

Some norms are not written or verbally spoken and are classified as **implicit norms**. These norms usually stem from the group's interaction over time (Engleberg and Wynn,

1997). Often, we are not aware of such implicit norms on our teams or in our groups until one of the members (or one of us) breaks or bends one of these norms. Where we sit during a team meeting may be an implicit norm that demonstrates the power arrangement in a group or with whom we are most aligned in a group. Students frequently sit in the same spot in a classroom and may even feel a little annoyed when they find their "favourite" spot taken by another student.

Norms can be further divided into the types of functions that they perform for the group or team. Teams' norms are usually more rigid than those of a less formal group. The four categories of norms are interaction norms, procedural norms, status norms and achievement norms (Englberg and Wynn, 1997).

Interaction norms are the rules around how group or team members will communicate with one another. Much of what we have talked about in this text would fall under this category of interaction with others. Some norms may centre around such issues as how personal are the relations to be among members or the extent of participation by members. How is conflict to be managed? Are conflicts tabled for the entire group to work out, or is conflict avoided?

Procedural norms are the expectations about how the group or team will operate to accomplish goals. Are members expected to attend and contribute to every meeting? Is it permissible to be late? Will there be an agenda and minutes, and who will be in charge of the proceedings? Are decisions voted on, or will the group need to arrive at consensus?

Status norms identify the levels of influence and the pecking order in a group or team. Assigning status means that an individual is given a certain degree of prestige, respect, influence or power within a group or team. How is status assigned in the group or team? Will status vary according to the current work of the group, and will the person with the most expertise in a current area have the highest status? Or will status be more rigid and assigned according to rank, authority or other external characteristics? Status may perhaps be based on personal characteristics such as communication and interpersonal skills, trustworthiness or intelligence.

Structure

All groups have some sort of structure that falls along a continuum from formal to informal to less structure. **Formal groups and work teams** are usually structured more rigidly, and membership may be more controlled. For example, to belong to an exclusive country club in some areas, you may need to be sponsored, be able to pay a very high price for membership and engage in other group rituals (such as the loser has to buy drinks for the entire group). Many youth gangs have a very rigid structure with a set of norms that govern conduct, dress, lines of authority and strict rituals to gain membership. The norms in a formal group may be more explicit with consequences for those who do not conform to the rules. Formal work teams are formed to accomplish specific goals or set of tasks within an organization (McShane, 1995). As part of a Morality Unit on a police service, your team's goals may include reducing prostitution in a specific residential area.

Informal groups are less rigidly structured, and membership may be more open. The purpose of these groups is usually to meet personal needs of the members (McShane, 1995). If you are new to your college, you may already be part of a friendship group that readily "let you in" because of similarity of interests and interpersonal attraction. In such a group, conforming to group norms may not be as strict, and you may be allowed to deviate more from the norms of the group. This does not mean that you can behave any way you please. There is just more latitude as to what is considered appropriate or inappropriate. Some groups at work may also be informal and based more on lines of friendship than on bureaucratic structure and formal roles.

Also, teams or groups may be structured according to some sort of **hierarchy** or along the lines of power and authority. Formal work teams may have supervisors, managers and captains who head the team and have formal authority over what team members do on the job. Larger teams may have more than one supervisor with various degrees of authority. Self-managed teams may rotate formal leadership in the team depending upon the tasks and goals on which the team is currently focusing its efforts. Informal groups may also have a hierarchy, but it is often not based on assigned positions. Rather, the structure may have a hierarchy based on talents of members, age of members, personal or social skills of members, expertise or other characteristics of the members themselves.

Cohesiveness

Another characteristic that groups and teams share is varying degrees of cohesiveness. Earlier, we stated that teams are more inclined towards higher cohesiveness than groups. In a highly cohesive group or team, members like each other very much, the goals are highly valued by all members and members often see this group as the best possible way to meet individual needs. As such, cohesive groups exert strong control over their members (Philipchalk, 1995).

Groups that are low in cohesion do not have as great an influence on their members. Perhaps you have belonged to a group where you did not like the other members, did not agree with the group goals and saw other and better ways to meet your needs.

Roles and Status

The third characteristic of groups and teams is the presence of distinct roles for members. Tied in with these roles is the status of group members in relation to others within the group. In the next chapter we will examine the various roles that members play within a group that foster or hinder group decision-making and problem solving. Here, it is important that you realize that each of us plays a specific role or set of roles in a group. In both formal groups and teams and in informal groups, members adopt various roles within the group setting. In formal groups and work teams, roles may be assigned, such as group leader, minutes taker and manager. Other roles may not be assigned but are products of the team and group interaction. For example, although not an "official role," one team member is very supportive of others and has a role of smoothing "ruffled feathers" during conflict and for easing tensions after a conflict.

For many of these roles, a certain amount of status is granted to that role by the group. In some groups and teams, these roles may be assigned by a higher authority. Police services have officers of different rank, and part of the duty of officers of lower rank is to carry out the instructions of higher-ranked officers. These are formal roles based on a structure or hierarchy, as mentioned in the previous section. In informal groups, status, like roles, may also not be assigned but develop through continued group interaction. In a friendship group, one person has more status because he or she organizes much of the group's social activities. Other group members look to this person to organize their social activities.

Patterns of Communication

Within groups and teams, patterns of communication are important aspects of group processes (Johnson and Johnson, 1985). The frequency and length of communication among group members is one pattern of communication. Does one person talk more than others? Does someone not talk at all? Who talks to whom is another pattern. Are all comments directed to the "leader" of the group or team? Does communication flow freely between members? A third pattern according to Johnson and Johnson (1985) is what is termed "triggering." When one person speaks or communicates, is there a pattern as to who speaks next and what is said? For example, is one person continually interrupted by the same person, and is this interruption always confrontational? Does one person always speak after another person and support the other's position? Is one person continually ignored? Viewing and understanding these patterns may tell you about the status and roles of members within the group or team.

INFLUENCES WITHIN GROUPS AND TEAMS: CONFORMITY, COMPLIANCE AND OBEDIENCE

Although rarely found in texts with chapters about team and group work, due to the nature of policing and its relation to society, conformity, compliance and obedience should be discussed in this chapter. In groups and in society, others influence us to behave in certain ways or not to behave in certain ways. Conformity, compliance and obedience are three different levels of social influence. Often we use the terms interchangeably, but they are actually very different, with conformity at one end of the continuum and obedience at the other end (Philipchalk, 1995). Entire books have been written on how to socially influence others, win friends, get your own way, even attract the perfect mate! Within teams and groups, members influence each other through a variety of overt and covert techniques. How can you get others to agree with your ideas? Second, how do we get group members to adhere to the group's rules or norms? The first question about getting others to agree with us will be explored in the next chapter under the heading Group Skills. Here we want to briefly explore the second question about adherence to group norms and rules.

Conformity is adhering to the norms of the group and going along with, or yielding to, perceived group pressures. When individuals in a group or on a team are pressured to conform, subtle techniques are used. Earlier in the text, we discussed nonverbal communication and nonverbal behaviour. A pursed lip or withdrawal of eye contact may be all that is needed to control a group member who is going against the norms of a group. Have you ever walked into a class or meeting late? No one said anything to you, but you immediately knew that the rest of the group was displeased with your behaviour. At the next meeting, were you on time or did you continue to "break" the rule or norm of punctuality?

Social approval and fear of social disapproval may be major reasons why we adhere to group norms (Alcock et al., 1998). This appears to be especially true in highly cohesive groups where membership is highly valued. When the situation is unclear to us, we also conform to the group. As a new officer, you may look to other officers and model some of your behaviour after their behaviour in various situations. We may also conform to group influence if we truly believe that the group is correct in its position. This leads to **private acceptance** where we change our ideas or behaviour because we see the group as right. This is very different from **public compliance** where we go along with the group even when we do not believe the group is right. We feel pressure to conform to the norms of the group. You may feel that being five or ten minutes late to a meeting is perfectly acceptable. You may change your behaviour, but your attitude may be "what's the big deal?"

Compliance is a stronger than conformity. With compliance, we yield to a direct request from another person. "Do not be late for meetings" is a direct request for you to change your behaviour. As police officers, you will be in situations daily where citizens are expected to comply with your requests to move vehicles, to stop loitering, to pull over or to answer questions. You may comply with the request of a fellow officer who has more experience than you or more expertise than you.

More importantly, for the purposes of group examination, as an officer within an organization of ranks, you will also be expected to comply with the requests of your superior officers. This type of compliance is actually obedience. **Obedience** is at the highest end of social influence and involves complying with a direct request of someone whom you perceive to be a higher authority. Lack of compliance may result in official sanctions and even expulsion from the group. Police officers also have the power and authority to demand obedience from the public when circumstances and the law make such obedience necessary. Ordering an individual to put down a weapon is done differently from requesting to see a driver's license. The first is a direct request for obedience; the latter is a request for compliance. It is important that officers differentiate between conformity, compliance and obedience so that communication can be adjusted accordingly. When obedience is an issue, tactical communication and the tactical use of force may be justified.

However, do groups and teams expect obedience from members? The answer is that it depends upon the type of group or team and what the team's tasks are at any given moment. In some youth gangs and other gangs, obedience to the leader is expected. At work, in jobs that are based on rank organizations such as the army and policing, obedience to superior officers is part of the job. In other groups and teams, to expect and demand obedience would probably result in the expulsion of the member who is attempting to get others to obey. Can you imagine how you would react if your best friend started to expect your unquestioning assent to his or her every request?

EFFECTIVE AND INEFFECTIVE GROUPS AND TEAMS

In the next chapter we will look at the skills you can develop to work effectively on teams and in groups. Before looking at these skills, we need to decide what is an effective team or group. If you survey job postings, they often include under the employee qualifications something to the effect of being a good team player or being able to thrive in a team-based environment. The new Police Foundations training in Ontario has several courses in it about communication, interpersonal skills and group skills. Think about some of these questions. What personal characteristics do you think are important for effective team and group work? Do you have to like fellow members or just be able to reach the goals of the group or team? What kinds of behaviours drive you crazy on a team or in a group? These are the same questions that researchers have been attempting to answer for years.

According to Johnston and Johnston (1985), effective groups have three core activities: accomplishing goals, maintaining themselves internally and developing and changing in ways to improve effectiveness. We might want to add a fourth activity: being able to respond and adapt to changing environmental conditions. While we do not want to use the entire model proposed by Johnston and Johnston, let's examine and summarize their nine dimensions of group effectiveness from their book, *Joining Together: Group Theory and Group Skills* (1985).

1. *Group goals* are clearly understood, relevant to the needs of the members, evoke commitment and promote positive interdependence among members.

2. *Group communication* is effective. Members freely express their ideas and feelings accurately to each other.

3. *Participation and leadership* is distributed among members. Everyone gets a chance to participate, *to be listened to,* and all members are "involved in the group's work, committed to implementing the group's decisions and satisfied with their membership" (p. 9).

4. Appropriate *decision-making* techniques are used based on the needs of the situation. The type of decision must be considered, the available resources accounted for and how the decision is to be made are all relevant. *Consensus* is the most effective way to make a decision. **Consensus** means that all members unanimously support the decision.

5. *Power* and *influence* should be distributed equally in the group based on such characteristics as knowledge, expertise, ability and so on rather than based on authority or seniority.

6. *Conflict* should be encouraged not discouraged when it is focused on ideas and opinions.

7. *Group cohesion* should be high. Liking and respecting other members maintains the desire to remain with the group.

8. *Problem-solving skills* and the ability to use those skills should be high.

9. *Interpersonal effectiveness* of members needs to be high. Effective interpersonal skills (from the first part of this book) are essential to being able to do well in a group.

10. This has been added. *Flexibility and adaptability* of the group is essential to continued success. The group must maintain an outward focus and adjust itself to outside changes that may have impact on the success of the group in accomplishing its goals or tasks.

Team effectiveness is the extent to which a team can attain it objectives or goals, achieve and meet the needs of individual members and sustain itself over time (McShane, 1995). This effectiveness results from a combination of the design and context of the team, the team characteristics, the interactive skills of its members and the quality and action skills of the members (Wellins et. al, 1991; McShane, 1995). An effective team is thus selected carefully, and the characteristics of the members are taken into account. As well, the type of skills and the quality of the work of the team members are also taken into consideration. Table 8-1 compares effective groups with ineffective groups on several of the dimensions above.

As you can probably ascertain by now, good teams and groups do not just happen. Training is at the heart of a functioning team. Such training in these team and group skills has also been a focus of research in policing and in the training of recruits. Several authors in the field of policing (Robert Stansfield, 1996; Chacko and Nancoo, 1993) have demonstrated that with the new focus on community policing, managing the increasing diversity of this nation and dealing with complex issues, recruits and current officers need extensive

TABLE 8-1	Comparison of Effective and Ineffective Groups	
Effective Groups	**Ineffective Groups**
Goals are clarified and changed so that the best possible match between individual goals and the group's goals may be achieved; goals are cooperatively structured.	Members accepts imposed goals; goals are competitively structured.
Communication is two-way, and the open and accurate expression of both ideas and feelings is emphasized.	Communication is one-way and only ideas are expressed; feelings are suppressed or ignored.
Participation and leadership are distributed among all group members; goal accomplishment, internal maintenance, and developmental change are underscored.	Leadership is delegated and based upon authority; membership participation is unequal, with high-authority members dominating; only goal accomplishment is emphasized.
Ability and information determine influence and power; contracts are built to make sure individuals' goals and needs are fulfilled; power is equalized and shared.	Position determines influence and power; power is concentrated in the authority positions; obedience to authority is the rule.
	Decisions are always made by the highest authority; there is little group discussion; members' involvement is minimal.
Decision-making procedures are matched with the situation; different methods are used at different times; consensus is sought for important decisions; involvement and group discussions are encouraged.	
Controversy and conflict are seen as a positive key to members' involvement, the quality and originality of decisions, and the continuance of the group in good working condition.	Controversy and conflict are ignored, denied, avoided, or suppressed.
Interpersonal, group, and intergroup behaviours are stressed; cohesion is advanced through high levels of inclusion, affection, acceptance, support, and trust. Individuality is endorsed.	The functions performed by members are emphasized; cohesion is ignored and members are controlled by force. Rigid conformity is promoted.
Problem-solving adequacy is high.	Problem-solving adequacy is low.
Members evaluate the effectiveness of the group and decide how to improve its functioning; goal accomplishment, internal maintenance, and development are all considered important.	The highest authority evaluates the group's effectiveness and decides how goal accomplishment may be improved; internal maintenance and development are ignored as much as possible; stability is affirmed.
Interpersonal effectiveness, self-actualization, and innovation are encouraged.	"Organizational persons" who desire order, stability, and structure are encouraged.

Source: Johnson & Johnson (1985). *Joining Together: Group Theory & Group Skills,* Prentice Hall Inc. p. 11.

training in team skills. The second half of this text is devoted to teaching you the skills for effective team and group work. Briefly, the skills are listed here:

- **Interpersonal Skills.** In the next chapter we will cover the interpersonal skills for working effectively in a group. Some of these will be a review of some previous skills but based on small group interaction rather than a person-to-person focus. We will examine interpersonal attraction as it relates to groups.

- **Goal-Setting and Decision-Making and Problem Solving.** There are several strategies that can assist in helping you in a group to set goals, solve problems and make decisions.

- **Developing Leadership Skills.** Effective teams share leadership. You need an understanding of power, leadership and skills to be a leader on a team.

- **Skills for Adapting to Change.** Groups and teams must be able to manage and adjust to change. Groups that remain static and do not change when the environment around them changes are doomed to eventual failure, or at the very least, a period of stress and upheaval. Understanding change and gaining knowledge of the changes in policing will be essential for your career.

"Armed" with these skills, you will fulfill the requirement for a good "team player" and will have a solid idea as to what it really means to be part of a team.

SUMMARY

In this chapter teams and groups were introduced as major ways that much of our personal and work goals and needs are met. With the increasing use of teams in our professional lives, it is important to understand what groups and teams are and the skills required for effective performance on a team.

First, groups and teams were defined. Major differences between groups and teams were discussed. Although the two terms are often used interchangeably, teams are characterized by stronger cohesion and a stronger sense of purpose with more clearly defined goals. Teams tend to be made up by more members with more diversity, have a stronger sense of identity, and leadership is a shared responsibility. Teams also operate within other systems.

We then examined the reasons why we belong and join teams and groups. We join for both personal and professional reasons. There are many types of groups and teams in the workplace including staff groups, ad hoc groups, task forces, work unit teams, self-managed teams, project teams and specialized units. There are advantages and disadvantages to group and team work. We also explored how teams and groups develop and some of the common characteristics of groups and teams such as norms, structure, cohesiveness, roles and status and patterns of communication. A special section on conformity, compliance and obedience was added to assist you in understanding the different levels of social influence that may exist within teams and groups. The chapter ended with a look at effective and ineffective groups and teams and how this part of the text will help you to become an effective team member.

JOURNAL AND DISCUSSION QUESTIONS

1. Now that you have completed this chapter on groups and teams, what are some strategies that you could try to improve concerning your performance on a team or in a group?

2. Norms can assist a group in meeting its goals, but norms can also interfere with goal completion. What are some norms that could develop in a group that would make reaching goals more difficult?

3. "In policing, being able to work effectively in teams is a critical skill." Discuss this statement.

WEB SITES

www.workteams.unt.edu

This is the site for the Centre for the Study of Work Teams from the University of Texas.

www.uiowa.edu/~grpproc

From the University of Iowa, this is the Centre for the Study of Group Processes. Of real interest is that from this site you can link to full text articles from the journal Current Research in Social Psychology.

www.theiapc.org

This is the site for the International Association of Chiefs of Police. There are several sites of interest here including a link to the magazine, Police Chief.

REFERENCES

J. E. Alcock, D. W. Carment and S. W. Sadava (1998). *A Textbook of Social Psychology,* 4th edition. Scarborough, ON: Prentice Hall Allyn and Bacon Canada.

James Chacko and Stephen E. Nancoo, editors (1993). *Community Policing in Canada.* Toronto, ON: Canadian Scholars' Press Inc. This book has several articles about teams and the new focuses in policing.

Isa N. Engleberg and Dianna R. Wynn (1997). *Working in Groups: Communication Principles and Strategies.* New York: Houghton Mifflin Company.

Brian D. Harrison, Henry P. Conn, Barrie Whitaker and James Mitchell (1994). "Mobilizing abilities through teamwork," *Canadian Business Review,* Vol. 21, pp. 20–27.

David W. Johnson and Frank P. Johnson (1985). *Joining Together: Group Theory and Group Skills,* 3rd edition. Englewood Cliffs, NJ: Prentice Hall.

Susan Kichuk and Willi H. Wiesner (1998). "Work Teams: Selecting members for optimal performance," *Canadian Psychology*, 39, pp. 23–32

Dennis Kinlaw (1991*). Developing Superior Work Teams: Building Quality and the Competitive Edge.* Lexington, MA: Lexington Books.

Marilyn E. Laiken (1994). *The Anatomy of High Performing Teams: A Leader's Handbook.* Toronto, ON: OISE Press.

Gay Lumsden and Donald Lumsden (1997). *Communicating in Groups and Teams: Sharing Leadership,* 2nd edition. Belmont, CA: Wadsworth Publishing Company.

T. R. McClernon (1991). One hundred percent participation: Key to team effectiveness, in R. A. Swanson and B. O. Knapp (Eds.), *Innovative Meeting Management.* Austin, TX: Minnesota Mining and Manufacturing, p. 157.

Paul F. McKenna (1998). *Foundations of Policing in Canada.* Scarborough, ON: Prentice Hall Canada.

Steven L. McShane (1995). *Canadian Organizational Behaviour 2nd edition.* Toronto, ON: Times Mirror Publishing Ltd.

Ronald P. Philipchalk (1995). *An Invitation to Social Psychology.* Orlando, FL: Harcourt Brace College Publishers.

John R. Schermerhorn, Jr., James G. Hunt and Richard N. Osborn (1994). *Managing Organizational Behavior,* 5th edition. New York: John Wiley and Sons, Inc.

Ronald T. Stansfield (1996). *Issues in Policing: A Canadian Perspective.* Toronto, ON: Thompson Educational Publishing.

Richard S. Wellins, William C. Byham and Jeanne M. Wilson (1991). *Empowered Teams: Creating Self-Directed Work Groups that Improve Quality, Productivity, and Participation.* San Francisco, CA: Jossey-Bass Publishers.

GETTING ALONG WITH GROUP AND TEAM MEMBERS

C h a p t e r

9

LEARNING OUTCOMES

After studying this chapter you should be able to:

1. Explain why we are attracted to some people.
2. Identify and explain several factors that influence team design and composition.
3. Explain several factors that influence team success.
4. Identify barriers to effective teamwork.
5. Explain several factors and steps that must be considered when building a team.
6. Use a variety of skills to enhance personal performance on a team.

Another typical team meeting:

Person 1: *Let's go through these ideas again. Should we focus on lighting in the park to deter these youths or get into something more involved like increasing youth activities during evening hours?*

Person 2: *It's getting late. I have to go so can we just decide one way or the other? Why do you keep going on about this?*

Person 3: *I know that you must be feeling tired too, but I can see that we need to carefully select among the alternatives. The first idea is easy but doesn't really resolve the problem.*

Person 1: *Exactly, the first idea is just a Band-Aid solution. The real issue is to get these kids off the streets and doing legal activities, not hanging out and getting into trouble.*

Person 2: *Well, isn't that up to the parents? My shift is over! You city agency types keep on haggling with your big salaries. I say let us do our work and get the little worms off the street with good old policing tactics. This committee is a waste of my time.*

Peterborough Lakefield Community Police Service

A containment unit requires members with specialized training

Person 3: *You are a valuable part of this group. Your experience in policing and dealing with young offenders is critical to our decision-making. But you are right, parental involvement is necessary. Do you have ideas about getting the parents more involved?*

Person 2: *Well, now that you mention it. I have been reading about ....*

If you look closely at the dialogue above, you can probably pick out the person who has some good communication and team skills. Now that you have a good understanding of groups and teams, let's move on to explore groups and teams in more depth. At the heart of team and group work are the people that make up the team or group. It is not enough to know the types of teams and groups, the goals the group is striving to reach and the tasks required to attain the goal. Being part of a group is an intricate balance of personalities that makes or breaks the team. Skills are required to be part of an effective team as you can see from this dialogue. In this chapter we will first examine interpersonal attraction. Interpersonal attraction is an important part of understanding why we get along with others, become close and intimate with others and why we do not like some people. Being attracted to team and group members can help establish positive relations within the group. Next, we will examine the factors and characteristics of what makes an effective team. As well, people assume behaviours and roles on teams; some of them enhance the group effort while other roles diminish group performance. We will examine the barriers to effective team and group work. Last and perhaps most important, we will finish by discussing the skills that will help you to play positive roles on a team and make you an effective "team player."

INTERPERSONAL ATTRACTION

Choosing policing as a profession means that you will spend a great deal of your professional life dealing with others. Unlike computer technicians, your client is not a machine but a human being. You will communicate with fellow officers, representatives from numerous agencies, lawyers, judges and the public. You will see people at their very best and people at their very worst, and out of all these people, some you will like and some you will dislike. Chances are you will meet people who will become your closest and most intimate friends, and many of these people will be fellow officers. An understanding of why we interact with others and the interpersonal attraction will assist you in understanding some of the complexities of interpersonal communication and interpersonal relationships.

Several researchers have pointed out that managers spend as much as 80 percent of their time interacting with others (Klemmer and Snyder, 1972; Penley et al., 1991). Adults spend 71 percent of their time interacting with others (Csikszentmihalyi and Figurski, 1982). Obviously, interaction and **social affiliation** are important parts of work and personal life. Team- and group-based work has its foundation in interpersonal interaction. Here, we will examine the factors that determine **interpersonal attraction**. How much we like others on a team or group may have an impact on its performance.

Determinants of Interpersonal Attraction

While many of the theories and factors of interpersonal attraction refer to romantic relationships, they can also be applied to friendships and our initial attraction to co-workers. These theories and factors are usually concerned with attraction to strangers and the beginnings of a relationship. Not all the factors will be discussed here. For further research and information, you may want to consult social psychology texts.

Proximity

We are more likely to interact with others with whom we can have contact. **Proximity,** or continued physical closeness, increases the likelihood of repeated exposures. This repeated exposure appears to facilitate attraction (Alcock et al., 1996). Increased exposure leads to more opportunities to learn about the other person, and it appears that this continued interaction leads to the comfort of familiarity. The officers that you work with regularly in a group or team thus become your friends due to this proximity.

Physical Attractiveness

While we may dislike seeming shallow, we tend to be attracted to people whom we find physically attractive. However, since we cannot all attract the most beautiful as friends, it appears that we tend to attract those who are roughly similar to us in physical attractiveness. This tendency to choose others who are similar to our own physical attractiveness is referred to as the **matching hypothesis.** Matching occurs among romantic partners and female friends. It is less common among male friends (Feingold, 1988).

Similarity

As well as similar in physical attractiveness, we are more attracted to those who have similar attitudes, interests and values to our own (Alcock et al., 1996). It may make sense that the people to whom you become attracted are others in the field of law enforcement as you are at least similar in your career choices. This foundation may lead to discovering further shared interests.

Reinforcement

In our dealings with others, we also like people who reward us and who do nice things for us. Some theorists believe that the principle of reinforcement is at the heart of all interpersonal attraction (Alcock et al., 1996). The **reinforcement-affect model** states that we are attracted to people who we associate with events or stimuli that arouse positive feelings. Not only do we like those who reward us, we also like those whom we have met or those with whom we have been in contact during events or situations that we find pleasing. For example, you may be more attracted to someone at a party or social event if you are actually enjoying yourself and having fun.

However, one limitation to this model concerns how much we give or get. If we get too much or give more than the other person, an imbalance occurs. We like **equity** or fairness in a relationship. We may feel guilty or angry if we perceive that the relationship is not equitable.

Social Exchange Theory

According to another theory, that of **social exchange**, human relationships are largely based on self-interest. Research indicates that we measure our social, physical and other assets against those of potential partners. Close matches tend to lead to long-term relationships. Again, as with reinforcement, a lack of fairness in the exchange can lead to hurt feelings if one partner feels he or she is being taken advantage of or if one person feels he or she is taking advantage of the partner (Dubrin and Geerinck, 1998).

How does all of this relate to working in groups and teams? One important way that attraction relates to groups and teams has to do with the formation of teams. Many workers are simply placed on teams or in work groups with little or no thought given to team or group makeup. Once on a team, the team develops through the stages of group formation that were discussed in Chapter 8. Team members who are attracted to each other may be able to develop more quickly into a cohesive and fully functioning team than a team whose members do not feel any attraction towards each other. Can you recall a team or group that you worked on where members did not like each other? The experience can be unpleasant, and trying to accomplish work can be significantly reduced on a team that suffers such discord.

Second, attraction to other members leads to positive feelings about the group experience. Cohesive teams invariably report that they liked the other members, liked being together and felt that what they were doing was important and meaningful (see Chapter 8). In essence, the team make-up is an important factor when differentiating between effective teams and ineffective teams. Here we will turn our attention to how to design an effective team and the important items to consider in team design. Even if you have no choice in your team composition, being aware of what these factors are will help you understand the dynamics of any team you are a member of currently and of those teams you will be a member of down the road.

FACTORS IN TEAM DESIGN AND COMPOSITION

With the increased use of teams in business and other organizations, a great deal of research has been devoted to trying to come up with effective techniques to ensure good teams: teams that work together effectively, achieve organizational goals, monitor their own performance and surpass management expectations. Teams share some common factors or attributes. Teams use some sort of selection process, have a heterogeneous or homogenous make-up, vary in size, develop a climate and develop a culture.

Selecting Team Members

Over the years, there has been research attempting to answer the questions surrounding team membership. This may be the most important question. "A team's effectiveness depends on membership composition" (McShane, 1995, p. 303). If an organization wants a team to be successful, then the first logical step is to select the right combination of people (Kichuk and Wiesner, 1998).

One method of assigning team membership is to use some sort of *screening* or *testing* to determine team membership. Many organizations rely on some sort of measure of personality to either predict potential success on a team or to assign employees to a particular team. This author was once on a team where members were assigned based on the personality types from the **Myers-Briggs Type Indicator (MBTI)**. The MBTI is an instrument used to help people identify their personal preferences and is still used for many job-related purposes such as human resource development, problem solving and team building as well as for personal counselling (Falikowski, 1996). Using various tests, potential members can be selected or not be selected to be part of a team.

Using tests or other instruments to assess **personality traits** and to assist in group member selection has gained popularity with newer and higher quality tests and "by the emergence of a widely accepted personality classification referred to as the 'Big Five' (Conscientiousness, Extraversion, Neuroticism, Agreeableness and Openness to Experience)" (Kichuk and Wiesner, 1998). According to Kichuk and Wiesner, personality may be one important factor for predicting future job performance. However, while these tests may measure personality and predict individual job performance, their use for team staffing is much more complex.

In their article, Kichuk and Wiesner (1998) do, however, summarize several studies that indicate that some personality traits affect performance for certain tasks in certain groups and situations. The following traits appear to affect individual performance within various types of groups and teams:

* **Conscientiousness.** Employees who are organized, dependable and responsible will help a group or team achieve its goals.

* **Need for Achievement.** Several studies that were summarized found that a group where members had a high need for achievement outperformed groups where members displayed a low need for achievement.

* **Extroversion and Sociability.** As being part of a team involves extensive social interaction, **extroversion,** or the ability to mingle and interact with others, may be an important characteristic or ability.

* **Dominance.** Used in many studies, this characteristic refers to both ambition and will as the degree of participation in the group.

* **Emotional Stability.** Emotional stability, or a lack of neuroticism, was positively correlated with group performance.

* **Agreeableness.** The results are mixed for this one! Some results did not find any relationship between group member likeability and group performance, while other studies found that group performance did suffer when members were not liked.

According to Kirchuk and Wiesner (1998), the use of personality to select team members requires further research and study and, if used, should be done very carefully so as not to disadvantage potential candidates. If personality or other characteristics or traits tests are going to be used to assign membership in a group or team, the next question then becomes whether we assign people to groups that have similar tests results or whether we assign people to groups to complement each other (different results).

In reality, selection based on some criteria may not happen. Another method of team selection is self-selection. For example, "Who would like to be a member of a task force examining student retention?" In other words, you may want to volunteer to be part of a team.

A third way of becoming a team member is to be assigned. For example, "John, as your manager, I think you would be an excellent candidate to be on this task force. Could you get going on it as soon as possible." Often, being a team member is not a choice but part of your job or role within an organization. Regardless of whether you like it or not, you may have little choice as to whether or not you will be part of a specific team or work group.

Team Heterogeneity

Homogeneous teams are comprised of members with things in common such as technical expertise, ethnicity, values or other personality constructs that were just discussed. **Heterogeneous teams** have members with diverse personal characteristics and backgrounds (McShane, 1995). It appears that which type of team is best depends upon the goals of the team and the types of tasks the members are performing.

When cooperation and coordination are essential, homogeneous teams may be the best choice for such work as emergency response teams (McShane, 1995). This also supports the notion of similarity as being an important factor in the mutual attraction of group members (Kirchuk and Wiesner, 1998). As well, such similarity may also lead to the other factors that affect interpersonal attraction. For example, if I share many common interests with you, I can more easily reinforce you and reward you for our shared interests.

On the other hand, heterogeneity of team members' personalities may also be beneficial in other situations. If the group or team is responsible for a large diversity of tasks, then a mix of personality types may be better (Kirchuk and Weisner, 1998). Also, diverse backgrounds may be beneficial in problem-solving groups as the knowledge and experience base may be broader (McShane, 1995). However, more diverse groups or teams may also be more prone to interpersonal conflicts that may negatively affect performance. When designing teams, the people responsible need to be mindful of the purpose of the team when determining whether the team should be homogeneous or heterogeneous. When forming teams, being aware of how people differ or how people are similar may help in team formation.

Some testing could be used to let team members themselves know how they score in relation to others on the team. When I was involved in the above team where assignment was based on the MBTI, group members were made aware of their own scores as well as the scores of other team members. During work problems or interpersonal conflict, we would jokingly refer to the different scores as the source. Such humour and understanding paved the way for good member relations for the lifetime of this task force.

Team Size

How large should a team be? The answer lies in the purpose of the group. Some decisions may require a large number of persons while some decisions only require one or two people. Larger teams may be more ineffective as it takes time to coordinate activities, and the potential for conflicts may also increase as the size of the group increases. In large teams not everyone may get a chance to participate, while in smaller teams people may become more involved and have more input. According to several sources, a rule of thumb is that a team should have no more than nine members (Johnson and Johnson, 1985). The important consideration is that the size of the group or team should be based on the goals and purposes of the team or group work.

Team Climates

Think again about your past team and group memberships. If you are like many others, some teams you thoroughly enjoyed being a part of while others you dragged your heels to every meeting. One significant difference between these two teams was the type of climate of each team. Teams meet, and as the team meets a **communication climate** develops. A communication climate "describes the conditions that people create and are, in turn, influenced by" (Lumsden and Lumsden, 1997, p. 89). Climates are created through the communication of team members and are similar to the defensive and supportive climates discussed in Part I of this text.

A *positive climate* is open and supportive. Members are attracted to each other and to the team. The climate is challenging. According to one researcher, such teams have members with strong feelings of inclusion, loyalty, pride, commitment and trust for each other (Kinlaw, 1991).

Conversely, a *negative climate* is closed and non-supportive. On this type of team, people withdraw, become defensive and engage in negative roles (see later in this chapter) and play manipulative games (Lumsden and Lumsden, 1997). Team performance and outcomes are poor.

Team Culture

Like other cultures, teams develop their own cultures over time. This **team culture** grows and develops in much the same way as any other culture, through continued interaction and learning. As the stages of group development indicated, the group goes through a process of norming where group rules and norms are decided upon. Team cultures are unique; you may belong to several teams all of which have very different cultures.

BARRIERS FOR EFFECTIVE TEAMS

Before moving on to the two most important topics of this chapter, team building and effective team skills, let's examine the barriers to effective team development and performance. Some of these barriers may be imposed upon the group by outside forces that the group may not be able to control. Other barriers are internal and result from group interaction and processes.

Time Constraints

When a work group or team does not have sufficient time to make a decision, complete goals or tasks, or solve a problem, the members may not put forth their best efforts. This type of pressure can create stress and work overload. Conflicts may erupt. As a result, the group or team may perform poorly.

Physical Barriers

Not all groups and teams work in environments conducive to structure. For example, in a course you may have had to work in groups during class. A room that is too small, too hot, too cold, too noisy and affected by other negative environmental barriers is a more difficult place for people to work. Teams that have members spread out geographically find it more difficult to get together. These types of barriers need to be dealt with before team formation so that these problems can be dealt with early in team development.

Inappropriate Group Size

Groups that are too large or groups that are too small, depending upon the purpose of the group or team, can create a barrier to effective performance. In a group that is too large, members may feel that they do not get enough opportunities for input, there may be more interpersonal conflict and individual resources may not be fully utilized. Groups that are too small may not be able to handle the heavy workload.

Conflicting Goals of Group Members

When people join a team or group, they also bring different motives or goals with them. Some members may be there to sabotage any group efforts. Others may want to assume leadership or display power. Some people may want to put in as little effort as possible. Some team members may have **hidden agendas** that may ultimately interfere with team performance. Hidden agendas are personal goals that a member keeps to himself or herself that may or may not be harmful to group efforts. The problem with hidden agendas is that they go against open communication in the group and destroy trust within the group. Even members with positive goals and motives in mind may have differences in such things as how the group should proceed, which goals should be given top priority and how various tasks should be divided up among members.

Roles That Interfere with Group Processes

In an earlier chapter we discussed that people may play games when interacting with each other. These games interfere with interpersonal communication and lead to defensive behaviour and interpersonal conflicts. Unfortunately, people also assume roles and play games in groups or teams that negatively affect the group. While labelled differently depending upon what research source you read, what the roles exemplify are the same. These roles hurt group members and hurt group performance. Some of these roles are summarized here (Engleberg and Wynn, 1997; Lumsden and Lumsden, 1997):

- **Dominator.** This person demands attention, tries to control the discussion, interrupts and tries to control others. He or she monopolizes the discussion and prevents the team from concentrating on its tasks.
- **Aggressor.** Similar to the dominator, this person wants control. However, he or she puts down other team members, uses sarcasm, name-calling and other negative means to get what he or she wants.

- **The Know-It-All.** This person knows everything (although he or she often doesn't) and tries to impose this knowledge on the group. This person uses age, experience, education or any other thing in his or her background to justify how he or she is correct and everyone else is wrong.

- **Distractor.** While distraction can be useful, when members are stressed, over-use of this role results in poor team performance. This person may clown around by teasing and joking, changing topics and getting the group off-task and generally "acting up." On a more aggressive side, this person can also distract the group by picking fights and watching "the fur fly" for fun.

- **Non-Participator.** This person can be a psychological deserter who may appear bored or above the pettiness of group interaction. He or she may doodle, daydream or in other ways nonverbally signal his or her lack of interest in the group work. These people can also be physical deserters by announcing they have to leave early, arrive late, do not arrive at all or arrive completely unprepared.

- **Recognition Seeker.** This person gets the group off-task by boasting about accomplishments and tries to be the centre of the group's attention. If not the centre of attention, this person pouts or becomes disruptive. He or she may try to hold side conversations or get recognition in other ways.

- **The Mean and Unethical Player.** This person can be unethical, dishonest, conniving, prejudicial and nasty and behaves this way consistently. He or she may lie, cheat, take credit for others' efforts, belittle others and engage in other unacceptable behaviours that harm team members, hurt team spirit and discourage group efforts. For example, a person who continually makes sexist comments after a person of that sex finishes speaking is belittling not only that person but the person's gender as well. The goal of such behaviour may be to get this individual to stop participating as it may be getting in the way of his or her hidden agenda.

- **Special Interest Pleader.** This person has outside interests and wants support from the group for these other interests. For example, as part of a task force, you set up the meetings over the dinner hour. Part of your responsibility is to provide supper. This person may attempt to get the group to use a family member or friend to do the catering.

- **The "Yes, but" Player.** This person is basically irresponsible for his or her part on the team. Usually not having something done, being late, missing meetings, obtaining the wrong data, doing the wrong thing is accompanied by excuses. At first, these excuses may sound legitimate, but as time wears on, it becomes obvious this person is an irresponsible team member who refuses to do his or her part. He or she might say, "I would have been here on time, but the traffic was bad," then at the next meeting say, "I tried to get here but the phone kept ringing," and at the following meeting say, "I was so busy with my other work, I lost track of time" and so on.

- **The Whiner/Complainer.** This person undermines the entire spirit of the group with continual complaining and whining. Every idea from others is met with a list of reasons why the idea would never work. This person may complain about personal problems and other injustices that he or she is currently managing in his or her life.

- **The Super-Agreeable Player.** This person never takes a stand. Perhaps afraid of hurting others' feelings or simply as a result of not caring, this person agrees with everyone. During discussions, this person will side with one person and then flip and side with someone else. This person has few original ideas and waffles on group decisions.

Competition Instead of Cooperation

In a society that values individualism, competitiveness and "doing your own thing," cooperation may be difficult for some people. A barrier that hinders team and group work is a structure that fosters competition among group members instead of cooperation.

In a competitively structured situation, communication may be lacking, distorted or misleading. Competition usually results in **defensive behaviour**. Defensive behaviour occurs when people feel threatened or when they anticipate being threatened (Johnson and Johnson, 1985). People will behave in ways to defend themselves against real or perceived attack. Energy is diverted from group tasks and is used to defend themselves. Members start thinking about how they look to others, how they can keep from losing, how they can win or dominate others and how they can protect themselves from attacks. The more intense the competition, the less constructive the communication becomes between group members. Information becomes inaccurate or missing as people try to win against their opponents. It can become next to impossible to move towards group goals.

Disregarding Individual Differences and Ethnocentrism

In Chapter 7 ethnocentrism was discussed as a barrier to effective intercultural communication. In a group, disregarding individual differences and making the assumption that your ways of doing things are better or superior than another member's ways is one quick way to promote disharmony within the group. In a heterogeneous group, there may be significant differences among group members based on difference knowledge, experiences, training, culture, values and interests. Differences need to be acknowledged (even celebrated) if a group is going to be effective. As well, while some strategies may be quicker, more effective, more creative and innovative, it does not mean that one is necessarily more "superior" than the others. In this group and at this time, one method may simply work better than other methods or ideas. Ideas or methods should not be dismissed simply because they are different or unusual. As we will see in the chapter on decision making, "weird" ideas may be at the core of a great idea!

Lack of Training in Team Building

Many organizations are getting on the "team bandwagon" and embracing the team concept. Unfortunately, many employees are not trained in how to work on teams, have little or no idea what skills are required and are often haphazardly thrown into work groups with little or no forethought by their well-meaning managers. How do you build a team, or do teams just happen? What are the specific skills that employees need to work on teams? Sometimes, these questions have not been answered prior to an organizational movement to a team-based organization. Before delving into teams, organizations need to train their personnel so that effective team building and teamwork can happen.

Evaluation Apprehension

Evaluation apprehension is anxiety that results from feeling that one's actions are being judged, monitored or evaluated in some way (Philipchalk, 1995). In some groups and in some teams, members may feel that they are continually being evaluated by other group members. Such anxiety can create stress and actually hinder performance in the group. In the face of such anxiety, some members may reduce their involvement for fear of looking stupid, not being correct or experiencing other negative side effects of evaluation.

Social Loafing

Have you ever been in a group or on a team where one or two members did very little work? These members were content to ride along for free and did very little to help the group obtain its goals. **Social loafing** is the tendency for people to perform at a lower level when working in groups than when working alone (Albanese and Van Fleet, 1985; George, 1992). Social loafers do not try as hard in a group as they do when they are alone. Social loafing occurs more often when individual contributions are not monitored or identified in some way and in larger teams where individual efforts are less noticeable (McShane, 1995; Philipchalk, 1995). Witnessing such loafing and lack of effort can demoralize other team members and reduce motivation.

Deviance

In Chapter 8 we discussed conformity as pressure, real or perceived, that individuals experience in a group. The group pressures the individual to conform to group norms and group rules, and such conformity is more likely in highly cohesive groups.

Deviance is a lack of conformity to other's expectations within the group or team (Lumsden and Lumsden, 1997). Depending upon the type of deviance, it can hinder or help the group. In the next chapter we will examine groupthink, a negative result of team cohesiveness, where deviance may be a positive factor in reducing the occurrence of groupthink.

Deviance may occur for a number of reasons and may have different results (Lumsden and Lumsden, 1997). Sometimes, deviance may lead to positive results. For example, a member who comes up with a new or different way of doing things can be classified as "deviant," but this may be "positive deviance" if it leads the group to better or more efficient means of working.

However, deviance can also lead to negative outcomes. A group member who insists on going against the group may lead the group into conflict and cause tensions among members. Other group or team members may attempt to change the other person's behaviour or ideas and increase the pressure for compliance. The person with the contrary views, ideas or ways of doing things may begin to feel like an outsider and not of any value to the group. This may lead to further negative behaviours or the adoption of a negative role by the "deviant" member.

DESIGNING EFFECTIVE TEAMS

To help avoid many of the barriers that we have just discussed, you must develop an understanding of **team building** that will assist you in becoming an effective team member. Team building is a formal intervention process that is directed toward improving the development and functioning of a work team (McShane, 1995). Outside consultants are often hired and use a variety of simulations with teams to assist those involved in developing the skills needed to be on an effective team. The results of such formal endeavours have been mixed, with some companies noting improvement but others noticing little, if any, improvement in team effectiveness (Woodman and Sherwood, 1980). An examination of some of these processes will give you some invaluable insights into how effective teams can be built within an organization.

In future employment you may be responsible to lead a team, share the leadership in a team or be given the responsibility of actually putting teams together. With the new emphasis on community policing, developing these skills may be essential for police work in the near future, if not already here (McKenna, 1998). According to McKenna (1998), police organizations, like other organizations, are feeling the need for high performance capacity work teams as a result of rapid and substantial change. Since empowered team development is a relatively new idea/concept within policing, we need to look at business for strategies used to develop high calibre and self-managed teams. This does not mean that such teams do not exist in policing, but little formal longitudinal research has been done to date. Check out the box below for some examples of Canadian businesses that have greatly benefited from the development and building of teams. We will now turn our attention to how effective teams are built.

CANADIAN PERSPECTIVE:

Successful Companies That Rely on the Team Approach

Here is a list of just some of the companies in Canada that rely heavily on teams, particularly self-managed teams. Many of these companies, such as Milltronics, did formal training of their employees to assist in the development of teams. These are not presented in any type of order.

1. Pratt and Whitney — Longueuil, Quebec — *PW500 turbofan engine*

2. Asea Brown Boveri Canada — Guelph, Ontario — *power transformers*

3. Milltronics — Peterborough, Ontario — *measuring equipment*

4. AMP of Canada — Markham, Ontario — *electrical connectors and interconnection systems*

5. Steelcase Canada Ltd. — Markham, Ontario — *manufacturer of office furniture and equipment*

Source: Adapted from Brian D. Harrison, Henry P. Conn, Barrie Whittaker and James Mitchell (1994). Mobilizing abilities through teamwork. *Canadian Business Review, 21,* pp.20-24. Steven L. McShane (1995). *Canadian Organizational Behaviour.* Toronto, ON: Richard D. Irwin Inc.

The Steps to Building an Effective Team

When an organization prepares to incorporate or design teams, the organization itself must undergo a transformation that includes developing a vision, determining what the new structure is going to look like, designing the new organizational systems (or re-modelling the old ones) including the teams, selecting and training members and finally monitoring the effectiveness of the teams (Wellins et al., 1991). For example, police services need to develop a vision around what is community policing and how it can best be accomplished now and in the future. Part of a vision is looking outwards at environmental and other external changes that have impact on the organization. For example, the increasing diversity in Canada, the increase in visible minorities, more emphasis on human rights, changes in the management of young offenders and Aboriginal policing are several changes that must be considered in any future vision and planning.

As entire books have been written on this very large and formal process of team build-ing, we would have little room to discuss all of these steps in any detail. What we are in-terested in here is some of the factors and steps that occur in all types of team building at the stage where the actual team has been formed. In other words, if you are assigned to a new team or volunteer to be on a team, what are some common steps that the team needs to con-cern itself with prior to and during the performing stage? Let's examine several of these factors:

- **Developing and understanding the purpose of the team.** Why was the team formed? What does the team do? While this may seem simplistic, the members need a clear idea of what the team is supposed to be doing. As well, members should make sure they are aware of how the team fits into the organizational structure. A Crisis Management team has as its purpose to assist in managing crises that occur in the community. A clear vision and sense of purpose must be established. The team also needs to be flexible enough to change when outside conditions change (Wellins et. al, 1991).

- **Setting team goal(s).** Goals are events, circumstances, objects, conditions or targets for which a team or individual strives. Goals are clearer than a purpose. A crisis man-agement team may have several goals. One goal is to assist other officers who are managing a potential suicide. Another goal is to assist other officers who may be dealing with a mentally ill individual. Assisting in hostage-taking situations may not be a goal of this team. Instead, another more specialized team may respond to this call. Conflict can occur between team members and teams as people are not clear about their team goals.

- **Establishing team roles.** Different members may have different roles within a team. Many teams may include a number of people from different departments, different organizations and other diverse areas. Part of team building is to establish who is re-sponsible for what. Will certain roles, such as leader, be shared? Will specific roles be established? Ensuring that all team members are aware of their roles and responsi-bilities will help the team establish positive relations. Confusion around who is to do what often leads to placing blame and to other conflicts when something goes wrong.

- **Establishing meeting times.** Some groups work together all the time while other groups and teams may see each other infrequently. Regardless of the frequency that members see each other, meeting times to go over the group processes is essential. Regular meetings to review how the group or team itself is functioning are essential to building and maintaining an effective team.

- **Establishing group norms.** How will the group manage inter-member conflict and controversy? How much work is each member expected to accomplish? How can group members support each other and assist each other in reaching established goals? If someone takes on a negative role, how will the group manage this behaviour? These are just a few of the questions that a team or group may want to examine prior to be-ginning work. As stated earlier, some teams and groups actually post their "norms" in a clearly visible location. By establishing norms, members are clear about what is acceptable and what is unacceptable. See the box below for an example of one group's norms were established for team meetings.

SKILLS PRACTICE:

Meeting Rules

Here is one example of meeting rules that a team established to help guide its regular meetings. Although not written down, all meetings could not last more than 90 minutes, there was a formal agenda, minutes were taken that included who would do what and when it was to be completed. These rules were posted on the wall in the meeting room.

1. Be punctual and prepared.

2. Treat all members with respect and dignity.

3. Allow members to finish talking before you have your say.

4. No swearing.

5. If you cannot attend a meeting, notify the team leader at least 24 hours in advance, and make sure that all your work is passed on to another member who

Another work group had their rules of conduct posted over the sink that they all used frequently. Another team had their rules taped inside their note binders that they all used on the job. However a team decides to conduct its business, it is important that all members have input into the rules and then abide by those rules. It should be noted that rules are not carved into "stone," and many groups change the rules over time by adopting new ones or discarding or rewriting old ones.

- **Develop a system to monitor individual and team progress.** Teams are made up of individuals, and part of building your team is to develop a system to monitor how people are doing on the team and how teams are doing compared to other teams (Wellins, et al., 1991). Are people completing their tasks on time, what is the quality, is anyone social loafing and is anyone having difficulty are the kinds of questions that can only be answered if you have some way of monitoring individual progress. The purpose of such a system is not to be punitive but to be supportive. If someone is experiencing some difficulties, measures to assist the person can then be implemented.

  Team progress also needs to be monitored for future evaluation. Have deadlines or goals been met? If there are several teams doing the same job, how does one team compare to the other teams? These systems do not have to be large and formal measurements. The key is that you have some system of seeing whether or not the group or team is being effective in its work

- **Accommodate different rates of progress.** Because people are different, not everyone will be ready and able to keep up with the team. Teams need to establish how they will cope with those members who forge ahead aggressively as well as with those who lag behind (Wellins et al., 1991).

SKILLS FOR EFFECTIVE TEAM INVOLVEMENT

Once a team has been built, your work is far from over. Effective teams need to be maintained over time. Some teams may be permanent work teams or self-managed teams. Other teams may only be set in place for a certain period of time, such as task forces or ad hoc committees. Regardless of how long the team is to be in place, skills are required to maintain team effectiveness. Team development is not a linear process (Wellins et al., 1991). Teams slip as new members come aboard, external pressures are felt by the team and lack of attention to the workings of the team all require skills to assist the team in getting back on track. In the next chapter we will look at techniques for team problem solving and decision making. But none of these strategies will work unless the team can maintain itself in a positive way. Here, we will discuss the skills that you can use to maintain your team's effectiveness, maintain a high level of involvement and support and to continue to build a positive team climate. Many of these skills you have already learned in Chapters 4, 5 and 6. You may want to review these chapters' skills. The difference is that in a group you use these skills in a larger setting. What you say and how you behave are witnessed by the entire group or team. The more people that are present increases the likelihood of misunderstandings, so it is very important that you be as accurate as possible with your communication.

Help Create a Positive Climate

One of the barriers to effective teamwork is a team that fosters a negative communication climate. To avoid the problems of a negative climate, team members need to develop a climate where **supportive behaviour** is encouraged. Team members can create positive climates or improve negative ones with their communication (Lumsden and Lumsden, 1997). Positive climates are characterized by openness, trust, empathy, willingness of members to take risks and to disclose their thoughts and ideas.

In their book on communicating within groups and teams, Lumsden and Lumsden (1997) offer the same suggestions as we explored previously in Chapter 5 on the differences between a supportive or positive climate and a non-supportive or defensive climate. Review these six dimensions, evaluation versus description, control versus problem orientation, strategy versus spontaneity, neutrality versus empathy, superiority versus equality and certainty versus provisionalism. Instead of a strictly interpersonal focus between two people, view these dimensions with a team or group focus as do these authors. If you demonstrate the positive side of these dimensions, you will be modelling the appropriate behaviours for others in the group or on the team. For example, a member of your team offers a rather controversial suggestion that had been dismissed earlier in the meeting as he feels strongly about the idea. Instead of immediately dismissing the idea again or evaluating it, you respond using description and some empathy. You say, "I'm not really clear about what you are trying to tell us. Perhaps, we should re-visit this idea. Could you re-word this for everybody?" Another example using this team focus would be if a group member is behaving as if he or she has more superiority or power than others; you can use this as an opportunity to voice the equality of all group members in a non-threatening way. As you go over these dimensions, try to think of ways that you could use them in a group or team setting.

Develop Your Ability to Assume Positive Roles

While some people assume negative roles on a team or work group, others assume positive roles that help establish a positive climate. We will briefly review a few of these roles. If you can adopt some of these roles on a team, you will help establish that positive climate. These roles can be divided into **task roles,** roles that focus on behaviour that is required for the group to achieve its goals, and **maintenance roles,** which are roles that affect how group members get along with each other while working on group goals (Engleberg and Wynn, 1997). Group members can and should play a variety of these roles although you may find that you tend to play some more than others do. These roles have been summarized and adapted below.

Task Roles

- **Initiator.** This person provides direction for the group, has ideas and suggestions.
- **Information Roles.** The *information seeker* asks for needed facts, figures and other relevant knowledge and points out gaps in information or data. The *information giver* has necessary information for the group. He or she will spend time researching and organizing necessary information.
- **Opinion Roles.** Like the previous role, there are two different roles: that of *opinion seeker* and *opinion giver*.
- **Clarifier/Summarizer.** This person can sum up what the group has just been talking about and helps to clarify what the group is attempting to do.
- **Evaluator/Critic.** An important role, this person can objectively assess the group's ideas and progress.
- **Motivator.** This person can keep the group going by helping to maintain enthusiasm and cheering the group on.
- **Technical support roles.** From keeping minutes to arranging meetings, this is a vital role for smooth group functioning.

Maintenance Roles:

- **Champion.** Comprising a variety of tasks, this person supports and encourages others, draws out those who are reluctant to speak, praises others for their input and listens with empathy. This is one role that every member on the team should learn how to do and learn how to do well!
- **Conflict Manager.** Again this person has several tasks. This person helps to resolve conflicts and emphasizes the need for teamwork. This person often comes up with solutions that are acceptable to everyone. This person's strength lies in negotiation and mediation skills.
- **Tension Releaser.** When tempers flare or tensions get high, this person may be the one with the friendly joke. Often this person has a great sense of humour and knows when to use it.

- **Observer/Interpreter.** This person can read nonverbal language well and tries to explain what others are trying to say in a positive way. This person expresses the group's feelings and paraphrases other members' contributions.

- **Follower.** This person supports the group and accepts others' ideas, opinions and solutions. This person readily accepts the undertaking of assigned tasks.

Develop Your Ability to Handle Others Who Have Assumed Negative Roles or Behaviour

What do you do when a group member starts to behave in ways that hurt the group's progress or challenges and treats other members poorly? Too often we may sit quietly, perhaps feeling guilty or not knowing what to do. We may launch into our own attack or even worse help the person out by supporting the behaviour. If you say or do nothing, you have by your lack of intervention supported the inappropriate behaviour. What should you do when this happens or if you are the target of such behaviour? Here are some suggestions to handle the negative group before a negative group climate becomes a reality (based on Johnson and Johnson, 1985; Lumsden and Lumsden, 1997; Dubrin and Geerinck, 1998).

1. **Accept the behaviour.** Sometimes, your best strategy is to simply accept the behaviour. Some behaviours are not critical to either group climate or group functioning. For example, while you may find a co-worker's green hair offensive, it probably does not affect the brain underneath.

2. **Use positive reinforcement.** All parents know this one! Sometimes you can ignore the unacceptable behaviour and reward the good behaviour. For example, a member who whines about things can be ignored when whining. When he or she says something positive, jump on it and praise it. Over time, the whining will disappear, and this person may become a more positive spirit in the group.

3. **Confront the individual on a one-to-one basis.** There are two ways to confront the person. The team leader (or assigned person) can talk to the person one-to-one outside of team meetings or work to attempt to find a solution or terminate the behaviour. For example, an aggressor who continually challenges one group member may be best approached alone. A responsible and assertive (and maybe brave) team member who is the victim of such inappropriate comments or treatment may confront the person outside of the team. For example, "In meetings, you continually make reference to my big salary compared to yours. I fail to see the significance of this in relation to what we are doing. In the future, do not make such references." This type of confrontation may also work for members who are continually late, do poor quality work or do not participate. If the reason for the behaviour is lack of understanding, lack of ability or personal problems, it is much less embarrassing to deal with this in a one-to-one meeting than if the whole group is looking on with eager interest.

4. **Confront the person as a team.** At times it may be appropriate to deal with the person as a team. If team members have discovered an individual with a hidden agenda or one who has been lying, cheating or in other ways acting unethically, group confrontation may be necessary. This may be especially important if this person has been playing team members off against each other. A united front may be your only recourse. Usually, a spokesperson is selected to start, but others may have information to share as well. For

example, "It has come to the team's attention that you have been lying to several of us about your progress with the computer support for this project. As a team, we would like to discuss this with you and come up with an acceptable way to resolve this as quickly as possible so that we can all get back to work." Team confrontation may work best when it is the entire team that has been affected by the negative role or behaviour. If a member has continually made sexist remarks to all the female members, the entire team needs to present a united front that this is unacceptable conduct of all team members.

5. **Go to management.** When the first four suggestions have failed, you may need to seek the help of a higher authority. Team members who consistently do not respond to other interventions may need more help to change their behaviour.

6. **Expulsion.** When all else fails, you may have to expel the group member. Your team may not have authority to do this, and in some environments this may be impossible. You do not want to resort to tricks like making his or her team life unbearable or taking on negative roles yourself, but many teams have been weighted down by poor team members. You may be able to expel the person by other sanctioned organizational methods. For example, a member who refuses to stop verbally making harassing comments may be dealt with by using the harassment policy of your organization.

Send Messages Effectively

These next few suggestions are a very brief review and adaptation of previous techniques on listening and responding. When sending a message to others in the group, make sure that what you said and what was received by the group are congruent. Solicit **feedback** to ensure that your message is properly received, particularly if the message is a complex one. Ask group members if what you have said is clear. For example, "I feel that I may be rambling a bit. Does everyone understand my point?" It also does not hurt if you are redundant and repeat yourself. Sending the message twice or more using different channels and ensuring that your verbal and nonverbal behaviour are also congruent will help team members to understand what you are saying (Johnson and Johnson, 1985).

Receive Messages Accurately and Check Out Your Perceptions

When you receive a message from another person, as the listener you really have two jobs to do. First, you need to communicate to the sender that you are interested in what the person is saying and that you are trying to understand the message. We all know what it is like when we talk to someone who stifles yawns or shuffles papers. The message we are receiving is "I am really not interested in what you have to say." In a group, focus may be more difficult. The sender may not be looking directly at you, what he or she is saying may not directly affect your tasks or you may be distracted by the behaviour of other group members. You have a responsibility to demonstrate interest.

Second, you need to understand and interpret the sender's message accurately. Here, you may need to use your skills of *active listening* and *paraphrasing*. For example, one member in the group voices agreement with another member's idea. However, you read from nonverbal cues that maybe there is not as much agreement there as the verbal side indicates. You can state something like, "You say that you agree, but I'm not so sure you do.

You sounded a little hesitant there. What are you really thinking?" You need to use the skill of *perception checking* to ensure that you have heard the message correctly. Remember that perception checking is tentatively stating back to the person what *you* think the person is saying and giving the person the opportunity to reply to your perceptions. Continue to discuss the issue until both you and the sender agree as to what the message means. The entire group needs to be clear about what members are saying.

Monitor Your Nonverbal Behaviour

When you are working with a group, what do you look like? Do you look interested? Do you fidget, doodle, chew gum, daydream, or do you look interested, lean forward towards the speaker, display enthusiasm in your tone of voice and express interest in the group? Some police officers on emergency teams have received criticism for their casual approach in emergency responses. They were nonverbally saying to the victims, "I'm really not interested in your problems."

Take time to monitor your nonverbal behaviour. Make sure that your verbal and nonverbal behaviour are congruent. Other team members or the public will pick up the discrepancies. A good team member will ask you about the apparent difference. On open and honest teams, you can say what you feel and think without censure. When dealing with the public, you have a professional image that you are required to maintain to effectively do the job.

Come to Meetings Prepared and Ready to Work

Although a very basic idea, how many times have you shown up to a group or team meeting and discovered that someone was unprepared (maybe even you!). Teams cannot work effectively unless everyone is prepared. You also have to come to group or team meetings prepared to work. This can be difficult as many organizations hold team meetings at the end of the day or in the evenings. However, if you want to be an effective team member, be ready and motivated to do your part.

Learn to Appreciate Individual Differences

The last suggestion is not new to you but worth repeating. Different beliefs, values and ways of doing things are part of our national diversity. Rather than fighting them within a group, learn to tolerate and even appreciate differences. Differences can be a source of strength in groups especially when the goals are varied, tasks are complex and creativity is needed to solve problems or make decisions.

SUMMARY

In this chapter we further explored teams and groups. Interpersonal attraction can be the basis for getting along with others in groups and teams. Several theories of interpersonal attraction were discussed including proximity, physical attractiveness and the matching hypothesis, similarity, reinforcement and social exchange theory.

All teams go through some sort of selection process. One way to select members is to screen or test applicants and base membership on some sort of personality assessments.

Traits such as conscientiousness, need for achievement, extroversion, dominance, emotional stability and agreeableness have been researched to determine their effect on team performance. All teams vary in their heterogeneity with some teams having diverse membership and some teams being more homogeneous in their makeup. Teams also vary in size, but smaller teams may be more effective than larger teams. As well, all teams create their own climate and culture.

Several barriers to effective team performance and functioning were discussed. These barriers included time constraints, physical barriers, inappropriate group size, conflicting goals of group members, members who play inappropriate roles within the team, competition among members, disregarding individual differences, lack of training in team building skills, evaluation apprehension, social loafing and deviant behaviour.

To establish productive teams or work groups, many organizations go through a formal process of team building. There are many strategies that groups and teams themselves can use to assist with building their own teams. These strategies include developing a purpose or vision for the team, setting team goals, establishing clear team member roles, establishing meeting times, establishing team norms, developing a system to monitor individual and team progress and accommodating different rates of progress.

Once a team has been established, members need to use effective interpersonal skills to maintain the team's progress and effectiveness. The most important skill is to establish and maintain a positive team climate. Other skills include learning and adopting positive group roles, developing an ability to handle others who have adopted negative roles or behaving inappropriately, sending messages effectively, receiving messages effectively and checking out your perceptions, monitoring your nonverbal behaviour, coming to team meetings prepared and ready to work and learning to appreciate individual differences. If teams are the "way of the future," you need to learn these skills for success in policing or in any other career.

JOURNAL AND DISCUSSION QUESTIONS

1. Many studies are being done to examine using personality traits as a method of selecting people for teams. Do you agree that using personality traits and developing tests to assess personality should be used to screen applicants for membership on teams? Why or why not?

2. In your community there are probably many businesses and organizations that are team-based. Interview several team members. Find out what they see as benefits of the use of teams as well as the problems with the use of teams. Is the company more successful since the implementation of teams?

3. What do you see as the major skills for being an effective team member? Are some skills more important than others? Why or why not?

WEB SITES

www.2hcom/Tests/personality.phtml

Here you can take different personality tests and learn more about yourself.

www.strategis.ic.gc.ca

A Canadian site about business in Canada, this site has many links to many organizations and businesses across Canada.

www.gov.on.ca/OPP/

This is the site for the Ontario Provincial Police. From this site you can access their "How Do We Do It" manual. This manual has a great deal of information on how teams are used in the OPP.

REFERENCES

R. Albanese and D. D. Van Fleet (1985). Rational behaviour in groups: The free-riding tendency. *Academy of Management Review, 10,* pp. 565–581.

J. E. Alcock, D. W. Carment, S. W. Sadava, J. E. Collins and J. M. Green (1996). *A Textbook of Social Psychology*, brief edition. Scarborough, ON: Prentice Hall Allyn and Bacon Canada.

M. Csikszentmihalyi and T. J. Figurski (1982). Self-awareness and overside experience in everyday life. *Journal of Personality, 50,* pp. 15–28.

Andrew J. Dubrin and Terri Geerinck (1998). *Human Relations for Career and Personal Success*, Canadian edition. Scarborough, ON: Prentice Hall Canada.

Isa N. Engleberg and Dianna R. Wynn (1997). *Working in Groups: Communication Principles and Strategies.* New York: Houghton Mifflin Company.

Anthony Falikowski (1996). *Mastering Human Relations.* Scarborough, ON: Prentice Hall Canada.

A. Feingold (1988). Matching for attractiveness in romantic partners and same-sex friends: A meta-analysis and theoretical critique. *Psychological Bulletin, 104*, pp. 226–235.

Jennifer George (1992). Extrinsic and intrinsic origins of perceived social loafing in organizations. *Academy of Management Journal, 35,* pp. 191–202.

David W. Johnson and Frank P. Johnson (1985). *Joining Together: Group Theory and Group Skills*, 3rd edition. Englewood Cliffs, NJ: Prentice Hall.

Susan Kichuk and Willi H. Wiesner (1998). Work teams: Selecting members for optimal performance. *Canadian Psychology, 39,* pp. 23–32.

D. C. Kinlaw (1991). *Developing Superior Work Teams: Building Quality and the Competitive Edge.* Lexington, MA: Lexington Books.

E. T. Klemmer and F. W. Snyder (June 1972). Measurement of time spent communicating, *Journal of Communication, 22,* pp. 142–158.

Gay Lumsden and Donald Lumsden (1997). *Communicating in Groups and Teams: Sharing Leadership.* Belmont, CA: Wadsworth Publishing Company.

Paul F. McKenna (1998). *Foundations of Policing in Canada.* Scarborough, ON: Prentice Hall Canada.

Steven L. McShane (1995). *Canadian Organizational Behaviour.* Toronto, ON: Richard D. Irwin Inc.

L. E. Penley, E. R. Alexander, I. E. Jernigan and C. L. Henwood (1991). Communication abilities of managers: The relationship to performance, *Journal of Management, 17*, pp. 57–76.

Richard S. Wellins, William C. Byham and Jeanne M. Wilson (1991). *Empowered Teams: Creating Self-Directed Work Groups that Improve Quality, Productivity, and Participation.* San Francisco, CA: Jossey-Bass Publishers.

R. W. Woodman and J. J. Sherwood (1980). The role of team development in organizational effectiveness: A critical review. *Psychological Bulletin, 88,* pp. 166–186.

PROBLEM SOLVING AND DECISION MAKING IN GROUPS AND TEAMS

C h a p t e r

LEARNING OUTCOMES

After studying this chapter you should be able to:

1. Differentiate between the two different processes of problem solving and decision making.

2. Set effective goals to assist in problem solving and decision making.

3. List the ways that groups make decisions.

4. Explain barriers to effective decision making and problem solving in groups and teams.

5. Use two models for improving problem solving and decision making in a group.

6. Explain three variations of group decision making.

7. Explain ways to improve group decision making and problem solving in a group or team.

Another meeting:

> Person 1: *Okay. Let's go with your idea 2. I think it will work.*
>
> Person 2: *Great!! Let's decide how we're going to do it.*
>
> Person 3: *Wait a minute. I don't think we have examined the potential side effects of this solution. I think we should take more time and examine all the alternatives in more detail.*
>
> Person 1: *Look, 3. There you go again. If you want to be part of this team, you simply have to go along. You're too worried about what might happen. We have always done the right thing in the past and no one has ever complained.*
>
> Person 2: *We don't have any more time! We're getting a lot of pressure. Are you for us or against us?*

While some teams and groups are simply work groups, the people that you work with on a daily basis, at some point the group will experience a problem or be required to make a decision. Other teams' sole purpose is to solve problems and/or make decisions. For example, a task force may have to make many decisions and solve many problems to attain specific goals that were the very reason for the set-up of the task force. If teams and groups are going to be the way you work in the future, groups and teams must come up with effective processes to solve problems and make decisions effectively. The dialogue above indicates some of the problems that occur when a team attempts to make a decision without proper skills and methods. If you have read anything about the Challenger Shuttle disaster, you'll know that this dialogue is very reminiscent of some of the conversations that took place prior to that fatal launch. Teams and groups that make poor decisions or solve problems in ways that create more problems are headed for disaster. Unfortunately, innocent people sometimes pay the price for such decisions. As well, organizations can pay the high price for faulty decisions including items that should never have been marketed, investments that never should have been made and so on.

In this chapter we will focus on decision making and problem solving in groups and teams. Teams and groups may do more than this, but for many groups these two processes take up a significant amount of group time and effort. Faculty teaching teams spend many meetings deciding upon curriculum, choosing textbooks, deciding who will teach what course or what group, deciding what new courses should be added, deciding what old courses should be dropped or changed, solving student retention problems, dividing up shrinking budgets and so on. Teaching is only part of a much larger picture of team teaching. For many professors, teaching is the easy part, and team decision making and problem solving is the hard part! The same holds true for many other professions out there, including policing. Hunting the "bad guys" may at times be much easier than partners trying to decide what they will do about a runaway from an abusive home or a police team deciding whether or not a curfew needs to be imposed in a specific area or neighbourhood.

First, we will discuss decision making and problem solving and how they differ. Then we will look at goal setting. Without being able to set good goals, you will have difficulty solving problems and making decisions in groups or on your own. In groups or on teams, decisions are made using a variety of methods. We will then examine barriers to effective decision making and problem solving. There are many different types of models used for increasing the effectiveness of decision making and problem solving in groups. In Chapter 6 a problem-solving approach was discussed as being one way to manage an interpersonal conflict. We will explore a very similar model that you can use when making a decision in groups. Last, several strategies will be introduced to help improve your effectiveness in problem solving and making decisions.

PROBLEMS VERSUS DECISIONS

Before moving on, let's discuss problems and decisions, as we often use the two terms interchangeably. A **problem** can be defined as a gap between what currently exists and what you want to exist. If you are hungry and there is no food in your fridge, you have a problem. When we encounter a problem, we try to solve it (or have somebody else solve it for us). What you want is food in the fridge, but currently none exists! There may be many solutions to this problem. If you have money, you can go to the store and purchase some food. If you can't wait that long and you have money, you can go to the nearest fast food restaurant and eat within minutes! You can go to your neighbour and beg. You can tell yourself that you are not hungry and that hunger is just a state of mind. Coming up with all the alternatives is part of **problem solving** and decision making. Problem solving is actually a complex decision-making process whereby a group or person analyzes a problem and develops a plan of action to solve the problem or to reduce the effects of the problem (Engleberg and Wynn, 1997). Not all problems will have a number of alternatives or solutions from which to choose. For example, if I get a sliver in my thumb, the only real solution is to get it out (and quickly). But many problems do have many solutions or alternatives, and this is where the decision-making process comes in.

When you choose from all of these options, you have made a **decision**. A decision is the solution, course of action or selection that you make from several alternatives. When you chose to go to a certain college out of a number of colleges, you make a decision. **Decision making** is selecting one or more alternatives from various courses of action that can be pursued.

When you have a number of alternatives available, you need (or the group needs) to pick the best one(s). Later, we will see how a model can help us in this process. Let's examine a current problem in policing today.

LAW AND JUSTICE PERSPECTIVE:

High-Speed Chases: Are They Worth the Price?

Recent newspaper articles and the nightly news on television have had several stories focused on high-speed police chases. It has become common knowledge that since February 1998 seven innocent bystanders have been killed during high-speed chases.

From a policing perspective, several factors have come into play. First, the number of dangerous high-speed chases has increased. Second, in recent years, vehicles themselves continue to be built for speeds far higher than necessary for ordinary transportation purposes. Does the average driver need a vehicle that can do up to 160 kph? Third, many police services have downsized and do not have as many vehicles on the road. With less police visibility, are people taking more chances?

The real dilemma is how police should apprehend suspects while still maintaining the safety of citizens. This is the problem: the gap between wanting to protect the public while still engaging in suspect apprehension. Several solutions have recently been proposed for examination and implementation. New provincial regulations in Ontario have been proposed for police pursuits that more carefully plot out when it is appropriate to begin pursuit and how long the pursuit should last. The Ontario Solicitor General and Minister of Corrections is handing out more funding for nine different services to purchase tire deflation devices. The province is also considering stiffer penalties for those who flee police by making amendments to the Highway Traffic Act. As well, the provincial government supports the federal private member's bill (Bill C-440) that would make it a criminal offence to flee police. Last, over $900,000 in grants is being offered for four helicopter evaluation projects. Whatever course of action is finally decided upon, it appears that this problem is not one that will quickly be solved. Police will still be faced with a vital question: No matter what guides are put in place, do we pursue? If police do not pursue, what are the consequences? If they do pursue, what are the consequences?

Source: Adapted from The Solicitor General and Minister of Correctional Services (April 1, 1999). New pursuit procedures will enhance public and police officer safety. *Government of Ontario Press Releases.* See the complete highlights of the proposed pursuit regulations at: www.newswire.ca/government/ontario/english/releases/April1999/01/c9373.html; and John Duncanson. Let's talk on chase rules: Union police want consultation with Solicitor General. *The Toronto Star,* November 27, 1998

GOALS AND GOAL SETTING

Being able to set goals is an integral part of decision making and problem solving as well as an important part of motivating you and the team towards larger organizational goals. Later, you will see that goals and reaching goals are important components of effective decision making. Here we will look at goals in general.

If you had not decided on choosing a career in policing, where would you be right now? When you chose to go into law enforcement, not only did you make a decision, but you also set a goal for yourself. Some students enter college or university with no real idea of what they want to do or where they want to be in five or ten years. Their goals are unclear. It is like the old saying, "If you don't know where you are going, chances are you're not going to like where you end up." **Goals** are events, circumstances, objects, conditions or purposes for which a person (or group or team) strives. Without goals, why and what you are doing becomes unclear and maybe even meaningless. Have you ever been to a meeting and sat there wondering why people were discussing what they were discussing, thinking to yourself what is the point of all this? This happens when we are unclear about goals. Goals serve the purpose of directing our behaviour. Effective goals help us or the group to get to where we want to be. Let's look at how we can design effective goals.

Effective Goals

Setting effective goals has several advantages. Goals can be thought of as motivational tools. Research indicates that setting specific and reasonably difficult goals actually improves performance. If we set effective goals, they serve as self- and group-motivators that energize us into action (Dubrin and Geerinck, 1998). Last, goals increase our chance of success as properly defined goals when we have achieved them. It means that we have been successful and have done what we were striving to achieve.

Guidelines for Effective Goals

Here are some guidelines to help you and your group or team set effective goals (adapted from Dubrin and Geerinck, 1998):

- **Formulate clear or specific goals.** When you formulate a goal, the group should have no doubt as to what the goal means. For example, if your task force wants to decrease youth crime in the area, the goal needs to state specifically by how much based on current statistics. For example, "The OPP in this area will reduce impaired driving by 20 percent over the next year."

- **Formulate concise goals.** Use a short statement that gets right to the goal. Goals that are too lengthy can become confusing to you, other group members and outsiders.

- **Describe what will actually be occurring when your goal is reached.** An effective goal states the outcome: what will actually be happening, how things will have changed or what the new event or object will look like. If your goal is to graduate from college with an average of 80 percent, you have a good idea what your final transcript should look like.

- **Set realistic goals for yourself and for the group.** On a good team, members understand each others' strengths and weaknesses. Teams will set goals that members know the group can reach. This does not mean that the goals are easy. On the contrary, while being realistic, the goal should also be challenging and stretch members' abilities, imagination and creativity.

- **Set goals for different time periods.** Part of planning a major goal is a series of smaller goals. Goals should range from short-term to medium-term and finally to long-term or long-range goals.

- **Allow some fantasy and dreams into the goal.** What would the ideal college look like? This was a question that was asked years ago on a committee at my college. Such visions of what could be can guide people to set their sights a little higher and diminish the rigid thinking that sometimes occurs as we plod along in our working life.

- **Specify the who, what, where, when and how of goal accomplishment.** Some groups and teams design great goals and then look at each other around the table. Each goal requires an **action plan** or a description of how the group is going to reach the goal(s). The action plan needs to include *who* is going to carry out the action. For example, if a police service management team decides that officers need more crisis intervention training, one person may be responsible for researching various related groups in the community. The *what* refers to the activities that each member will carry out. The *who* is the identified officer, and the *what* is the research. *Where* refers to location, although this may not occur in all goal setting. But if you choose a specific college, this is the *where* of your location of goal attainment. *When* usually refers to the deadline of when the goal activities should be accomplished. For some goals, one person may have to wait and rely upon another member's task completion before doing his or her portion of the activities to reach the goal. Using the above example, one officer researches the available training in the area. Another officer may be responsible for advertising or designing a process of who will attend the training based on the numbers the chosen training group can train at any given point. Can the training group train 30 at once, 40, 80 or 100? The *how* is about the methods used for achieving your goal. In this example, the *how* is formal training. There are other methods such as arranging time for officers to do self-study or having officers pay for their own training during their time off. Usually the methods that the group chooses are the ones that should lead to the best probability of reaching the goal.

- **Review your progress.** As stated in the last chapter, groups need to monitor both individual and group processes. Part of this review is examining the time lines of tasks and activities to ensure that the group is on track and to handle difficulties before they become major barriers or group problems.

- **Review your goals at specific times.** Sometimes, as a group (or only you) works towards a goal, questions start cropping up. Why are we doing this? Is this goal still relevant? For example, outside influences can change the environment of the group and its goals. While the group is busily arranging the crisis intervention courses, the department experiences a massive budget cut that affects the training budget. The group may have to change its strategy and, worst of all, maybe cancel its activities. Goals need to reviewed in order to assess their continued relevancy, to see whether they can still be managed and to determine whether the group or team can still continue to proceed.

Below is an activity for you to try. The goals need some work to meet the above criteria.

SKILLS PRACTICE:

Personal Goal Setting

Personal goal setting is similar to group or team goal setting. By practicing personal goal setting, you will be more able to assist a group or team in setting and achieving goals. Below are several goals that do not adhere to the previous guidelines. Rewrite the goals to meet the criteria above. Remember that effective goals are specific, concise, have specific time lines, are realistic and describe what you will actually be doing when you achieve the goal. Feel free to use your imagination!

1. I want to do better at school.

   Revised goal:

2. I'm going to get into better shape.

   Revised goal:

3. I'm going to save money for a new car.

   Revised goal:

Share your goals with other classmates. Were your goals identical? Did the goals meet the criteria of being an effective goal? How could you improve your goals?

GROUP DECISION-MAKING PROCESSES

How do groups come up with goals, decide upon action plans and move towards the identified goals? Groups and teams continually make decisions and solve problems and have to decide which solutions they will choose to implement or to decide upon a given course of action. Let's briefly review some of the ways that groups make these decisions from a variety of different sources. Not any one method is the "best" method; the method used may be better or worse depending upon the circumstances, the amount of time available, the type of decision, the group's resources and so on. This list does not include all of the ways that groups make decisions but will give you some ideas as to the diversity of methods (Johnson and Johnson, 1985; Engleberg and Wynn, 1997; Lumsden and Lumsden, 1997).

Voting or Majority Rules

This is the most common method of group decision making (Johnson and Johnson, 1985). The group or team will usually continue to discuss an issue until at some point the group either takes a vote or uses some other means to find out who is against or who agrees with a course of action. If 51 percent or more vote in favour, then the decision is supported.

Decision by Authority after Group Discussion

Some teams or groups have a leader who listens to the group's discussion and, based on this discussion, makes the final decision.

Decision by Authority without Group Discussion

The leader makes a decision without any group input. This method is still quite common in organizations (Johnson and Johnson, 1985).

Decision by Group Consensus

Consensus "is the most effective method of group decision making, but it also takes the most time" and the most individual member motivation (Johnson and Johnson, 1985, p. 102). **Consensus** is achieved when all group members agree with the decision and are committed to the decision (Engleberg and Wynn, 1997). When achieved, consensus can bring a group together and energize the group. Discussions can promote critical and careful analysis of contributions (Wood, 1997). In an effective group, such discussions that simulate each other's thinking can lead to **synergy**. Synergy is a special kind of energy that enhances the efforts and contributions of individual team members (Lumsden and Lumsden, 1997). The group product is far superior to what could have been achieved by any one member.

Consensus should be used when an innovative, creative decision is needed and when group member's commitment is necessary for implementation. In order for consensus to be achieved, all members must contribute their ideas and views. Members must feel free to voice their opposition and be given the time for a full discussion (Johnson and Johnson, 1985).

BARRIERS TO EFFECTIVE GROUP PROBLEM SOLVING AND DECISION MAKING

When groups get together to solve problems and make decisions, a number of problems can influence the process. In the last chapter we concentrated on personal characteristics, time constraints and several individual factors that create barriers. Here, we want to concentrate on processes that effect the group processes themselves. First, we will examine group polarization. We will then look at groupthink, organizational and external pressures, politics, pre-existing preferences and power differences.

Group Polarization

When groups make a decision or choose a solution, many of the choices may involve some sort of *risk*. Some alternatives may be very risky while, on the other hand, some decisions have very little risk and are extremely conservative. Think of some of your own personal decisions. At times you may have chosen the more risky alternative, going to college in a foreign country where you do not know anyone, for instance. Much less risky would have been to stay in your hometown and attend the local college. There were many alternatives in between theses two extremes, such as a college in a neighbouring city or province. Groups engage in the same process of choosing from a set of alternatives.

In a group, the group processes may lead to the group making a more extreme decision than individuals would have made if they had been working alone. This process is known as **group polarization**. Why does this polarization occur in some groups?

First, members engage in using persuasive arguments. These arguments help to convince doubtful members. Remember public compliance and personal conformity? Some members actually change their beliefs to go along with the dominant group members' persuasive information.

Second, when a decision is made by a team, members may feel less personally responsible for the outcome and consequences of the decision.

Third, people compare themselves to others in the group. In the process of **social comparison,** we try to see ourselves and present ourselves favourably (Alcock et al., 1998). In order to maintain this favourable image, we carefully observe ourselves and others in the group. When we see the group shifting its decision, we go along with the shift.

Last, the process of **social identification** may also account for polarization. Social identification is a process whereby we define ourselves in relation to others and thus conform to the norms and stereotypes of the group. Individuals may hold a stereotype of their group that is more extreme than it actually is and are motivated to conform to this perceived extreme norm (Alcock et al., 1998). For example, if you see your decision-making group as extremely creative and innovative, you will go along with decisions that are "far-out" and "weird" to maintain this image. All of these processes operate to push a group toward more extreme attitudes and more extreme decisions.

Groupthink

In the early seventies, the research of Irving Janis (1972, 1982) led to the popular use of the term **groupthink** to identify a process of faulty decision making in a group. Groupthink is the tendency for cohesive groups to value consensus more highly than making effective decisions. As a result, the group experiences a deterioration of mental efficiency, a lack of reality testing and assumptions about the morality of the decisions. See Table 10-1 for a summary of the eight symptoms of groupthink. A good example of such faulty decision-making processes was the final decision to launch the Challenger in January 1986 (Philipchalk, 1995). There had been problems in the past with the O-rings under cold conditions. The launching was the coldest on record. The O-rings could not seal correctly under such cold conditions, which led to the explosion of the shuttle as fuel ignited and blew back into the engines. The inquiry into the disaster indicated many examples of poor group decision-making processes (Moorhead et. al, 1989).

TABLE 10-1 The Eight Symptoms of Groupthink	
1. **Illusion of invulnerability**	A belief that the group is above attack and reproach.
2. **Collective rationalization**	Rather than exploring the decision, the group justifies its actions.
3. **Illusion of morality**	The group members believe that they are right, and therefore their actions are moral.
4. **Shared stereotypes**	The group shares stereotypes of outgroups such as "They are just scientists."
5. **Direct pressure placed on dissenters**	In order to preserve cohesiveness, pressure is applied to those who express contrary views.
6. **Self-censorship**	Rather than expressing their doubts and assuming everyone else is in agreement, members go along with the decision.
7. **Illusion of unanimity**	By suppressing dissension, the group produces the appearance that everyone is in agreement.
8. **Mindguarding**	Certain group members act as mindguards, making sure that the group is protected from dissenting information.

Source: Irving L. Janis (1982).*Groupthink: Psychological Studies of Policy Decisions and Fiascoes,* 2nd edition. Boston: Houghton Mifflin Company. Used with permission.

Organizational and External Pressures

Many external pressures are experienced by a group or team that affect what goes on inside of the team. Some of these pressures come from within the organization itself. Managers may be impatient or may pressure the group into making a decision or coming up with a solution when the group is not yet ready. Other groups may also exert pressure on the group. One group may have to wait until this group has completed its task before it can continue with its work.

Pressures can also be exerted from outside of the organization. There is the media and the families of the victims pressuring the office of the solicitor general for new guidelines and methods of pursuit. Minority groups have successfully pressured the government at all levels for changes and for recognition of their rights as citizens and human beings. Special investigation units often feel the stress from outside parties as these parties wait for their decision regarding a shooting or any other areas necessary for investigation. Groups may be fearful of what the reaction to their decision may be especially given the history of some past results, such as the jury decision in the beating of Rodney King and other controversial decisions. When a group's decisions affects members external to the organization, there is bound to be reaction to the decision. This reaction may be positive or negative. For example, as part of a hiring committee, those who were not hired may come back to question why him or her and not me.

Politics

Some of the previous examples illustrate a significant barrier for groups and teams. There are usually political components in all decisions. There are organizational politics. Members may react and come into the group with political interests as well as the usual set of hidden agendas. For example, in a political climate of cutbacks, it may not be prudent to make decisions that involve large pay raises or other perceived extravagances.

Pre-existing Preferences

No matter what method the group or team uses to make its decision or solve its problem, there may be people on the team who have their minds made up from the very first day. As a teacher, I may favour a particular textbook for a course. I may go through the "motions" of examining other texts with the group although my mind is already made up.

Power Differences

Individuals differ in the amount of **power** they hold within a group. These power differences will effect the problem-solving and decision-making processes within the group. In the next chapter the different sources of power will be discussed. As power shifts, members may change their minds or have difficulty committing to one member's ideas over another member's ideas. This is one reason why ideas need to be separated from ownership of ideas. In other words, members need to commit to ideas and not to the people who voice them.

IMPROVING GROUP DECISION MAKING AND PROBLEM SOLVING

In the last chapter we examined many ways that you can help to improve team and group work. Again, like the barriers, many of these suggestions could be done on an individual basis with or without group consultation. We also discussed creating a positive climate, which can be undertaken as a group, and developing group norms and rules that foster such an environment. But these processes may not be enough. After all, groupthink occurs in cohesive teams and groups. Here we will examine ways to reduce polarization, groupthink and other group processing problems. Another major strategy for effective decision making and problem solving is to rely on a model to guide the group through the process. Although using a model is a method to improve group and team decision making and problem solving, we will discuss models as a separate topic.

Encourage Constructive Controversy

When discussing problems, solutions and making decisions, teams should encourage constructive controversy. With **constructive controversy,** team members feel free to openly debate their different opinions regarding an issue (McShane, 1995). One person or part of the team could also be appointed to play "devil's advocate" and, using constructive criticism, point out flaws or weaknesses of a team decision, solution or action plan. The emphasis here is on "constructive." Constructive controversy is issue-oriented, not person-oriented. People on the team share ideas and critique those ideas. Personal feelings of idea-ownership are not part of this process.

Use Brainstorming and Other Methods to Encourage Creativity

Often unique problems or difficult decisions are a challenge to even the best teams or groups. Everyday problem solutions and decisions can often be found in pre-existing policies and procedures. Police officers have standard procedures for much of everyday activity as do many jobs. Police services, like other organizations, have been struggling with many new issues and will continue to do so in the near future. For example, the increase of bystander deaths in car pursuits has created the need for new guidelines for pursuits and an examination and creation of new methods for apprehension of fleeing suspects. An older example was when bulletproof vests were first issued. There were no vests designed for women! This is another problem that has been solved, much to the relief of many female officers. Many good ideas and solutions have not always come down through the channels. Many ideas are thought of by front-line workers: those people who are dealing with customers or clients on a daily basis. If organizations want their workers to think of solutions and make important decisions, organizations need to provide resources to encourage such creative thinking.

Creative thinking is an ability to process information that results in a product that is new, original and meaningful. The product can be an actual product, like velcro, or it can be a new procedure, a novel solution, a different angle and so on. Edward De Bono (1972) coined a term for creative thinking, "**lateral thinking**." Lateral thinking is non-logical, non-sequential, generative, explores unlikely paths and escapes traditional patterns. "**Vertical thinking**" is analytical, sequential, logical, stays on tried and true paths and stays within traditional and rigid patterns. Vertical thinking is often referred to as "left-brained" thinking as it is the left hemisphere of the brain that controls such functions as speaking, numerical skills and is the analytical half of the brain. Creative thinking is more of a "right-brained" process as the right brain is non-analytical and is the more feeling side of the brain. So how can organizations encourage employees to be more creative, to get away from vertical and rigid thinking when the organization needs to solve problems and make decisions?

One strategy is to encourage brainstorming. Brainstorming is an excellent tool as well as a process for coming up with alternatives in a group or team and for improving group creativity. **Brainstorming** is a process whereby a team meets and generates as many alternative solutions to a problem as possible. Most models of decision making and problem solving rely on brainstorming during the stage of generating alternatives. The primary goal of brainstorming is idea generation; evaluation and other analyses are done at a later time. Because there is no evaluation component in brainstorming, even the quietest group members may feel free to participate without any evaluation apprehension. There are four main rules in brainstorming (Adams, 1979):

1. There is no criticism, defense, evaluation or judgment of ideas. The focus is to generate as many ideas as possible within a given amount of time.

2. Free association is encouraged. All ideas are to be voiced no matter how "far out" or "wild" or "weird" the ideas are.

3. Quantity is the goal, not quality. The more ideas there are, the more likely there may be more ideas to evaluate later on.

4. Building on ideas or "piggybacking" is encouraged. Ideas can be expanded and be put together with variations on the ideas.

It is best if all the ideas are written down so that the whole group can see them, and time limits may be useful. Brainstorming stimulates creativity, an essential part of effective problem solving and decision making. Try the exercise below, preferably in small groups, and you will get a better understanding of how creativity is enhanced when using brainstorming. Many activities can be found similar to this one in books on enhancing creativity.

SKILLS PRACTICE:

Stranded on a Desert Island

For this exercise you will need some large pieces of paper taped up somewhere, or a blackboard or other space where ideas can be quickly written. Assign one person as writer (although this person can also participate). One person will also need to keep time. After reading the exercise, you will have 10 minutes to complete it.

Your group is stranded on a desert island. There is water on the small island, some fruit and, of course, ample food in the ocean around the island. Unfortunately, when your small craft hit a reef you were all in your bathing suits except for one person in shorts with a belt. You realize that you will probably be rescued in the next few days, but until then you will have to eat and drink. The belt will have many uses for your group.

Set a timer or have someone monitor a 10-minute time limit. Write down as many uses for the belt as you can think of. Adhere to the rules for brainstorming.

When you are done, answer these questions:

1. Did your group start out with vertical thinking ideas first? Some examples of vertical thinking would be to use the belt to tie up fruit or use the buckle to dig for clams.

2. When did the creative ideas start? Was there a transition point for the group?

Some examples of creative thinking are shining the belt buckle to signal a rescue plane and using the belt for a "spin the bottle game" to alleviate boredom.

3. Can you think of current uses for brainstorming in your lives right now?

Get an Outside Opinion and Have Outside Experts Join the Group

Groups and teams may benefit from outside expertise at times. Rather than protecting the group from outside interference or mindguarding, outside experts may give the group new ideas or new perspectives. An outsider may be able to point out fresh approaches or fresh ideas. Also, an outsider may be able to more objectively assess group ideas or solutions. For example, a police committee, may have members of a particular social agency join the committee when making decisions about new educational initiatives.

MODELS FOR EFFECTIVE PROBLEM SOLVING AND DECISION MAKING

Recall from our earlier discussion the differences between problem solving and decision making. Problem solving differs from decision making in that the problem is analyzed to determine causes and effects. Decision making, although it is certainly an important part of problem solving, is choosing one alternative from several alternatives. To improve a team or group's ability to solve problems and make decisions, models or processes have been developed and used by many researchers and organizations. For example, the Ontario Provincial Police uses P.A.R.E. analysis, which is a variation of the problem-solving model presented here. Later, this OPP model is briefly presented for you to look at. The models below will have some common components. First, a model of problem solving will be presented as it shows the more complex steps in the beginning. The model of decision making will then be discussed.

A Model for Problem Solving

The model presented here is an adaptation based on a variety of material and research from many sources such as, for example, material presented by Quinlivan-Hall and Renner (1994), Dubrin and Geerinck (1998), Kaufman's Six-Step Model (1982) and Kepner and Tregoe (1981).

Step One: Problem Identification

Sometimes a problem can start as a nagging in the back of your mind that something is not quite right or things are not the way they should be. For example, an officer notices more than the usual number of calls for loud activity and vandalism in a neighbourhood park. Almost every shift seems to include a call to this park. Although not realistic in many ways, let's use this "problem" for the purpose in aiding your understanding of this model.

Your fellow officers also report that they have had more calls for intervention at this park. The calls have included loud parties, the witnessing of drug transactions, children being bullied and assaulted, two incidents of beatings, one sexual assault, several "muggings" and three concealed weapons charges. This officer brings this problem to the attention of the captain. The captain, in her great wisdom, states, "Yes, the community has noticed that this has indeed become a major problem area in the city. There is a new task force that will be meeting later this week, and the park is on the agenda. Would you like to join a task force that is looking at ways to reduce crime in the city?" The officer says, "Yes."

Now the officer has joined a team, a task force that sees the park as part of a problem of increased crime in the city. As a team, they identify the park as a major problem with input from the officer who comes with statistics about recent police interventions in the park. If there are several different problems, a system of prioritizing may be used to determine which problem will be addressed first.

The job is not done here. To correctly identify a problem, it needs to be stated as a goal using some of the goal-setting guidelines outlined earlier. It would not be clear enough for the team to say, "Let's get rid of the crime in the park" as this is a fairly sketchy goal. How could you word the problem better? "One of the goals of this task force is to take the appropriate measures to reduce violent and drug-related crimes in the park (name it) by 100 percent by December 2000." This is clearer, and the goal may need further clarification as the team proceeds. Remember that goals are not inflexible and can be changed if necessary.

Correct and realistic problem identification is essential to effective problem solving. Sometimes problems are really symptoms of a much larger problem. For example, I may claim that employers are biased because I am a woman and that is the reason I cannot get a job. This may not be correct. I am addressing the wrong problem, and I should perhaps be examining my skill base. Not getting the employment I desire may be rooted in inadequate skills rather than my gender. On the other hand, all you may be able to manage as a team is to correct symptoms. A philosophical team member may point out that the real problem is the decay of morality in the nineties. While this may or may not be true, chances are your group will not be able to solve this one!

Step Two: Problem Analysis—Determining Possible Causes

What is the cause of this "crime wave" in the park? Armed with their different knowledge and experiences, the task force may want to engage in some brainstorming around what the potential causes could be or how things are different from two years ago when the park was not a problem area. They may come up with a very diverse list, such as city population changes, neighbourhood population changes, youths with too much time on their hands, influx of street gangs, lack of parental supervision, lack of funding for youth programs, increase in drug use, increase in drug-related crimes and so on. If the causes can be determined, then eliminating the causes or reducing the impact of the causes may help to solve the problem. For example, if the cause is youths who do not have enough to do, then increasing programs for youth may be a solution.

Step Three: Determine Solution Requirements

Once there are some ideas around possible causes, the group also needs to look at requirements for the solution. If the goal is to achieve a reduction in two years, solutions must be able to be up, ready and running in just a few short months. Therefore, for this problem, one of the solution requirements is that the solution must be implemented within three months. Other solution requirements for a variety of problems may be budget constraints or how much can be spent on the solution. Another solution requirement may be that the solution may be limited to what can be done by the organizations represented by the task force. The solution requirements will vary depending upon the nature of the work, the type of group that is examining the problem and the type of problem. For example, a committee that only makes recommendations may not have to worry about budget considerations unless that has been explicitly stated.

Step Four: Identify Possible Solutions

Once you have reached a consensus about causes and have determined the requirements for your solution, you can now identify possible solutions. Brainstorming or methods of coming up with strategies can be used by the group. At the early part of this stage, quantity may be the goal, and you may even want to ignore the solution requirements as the group engages in a creative process of idea generation. Using our example, the group may brainstorm some of the following: close the park, increase lighting, have more patrols, use a neighbourhood watch system, close the park at night only, cut down all the shrubs and bushes that provide cover for would-be assailants, post warnings about the dangers in the park so law-abiding citizens won't enter, keep young people busier so they will have less time to hang out at the park, make the park a parking lot and so on.

Step Five: Select Solution Strategies Based Upon an Agreed-Upon Selection Method

Now that there is large list of possible solutions, you need to evaluate those solutions based on the solution requirements. Some solutions will be quickly discarded as not being appropriate or being downright silly! But remember, someone may have "*piggybacked*" on a silly solution and come up with a good one. For example, making the park into a parking lot may have led to someone saying something about redesigning the park in such a way as to discourage it as a "hangout." Once all solutions have been evaluated, you may end up with several good ones that meet all the criteria.

Step Six: Implement Solution Strategies

At this stage you may also need to prioritize the solutions if your group is the one that will actually implement these solutions. You may not be able to do all of them all at once. You will need to develop a method to do this. The OPP prioritize based on how easily the solutions can be implemented, and they do the easiest ones first. For example, one solution to reduce bushes is relatively easy and can be done quickly by the city's park and recreation workers. As well, lighting has also been classified as easy and will be taken care of simultaneously with the brush cutting. Other solutions such as reorganizing the park with a ball field for night games may be more long-term and will take more planning by a sub-group or sub-committee.

It is important at this stage to ensure that you outline who will look after the various components of the solution. Second, timelines also need to be established as to when things will be completed. The group will need to continue to meet in order to monitor and evaluate progress.

Step Seven: Evaluate Solution Strategies for Effectiveness

The problem-solving process seems to end here for most people. With solutions in place, we go on our merry way until we encounter a difficulty with the solution. Groups often come up with great solutions, identify who will do what and then assume everything will go according to plan. A system of evaluation is essential to measure the success of the solution. After measures such as lighting, reorganizing the park and so on have been completed, the police should continue to monitor the crime activity in the park. If it decreases, it means that perhaps the solutions are working. What if it increases or if there is no change? The group will need to backtrack based on data from the evaluation.

Below (Figure 10-1) is an outline of this model. Notice that is has been designed as a circle. If you see problem solving as a cycle rather than as a linear process, you will be a better problem solver. Groups can go back to any part of the circle and identify where they went wrong or conversely where they went right to adopt and use some of this process again. See the box below for a brief outline of the Ontario Provincial Police and its use of P.A.R.E. analysis.

FIGURE 10-1 Problem Solving Model

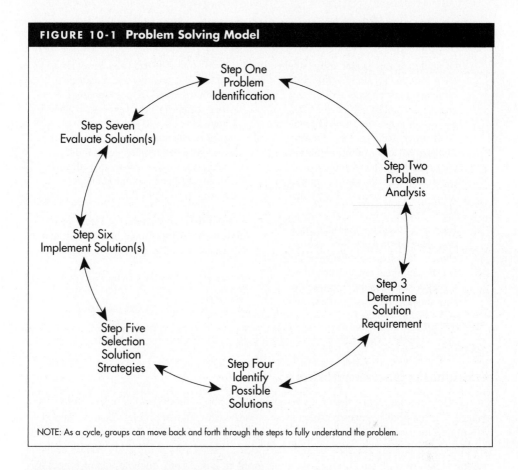

Step One
Problem
Identification

Step Seven
Evaluate Solution(s)

Step Two
Problem
Analysis

Step Six
Implement Solution(s)

Step 3
Determine
Solution
Requirement

Step Five
Selection
Solution
Strategies

Step Four
Identify
Possible
Solutions

NOTE: As a cycle, groups can move back and forth through the steps to fully understand the problem.

CANADIAN PERSPECTIVE:

The OPP and Problem Solving

With the new emphasis on community policing, police and members of the community are responsible for solving crime-related problems. New partnerships have developed that are bringing together diverse teams made up of police and representatives from communities. These new teams jointly identify the issues and outline processes to manage the issues around crime. The Community Policing Development Centre has developed a problem-solving model referred to as The P.A.R.E. Problem Solving Model. For a complete look at the model, visit the web site listed below. Here is just a very brief synopsis of the model.

The model consists of four steps:

1. **P**roblem Identification and Analysis. This step includes listing everyone's perceptions of the problem or events. Continue to discuss these perceptions by asking "why" questions.

2. **A**nalysis. Examine the problem using the five Ws: who, what, where, when and why. Obtain information on the victims, offenders and the situations.

Of interest in this model, the problems are prioritized (given weight) by determining their impact, seriousness, complexity and solvability. At this end of this stage, the "target" problem is identified and a goal(s) developed. The goal has one of four intentions: eliminate the problem, reduce the problem, reduce the harm or impact of the problem or redefine the problem responsibility.

3. **R**esponse. Based on your goal, an action plan is developed. Strategies are chosen. This document lists nine different strategies that range from enforcement and investigation responses to educational responses to community and social development.

4. **E**valuation. The team also develops a system of evaluating and monitoring the effectiveness of the responses. Evaluation consists of process evaluation where an analysis is done on the implementation strategies (was it difficult, were there easier ways) and impact evaluation, which is an evaluation about whether or not the strategies worked (had impact).

A final note is that the results of a team's problem-solving efforts should be stored so that they can be shared by other interested parties.

Source: Adapted from The OPP Community Policing Development Centre, "How Do We Do It" Manual, May 1997. Web site: www.gov.on.ca/opp/english/cpdc/howto/index.htm

A Model for Decision Making

This model shares many of the characteristics of the above model and is based on the same sources. The major differences between these models is the stage of problem analysis and identification of the causes of a problem. The real concern with decision making is to generate alternatives, evaluate the alternatives and then decide upon a course of action. While decision making is part of problem solving, often the problem has already been solved or a goal formulated that begins the rest of the decision-making process. For example, you have decided that your goal is to go to college to earn a diploma in Police Foundations Training. The decision then is to decide which college you will attend. As another example, a police service feels that police officers need more training and sensitivity when dealing with people with disabilities.

Step One: Formulate a Goal(s) or Decision Statement

Formulate a goal or decision statement using the criteria for effective goals. In a group, once the goal statement has been specified, it is now the focus of discussion. The group responsible for the training makes a goal statement about training. By 2001, 60 percent of the frontline officers will be better trained to more effectively manage calls that involve a person with disabilities. To be even more effective, the types of disabilities should be outlined as "disability" as a very global term.

Step Two: Identify Criteria for Selection

Based on the goal statement, the group now establishes what criteria are important and necessary to meet the goal. If you are choosing a college for Police Foundations, your choice will be limited to the colleges that currently offer that particular training. Other criteria may be that it is close to your hometown as you have a part-time weekend job, perhaps no more than a two-hour drive. You may also wish to select a college that has a residence, a pool or a gymnasium. The criteria that you establish will influence the rest of the process. As such, groups should spend enough time here so that all criteria are established. With the training example, what might be some of the criteria here? Some criteria may be the length of the training (a college course on diversity may be nice, but it also may take 15 weeks), the cost of the training, the timing of the training and how candidates should be selected for training.

Step Three: Generate Alternatives

Using the criteria, you can now generate some alternatives. Some decision-making tools such as the work of Kepner and Tregoe (1981) use criteria of go/no go and a weighted system for criteria. If an alternative does not meet a "go" criteria, it is automatically eliminated from all further discussion. If residence accommodation is essential, then some colleges will automatically be eliminated from your list. If cost is a factor and there is a ceiling on cost, some training alternatives may be eliminated.

Step Four: Evaluate Alternatives Based on a Weighting or Rating System

After selection is done, you may still have several alternatives that meet your criteria. You may now want to rate them as to how good each one is according to the criteria that were developed. For example, some colleges may have better (or cheaper) residences than others. If there are several training alternatives that fall below a certain cost, which one is the cheapest and by how much. If cheap, is the quality still there? One of the criteria may have been recent and practical training information for officers. Although one trainer is inexpensive, his or her outline brochure appears to be outdated.

A rating system can be developed for each piece of criteria prior to evaluation. The Kepner and Tregoe method relies on a weighted score system (Kepner and Tregoe, 1981). You can use a one–ten or one–five system. The group can then "grade" each alternative as to how well they meet the criteria.

Step Five: Make and Implement Selection

After evaluation, the group makes its choice. If you have used a number system or rating system, you would chose the alternative with the best rating. Now implementation begins. The group hires the trainer or sends officers to the training. More complex models sometimes add a stage of analyzing potential problems or adverse consequences that may result from the choice (Kepner and Tregoe, 1981; Von Winterfield and Edwards, 1986).

Step Six: Evaluate Selection

Was the decision a good one? Is it meeting the goals of the group? As with problem solving, evaluation is a critical component of decision making. You may set up a couple of systems for evaluation. You may have a questionnaire that officers fill out after training to assess whether the officers themselves found the training useful. Your group may also set up a system of monitoring calls that deals with individuals with disabilities. Whatever the group decides, evaluation must be included.

Similar to our model of problem solving, the model of decision making (Figure 10-2) is also designed as a circle. Groups can go through the process several times and, if problems occur, can re-visit what they did at any one stage.

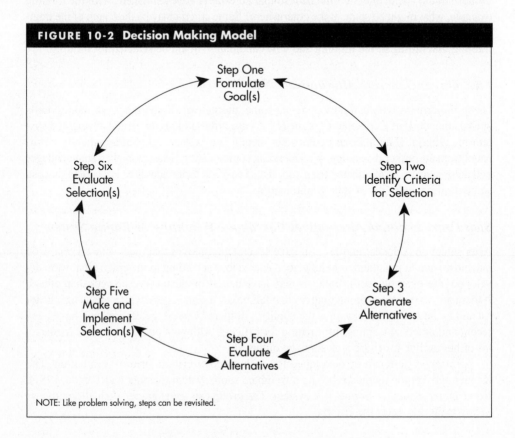

FIGURE 10-2 Decision Making Model

Step One
Formulate
Goal(s)

Step Six
Evaluate
Selection(s)

Step Two
Identify Criteria
for Selection

Step Five
Make and
Implement
Selection(s)

Step 3
Generate
Alternatives

Step Four
Evaluate
Alternatives

NOTE: Like problem solving, steps can be revisited.

VARIATIONS ON GROUP DECISION MAKING

It is not always possible to bring people together to meet face-to-face, or there may be situations where it is unnecessary or too inconvenient for people to meet as a team. For instance, when dealing with large groups with diverse members who normally do not work together or who are geographically too far apart, other methods may work more effectively.

Nominal Group Technique

The **nominal group technique (NGT)** combines the benefits of team and individual decision making (Delbecq et al., 1986). There are four basic stages in NGT. First, the problem is described to the group. Next, individuals silently and independently write down their solutions to the problem. The third step involves the group being brought back together. Participants, usually taking turns in a round-robin format, share their solutions. As with brainstorming, there is no evaluation or critiquing during this stage. However, questions for clarification may be asked by team members. The fourth and final stage is again done on an individual basis. The participants rank order or vote on each proposed solution. For example, if there are 10 solutions, the most preferred solution could be scored as a 10 and so on down to one. Or members' votes can be pooled to tally which idea received the most votes.

Delphi Technique

In situations where face-to-face meetings may be impractical or impossible, the **Delphi technique** can be used to pool the knowledge of a group of experts on a particular topic or area. If you remember from mythology, the oracle at Delphi could predict the future. Delphi groups can be used to make decisions, predict future trends or events or identify opposing views on a particular issue. For example, a group of experts from all over Canada could identify future issues that will concern young people in the year 2000 and up.

The Delphi method involves five stages that may be repeated several times (Linstone and Turoff, 1975). First, a central chairperson forms the panel of experts. Next, the problem is clearly described to each panel member. This may be done as a questionnaire. Each panel member then independently and anonymously submits his or her solutions, comments or ideas. Fourth, the chairperson records all of this information and returns the compiled results to panel members. Then, each member replies again (independently and anonymously, again) to the compiled results. Further suggestions, thoughts, ideas and explanations are provided. The process is then repeated several times until some degree of consensus or **dissensus** is reached.

This method is very time consuming although with the Internet and electronic mail, the process can be speeded up. Still the chairperson has the onerous task of choosing panel members and organizing and getting the results back to the members. If the chairperson does not choose appropriate panel members, does not understand returned comments or misinterprets them, this process can be a faulty one.

Groupware

With the advent of the computer era, an interest in using software to enhance decision making and problem solving surged in the seventies and eighties. **Groupware** is software designed for use by teams and groups to enhance a variety of group experiences including such group processes as decision making and brainstorming. Groupware has also been designed for uses such as **electronic brainstorming**. Instead of meeting as a group for brainstorming, individuals can meet in rooms designed with computers that have programming ready for the participants to brainstorm within the room network. Ideas can be posted anonymously and randomly on the screens of all the participants (McShane, 1995). Participants could be located throughout the organization and could post their ideas any time during an ongoing brainstorming "session." For example, at any time during the day, a participant could access the brainstorming program, review previous ideas and add his or her own.

SUMMARY

In this chapter we examined how teams and groups make decisions and solve problems. Problems and decisions were defined with problem solving being a more complex decision-making process. To assist in problem solving and decision making, effective goal setting and its steps were discussed. Setting effective goals with an action plan is an important skill for individuals to develop as well as for teams.

Groups and teams arrive at a decision in a number of ways: voting, decision by authority with or without discussion and by consensus. There are many barriers that interfere with effective group decision making and problem solving, including group polarization, groupthink, organizational and external pressures, politics, pre-existing preferences and power differences. To improve group decision making and problem solving and to reduce these barriers, groups and teams should encourage constructive controversy, use brainstorming and other techniques to encourage creativity and get an outside opinion and have experts join the group.

Two models were presented to assist in group and team decision making and problem solving. The problem-solving model consisted of seven steps: problem identification, problem analysis, determine solution requirements, identify possible solutions, select solution strategies, implement solutions and evaluate the solution effectiveness. The decision-making model consisted of six steps: formulate a goal statement, identify criteria for selection, generate alternatives, evaluate alternatives, make and implement selection and evaluate the selection.

When it is not feasible to bring groups together to solve problems or to make decisions, the nominal group technique and the Delphi technique are options. Groupware is another option to utilize group input without face-to-face meetings. With more focus on the use of teams and groups in the workplace, including police forces, skills for effective group problem solving and decision making will be essential tools.

JOURNAL AND DISCUSSION QUESTIONS

1. This chapter offers models for problem solving and decision making. What do you see as advantages of using models? What do you see as disadvantages of using models?

2. Use either of the two models and design a simulation for a real problem or decision that you feel is required to be made or solved in policing. Some ideas are increasing the number of women and visible minorities in policing, new decisions around police chases, youth involvement in crime or amalgamation of police forces.

3. You and your team have been selected to identify the characteristics of the "ideal" policing candidate. How will your group do this? Plan a strategy that your group can use to identify what the ideal candidate will be like.

WEB SITES

www.lineofduty.com

This is a really interesting site with a number of links. One of the links, From the Blotter, has articles from the United States and Canada about policing actions and issues.

www.carslisle.ac.uk/students/bm304

This is the site for a course on problem solving and decision making. The Kepner and Tregoe method is here in detail as is another model called the SMART approach.

www.che.umr.edu/che/faculty/dludlow/fall97/111/kt.htm

❚ *Try this homework assignment using the Kepner and Tregoe method.*

www.gov.on.ca/OPP/

❚ *This is the site for the Ontario Provincial Police.*

REFERENCES

J. L. Adams (1979). *Conceptual Blockbusting: A Guide to Better Ideas*, 2nd edition. New York: Norton.

J. E. Alcock, D. W. Carment and S. W. Sadava (1998). *A Textbook of Social Psychology*. Scarborough, ON: Prentice Hall Allyn Bacon Canada.

Edward De Bono (1972). *Lateral Thinking: Creativity Step By Step*. New York: Harper and Row.

A. L. Delbeque, A. H. Van de Ven and D. H. Gustafson (1986). *Group Techniques for Program Planning: A Guide to Nominal Group and Delphi Processes*. Middleton, WI: Green Briar Press.

Isa N. Engleberg and Dianna R. Wynn (1997). *Working in Groups: Communication Principles and Strategies*. Boston, MA: Houghton Mifflin Co.

Andrew J. Dubrin and Terri Geerinck (1998). *Human Relations for Career and Personal Success*, Canadian edition. Scarborough, ON: Prentice Hall Canada.

Isa N. Engleberg and Dianna R. Wynn (1997). *Working in Groups: Communication Principles and Strategies*. New York: Houghton Mifflin.

I. L. Janis (1972). *Victims of Groupthink*. Boston: Houghton Mifflin.

I. L. Janis (1982). *Groupthink*, 2nd edition. Boston: Houghton Mifflin.

David W. Johnson and Frank P. Johnson (1985). *Joining Together: Group Theory and Group Skills*, 3rd edition. Englewood Cliffs, NJ: Prentice Hall.

Roger Kaufman (1982). *Identifying and Solving Problems: A System Approach*, 3rd edition. San Diego, CA: University Associates.

C. H. Kepner and B. B. Tregoe (1981). *The New Rational Manager*. John Martin Publishers.

H. A. Linstone and M. Turoff, ed. (1975). *The Delphi Method: Techniques and Applications*. Reading, MA: Addison-Wesley.

Gay Lumsden and Donald Lumsden (1997). *Communicating in Groups and Teams: Sharing Leadership*. Belmont, CA: Wadsworth Publishing Co.

Steven L. McShane (1995). *Canadian Organizational Behaviour*, 2nd edition. Toronto, ON: Times Mirror Professional Publishing Ltd.

G. Moorhead, R. Ference and C. P. Neck (1991). Group decision fiascoes continue: Space shuttle Challenger and a revised groupthink framework. *Human Relations, 44,* 539-550.

Ronald P. Philipchalk (1995). *Invitation to Social Psychology*. Orlando, FL: Harcourt Brace and Company.

David Quinlivan-Hall and Peter Renner (1994). *In Search of Solutions: Sixty Ways to Guide Your Problem-Solving Group*. Vancouver, BC: PFR Training Associates Ltd.

Richard S. Wellins, William C. Byham and Jeanne M. Wilson (1991). *Empowered Teams: Creating Self-Directed Work Groups that Improve Quality, Productivity, and Participation.* San Francisco: Jossey-Bass Publishers.

D. Von Winterfield and W. Edwards (1986). *Decision Analysis and Behavioural Research.* Cambridge: Cambridge University Press.

Julia T. Wood (1997). *Communication in Our Lives.* Belmont, CA: Wadsworth Publishing.

Patrick M. Wright (1990). Operationalization of goal difficulty as a moderator of the goal difficulty-performance relationship, *Journal of Applied Psychology.* June, p. 227.

C h a p t e r

DEVELOPING LEADERSHIP AND SKILLS FOR DEALING WITH SUPERIORS

11

LEARNING OUTCOMES

After studying this chapter you should be able to:

1. Define leadership and differentiate leadership from management.

2. Explain three approaches to leadership.

3. List and explain the sources of power.

4. Explain various styles of leadership.

5. Explain effective leadership skills and behaviours.

6. Demonstrate effective skills for dealing with superiors.

7. Discuss the issue of leadership from a policing perspective.

This chapter will explore the area of leadership. Leadership occurs within groups, teams and organizations. Many of us answer to more than one leader. You may have a team leader, a staff sergeant, a sergeant and a captain. To make matters even more complex, some work teams have more than one leader! Some of us have had good superiors/managers, and some of us have had bad superiors/managers. Our managers have inspired us to do great things or have diminished our motivation and left us feeling angry and frustrated. In this chapter we will examine what leadership is and how it differs from management. Then we will examine some theories and research on leadership and leadership styles. Power or the ability to influence others is part of leadership, so power and the sources of power in a group or organization will be discussed. As this is a skills-based text, effective leadership skills and behaviours will be examined from various perspectives. Using police research and ideas from police experts, we will end the chapter by discussing leadership from a police perspective.

Sr. Constable Brad Filman, Ontario Provincial Police, Peterborough Detachment

Police officers require leadership skills as well as skills to deal with superiors.

LEADERSHIP AND MANAGEMENT

There are many definitions of **leader** depending upon what book or area of research you are examining. It appears that **leadership** is an ability or a process of influencing people, and leaders have these qualities, characteristics, abilities or capabilities to influence people towards attaining goals of the organization or team (Hollander, 1985; McShane, 1995; Bergner, 1998). Other researchers identify leadership as a process that empowers followers and provides an environment where goals can be achieved (McShane, 1995; De Paris, 1998). Leadership can occur anywhere in an organization and is not necessarily an assigned position (Portnoy, 1999).

On the other hand, **management** refers more to the actual tasks and the more "technical aspects" of managing, such as budgets, time management and so on (Bergner, 1998). Managers are people who are selected to fill a certain spot in an organization, and this position gives them a certain amount of authority to manage and organize certain activities (Portnoy, 1999). To train people in these technical tasks is not difficult, and often it is the police organizations and the police leaders themselves that confuse management with leadership (Bergner, 1998). According to Laurie Bergner (1998), a law enforcement trainer and consultant, leadership is something that cannot be measured by a paper and pencil test like the many skills of the manager. McKenna (1998, p. 93) succinctly states that "a leader is someone who is equipped to move people and events toward some goal or objective." Part of effective police leadership is management and the ability to manage information in a number of ways (McKenna, 1998). Therefore, in essence, leadership is a process undertaken by an individual with specific characteristics and abilities that include the ability to also perform management functions. Ideally, what organizations may really be reaching for is an individual who can also lead. The real question may not be how can we train effective leaders, but rather how do we train people in leadership and then have them assigned to positions in an organization where they can use their leadership skills.

THEORIES OF LEADERSHIP

If you look at the great leaders in history, they were very different people. Pierre Trudeau, Martin Luther King, Genghis Khan, Joan of Arc and Winston Churchill are just a few of the great leaders in history. Social psychologists and other researchers have long been trying to come up with the answer as to how a person becomes a leader. Does a leader in one situation or set of circumstances maintain that leadership in a different situation or set of circumstances? Would Genghis Khan make a good president at your learning institution or chief of your local police service? Likely not! Before we look at leadership today, we have much to learn from past (and still present) theories. These theories have provided much of what we know today about effective leadership.

The Trait Approach or "The Born Leader" Approach

The "Great Person Theory" or **trait approach** suggests that leaders have unique traits, or characteristics, that qualify them to lead. In the early 1940s to 1950s, there was a number of studies done, and a bewildering number of characteristics were discovered. This approach declined until computer technology improved, which allowed for faster and more efficient analysis of results. Three areas of trait research have been of recent interest. These characteristics include charisma, self-monitoring and gender (Philipchalk, 1995).

Charisma, or the unique leadership quality that inspires followers, has been studied intensely by one pair of researchers, Conger and Kanungo (1987, 1988, 1992). Several common behaviours were identified as making up charisma, such as sensitivity to follower needs, striving to change the status quo and taking personal risks and engaging in self-sacrificing behaviour. A very important feature of the charismatic leader is the ability to articulate a vision of radical change.

Self-monitoring is the degree to which people change their behaviour according to their perceptions of the social demands of a situation. It is really a continuum from low to high. Low self-monitors are relatively unaffected by social demands and continue to act according to their inner dispositions and tendencies. On the other hand, high self-monitors strive to adapt to the social demands and change their behaviour accordingly. High self-monitors are very conscious of how other people are reacting to them and have a high ability to adjust their behaviour based on these reactions (Philipchalk, 1995). In studies of groups and leadership emergence (for example, Cronshaw and Ellis, 1991), high self-monitors or those who could be classified as high self-monitors have emerged as leaders. Apparently, leaders tend to be high self-monitors. It should be noted that this was research done with male subjects and may not hold true for female leaders. More research needs to be done with female subjects.

The third area of trait research is the area of gender. For many years, leadership was considered to be a masculine trait (Philipchalk, 1995). Do women lead differently from men? If so, what is the best leadership style: the male style or the female style? Several research studies have tried to answer these questions (Eagly and Johnson, 1990; Eagly et al., 1992; Rosener, 1990).

According to this research, there appear to be a couple of differences between how men and women lead. Women tend to be "transformational" leaders by motivating their subordinates to transform their self-interest into interest for the welfare of the larger group. Men are more inclined to be "transactional" leaders and see leadership as a series of job transactions with subordinates. Women also tend to more democratic or participatory in their leadership style and use a less autocratic or directive approach than men. The answer to which style is the best style led to further questions as women are still under-represented in positions of leadership. Obviously, the environment and situation also have much to do with leadership.

The Behavioural Approaches to Leadership

Before examining the situation, when we looked at charisma and gender some of the results of the research had to do with the behaviours of the leader. A person may have specific characteristics or traits, but he or she can be identified only through the actual behaviour. What behaviours make a leader effective?

Several different groups of studies examined two specific behaviours of leaders: the degree to which a leader was concerned with people (called in different studies employee-centred, people orientation, consideration, concern for people) and the degree to which a leader is concerned with production (called in different studies production-centred, task orientation, initiating structure, concern for production). (For a brief summary of these studies, examine organizational behaviour texts such as Schermerhorn et al., 1994).

A people-centred leader is concerned with employees' feelings and employee welfare. A production-centred leader is concerned with getting the work done. The leadership grid developed by Robert Blake and Jane Mouton (1978) uses both of these styles and plots them on a graph. Thus a leader can be high in both, low on both, in the middle on both or at the extreme of each behavioural style. For example, a leader who is highly concerned with both people and production has a team management approach. A leader who is concerned with neither has adopted an impoverished style.

The Situational Approaches to Leadership

The major problem of the behavioural approaches to leadership is that these approaches did not really address the environment where leadership takes place, especially the type of subordinates or followers. Several theories were developed that examine the situation where leadership occurs. The results all indicate that no one style is the best of style of leadership, and, in order to be effective, a leader must pay attention to the external environment, including the capabilities and motivation of employees. Successful leaders adapt their behaviour (high self-monitoring) to meet the needs of followers and the demands of the situation. Leadership effectiveness depends on the leader, the followers and all the elements of the situation (Blanchard and Hersey, 1996). We will briefly discuss the popular theory of Paul Hersey and Kenneth Blanchard (1988,1996). This theory has become the basis for much training in both Canada and United States.

Hersey and Blanchard's Situational Leadership Theory

While we do not want to go into great detail about this theory, some important components of this theory can be reviewed to increase your understanding of the complexity of leadership. The emphasis in this theory is that the leader changes his or her leadership style based on the level of maturity or "readiness" of employees. According to Hersey and Blanchard (1988), maturity or readiness is based upon the ability and willingness of an employee to accomplish a specific task. Figure 11-1 can be used as a visual guide to enhance understanding. Followers fall into four categories of readiness from low to high. The leader adjusts his or her style to manage this person and chooses from four different styles of leadership: *telling, selling, participating* and *delegating*. Let's review each one using the level of readiness from low to high.

- **Telling or Directing Style for R1 followers.** The leader has a high-task orientation and provides specific instructions and closely monitors performance. This might be the type of behaviour most appropriate when a person is first hired on a job with little or no experience. A Field Training Officer with a new rookie would be a good example in policing.

- **Selling Style or Coaching for R2 followers.** The leader maintains a high-task orientation while increasing support behaviour. Here the follower is more willing to perform the duties but may still lack many skills. There is still a lot of explaining and directing, but the leader also reinforces the willingness of the follower. The Field Training Officer, although very directive, can praise the rookie for properly handling an incident.

- **Participating or Supporting for R3 followers.** The leader increases support behaviour and decreases the amount of guidance and instruction. The employee is now able to do the task, but is still unwilling or insecure. The Field Training Officer continues to offer encouragement to the rookie and allows the rookie to do more tasks independently.

- **Delegating for R4 followers.** The leader decreases both supportive and task behaviour as the follower is now both willing and able or confident to do the tasks. At this stage, the Field Training Officer may make his or her final assessment of the rookie, and the rookie may now be able to go out on his or her own.

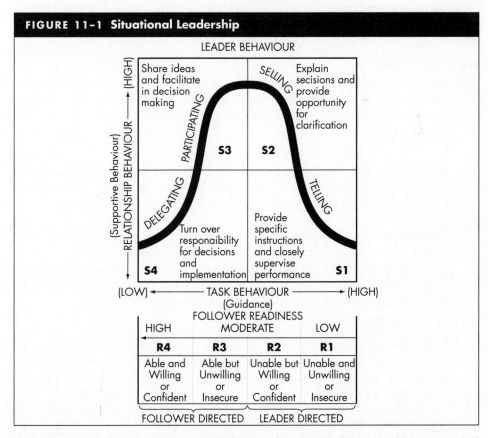

FIGURE 11-1 Situational Leadership

These two researchers have changed the model somewhat since their original ideas (Blanchard and Hersey, 1996). However, the premises are the same in that leaders need to determine where their followers "are at" and adjust their behaviour accordingly.

This theory also points the way to several key ideas in training people to be effective leaders, which we will discuss in the section on developing leadership skills. The most important idea from this situational approach is that an effective leader can assess the needs of subordinates and can vary his or her leadership style accordingly.

POWER

If leaders (or managers or captains) are going to influence followers towards achieving organizational goals, they have to have some sort of power. **Power** is the ability to get someone to do something that you want him or her to do; in organizations, having power influences subordinates to achieve the goals that the leader has defined. In other words, if I have power over you, I can get you to do the things that I want done in the way I want them done. Leaders use power to accomplish organizational goals. Organizational leaders and managers derive power from five different bases that come from two different sources. The sources are *position power* and *personal power* (French and Raven, 1959; Raven, 1993). Not all of these sources are strictly controlled by those in managerial positions. Group and team members and other employees may also have power. Police officers have power to influence a large number of people in their daily duties granted by law. Here, however, we want to examine power as it occurs within organizations or within police services.

Position Power Sources:

- **Reward Power.** Reward power is based on the ability of the leader or manager to control rewards. Rewards can include money, promotions, compliments, time off, vacation schedules, work assignments and so on.

- **Coercive Power.** As well as using rewards to influence others, punishment can also be used. Coercive power is the extent to which a leader or manager can deny rewards or use punishment. Withholding a pay raise, threatening a transfer, demoting, threatening to fire, personnel file letters, threatening to stop a promotion are all examples of punishments. The manager who relies solely on coercive power is often not well liked by subordinates.

- **Legitimate Power.** Legitimate power is the perceived right of a manager or leader to influence others through the use of formal authority. The chain of command consists of a formal authority structure in police services and other organizations. However, even legitimate power is subject to rules, such as the policy and procedures of an organization and other codes of conducts such as laws against harassment.

Personal Power Sources:

- **Expert Power.** Expert power is the ability to influence another person's behaviour through the possession of special talents, knowledge or abilities that the other person does not have but needs. In a group performing a specific task, the person that has the most knowledge in that area may lead and direct the group through this task. Access or control over specific information is important in building and maintaining this power base. If the knowledge that this person possesses is out of date, then this person will no longer have this as a base for power. In an organization, both leaders and employees may have this source of power.

- **Referent Power.** Referent power is the ability to influence another person's behaviour by being liked, respected or having the person identify with the leader. Referent power is related to our earlier discussion of charisma. Those who have referent power have good interpersonal skills (Yukl, 1989). Again, in an organization both leaders and employees may have this type of power. For example, an employee who is well liked by his or her manager may receive better job assignments than co-workers who are not as well liked.

It should be noted that any person can have more than one source of power. A manager may have legitimate power, be well liked and respected by employees (referent power) and have the knowledge needed to orchestrate a major organizational restructuring project (expert power). Also, power can change in organizations in response to personnel changes, organizational restructuring, responses to external and internal changes and any other factors that change the environment where the power is based. However, effective leaders do have the ability to influence others and have an understanding of how to use their power in ways that empower subordinates to continue to meet organizational goals and challenges.

LEADERSHIP STYLES

Building on some of the styles from our models, let's briefly review some of the styles that leaders and managers adopt. There is no one best style of leadership, but nevertheless, many managers tend to favour one style over the others. This is certainly not a complete list, and other styles are included in the previous theories. This list will give you just a notion of the radically different ways leaders "lead."

The Authoritarian Leader

This style is exactly what it sounds like. This type of leader keeps tight control over his or her staff and their functions. This leader may use reward and coercive power to influence subordinates (Lumsden and Lumsden, 1997). This type of leader or manager is a "by-the-book" leader and sticks to policies and procedures. This leader believes that the job of employees is to do exactly what they are told, and the goal is success and perpetuation of the organization.

The Laissez-Faire Leader

This leader lets things happen and allows employees to do what they please. Although this type of leadership works for teams of experts who do not require leader involvement, it is rarely effective in the long run (Lumsden and Lumsden, 1997). If jobs get done, their completion has little to do with input from the leader. The jobs get done because the team is competent enough to work without leadership (at least for awhile).

The Person-Centred Leader (Coach)

This leader is concerned with people and issues about people. Sometimes referred to as the human relations style manager (Dantzker and Mitchell, 1998), this leader recognizes the importance of the human element in the workings of the organization. This leader wants to have input from others when making decisions and solving problems. This type of leadership also recognizes the importance of coaching and mentoring as leadership practices.

The Transactional Leader

The transactional leader (Bass, 1990) uses negotiation and rewards to influence followers. As stated previously, this type of leader views leadership as a series of "jobs" or transactions. Followers participate in decision making, but unlike the tranformational leader, there is not as much inspiration gleaned from this style for followers.

The Charismatic Leader

This type of leadership is characterized by an intensely personal relationship between the leader and followers. Charismatic leaders provide followers with visions of tranformation; they are innovative and creative and try to change the status quo (Conger and Kanungo, 1992).

The Transformational Leader

The transformational leader is one of the most contemporary styles of leadership that has some of the characteristics of the charismatic leader. This type of leader motivates, inspires and develops the team like the charismatic leader. The difference is that the transformational leader does this within the team and organization. This leader helps members to achieve their own goals while also fulfilling the vision and goals of the team and organization (Lumsden and Lumsden, 1997).

Transformational leaders have charisma, have the ability to inspire others with high expectations, stimulate team members intellectually and treat people as individuals by giving personal attention (Bass, 1990). The focus of a transformational leader is two-fold: a high concern for people and a high concern for achieving goals.

DEVELOPING LEADERSHIP SKILLS

Now that we have some ideas about what leadership is, what leaders do according to theory, where their influence comes from and some ideas about leadership styles, the questions that remain are what are effective leadership skills and behaviours and how are they developed? Unlike the earlier Great Person Theories, great leaders are not born but develop their skills over time. Leadership is a process that enables people to achieve goals, but what is this process? In reality, leadership is a "series of behaviours that enable a group or organization to accomplish commonly desired goals ... to enable organizational members to choose to move in a common direction and to accomplish their organizational tasks" (Ray, 1999).

The process of leadership is choosing and using specific behaviours to influence others. There is an incredible amount of research in this area and a great deal of controversy, but there appears to be one solid conclusion: there is a great need for good leaders, including leaders in policing. Second, the characteristics of the transformational leader appear to be those characteristics credited to effective leaders and may be the ones that potential leaders, need to learn in the current environment of change. Most writers agree that times are chaotic with fast-paced changes occurring, and according to one pair of researchers, a "leadership void" is occurring (Bennis, 1989). Many law enforcement writers are echoing these same sentiments (Nancoo, 1993; Bergner, 1998; De Paris, 1998).

Because of the team and group approaches in organizations, leadership is not just something that occurs at the top. Leadership occurs at all levels in an organization, in that leadership behaviours are behaviours (including verbal and nonverbal communication) that "facilitates a team's transactional and task processes in achieving members' and the team's needs and goals" (Lumsden and Lumsden, 1997, p. 31). Leadership addresses both how the group functions (transactions) and what the group does (tasks). It is this approach that the rest of this chapter will reflect. All of us can be leaders in organizations even though we may not all be managers or leaders in the hierarchical sense of the words.

Leadership Skills, Behaviours and Abilities

While not a complete list, these are several skills, behaviours and abilities that leaders have and know how to use. Many of these skills can be used by anyone within any team or organization. A few are based on an existence of the individual holding a formal position of authority. Each of these 13 skills was found in at least two sources. For most of these skills, at least one reference is from law enforcement sources.

1. **Leaders have vision and can clearly articulate that vision.** It is difficult to lead if you have no idea where you are going. The vision is a clear idea of where the organization is headed as well as the set of actions required to get there (De Paris, 1998; Ray, 1999). In a climate of organizational change, the change processes need to come from the top down (De Paris, 1998). Leaders who have positions of management and authority need to develop their abilities in that particular area. Not only does the leader need to have a vision, but he also needs to break down this vision into "doable" components so that all employees can take their lead and do their part. For example, the vision of community policing is with us today, but what does it really mean and how is it really done. For many services, it has meant a complete restructuring process of how they do "business." Effective leaders, by articulating the vision, can excite other group members and provide the impetus and can move the organization forward. Martin Luther King, Jr., in his many speeches, gave a clear image of what the social order should be with all men being equal.

2. **Leaders communicate effectively.** For future police leaders, communication skills "will be paramount." (Lunney, 1989, p. 210). Leaders can communicate effectively both verbally and nonverbally (Sewell, 1996; McKenna, 1998; Portnoy, 1999; Ray, 1999). Using strategies for listening and responding (see earlier chapters), leaders work hard at both understanding others and assisting others in understanding them. This also includes sharply honed writing skills (Sewell, 1996).

3. **Leaders manage and know themselves.** James Sewell, in his article about the four R's for police executives, refers to one of the R's as "Roots." Roots are grounded in who you are: your professional and personal philosophies, values and experiences. These roots form the basis for your decisions, actions and other visible displays of leadership (Sewell, 1996). Leaders take time to develop their own philosophies, to understand who they are and to identify what it is that they stand for and support (Lunney, 1989; Sewell, 1996).

4. **Leaders know how to get attention.** Effective leaders also draw others to them (Bennis, 1989). These leaders attract people who want to work with them and can gain the commitment of other group members. According to Lunney (1989), future police leaders will have a hands-on style and be action-oriented. They will be adept at being highly visible within their organizations. Leaders will therefore need to develop skills such as effective public speaking, effective listening and the capacity to talk to a broad spectrum of people.

5. **Leaders recognize and encourage others in skill development.** Effective leaders help to develop people (Ray, 1999). While modeling effective behaviours and skills, the leader also teaches these skills to anyone who wishes to learn them. The leader demonstrates and teaches the skill using learning methods suitable for members and then gives feedback when others practice these skills. Feedback must be clear, describe the behaviour and not evaluate the person (Ray, 1999). Being able to give feedback is an essential leadership skill. Try the exercise below to improve your skill at giving feedback.

6. **Leaders work to establish positive climates.** Effective leaders use many techniques to create positive work and growth environments. With your knowledge of establishing supportive and positive climates, you will be able to use this knowledge in a leadership role. They create opportunities for group and team decision making, reward effective team work, discipline lack of team work and know the skills to establish effective and com-

SKILLS PRACTICE:

Giving Feedback

Many managerial and other leadership positions involve giving feedback on performance to others. This may be done as a formal performance review or evaluation or a simple question such as "How am I doing?" or "Do you think I'm getting the hang of this?" Before attempting the exercise below, let's briefly review the skills for effective feedback.

1. Feedback focuses on the behaviour, not the person.

2. Feedback must be clear and descriptive.

3. Try to lead your feedback with a positive statement first or demonstrated strengths of the person.

4. Be aware of why the person is soliciting feedback. In formal performance evaluations, this is not an issue. However, in informal situations, there may be more than the goal of improvement on the person's mind. The person may be fishing for a compliment or for increased attention. The "compliment

fisher" may just need some reassurance that he or she is a valuable team member (if he or she is). It is appropriate to ask the individual what the goal or purpose of the feedback is. For example, "I'm curious as to why you would be asking me about your target shooting skills?"

5. Feedback should occur in a timely fashion and in an appropriate place.

6. Use "I statements" if the feedback is about your impression of performance. It is your perception, you own it, not the person. For example, "I think that your writing has improved considerably.

There are still several grammar errors that I would like to go over with you, but I saw only a couple of spelling errors."

7. Feedback should include specific ideas or alternatives about how to improve or where to go to access information for improvement. For example, "Since it appears that grammar is the really big problem, may I suggest the on-line grammar course at the Learning Centre. You can do it when you have time and work at your own speed."

8. For ongoing development, such as field training or other evaluations, set a goal for improvement and a time for completion and a specific time for further feedback. For example, "You still have three weeks before the paper is due. Why don't you amend the errors that I have underlined using the program, and come and see me the at same time next week?"

9. The feedback session should end on a positive note. For example, "Thanks for letting me help you with this. I think with a bit of work, you will be a very competent writer."

Try these exercises (use your imagination):

1. You are a teacher. A student has asked you to quickly proofread a paper. There are many spelling and grammar errors. The topic and the development of ideas are good.

Your Feedback:

2. You are a Field Training Officer. The rookie under your guidance just issued her first ticket without any help from you. You stood back and watched. While she politely issued the ticket, you noticed several nonverbal indicators of nervousness. You noticed a nervous laughter, and she used lots of "ums."

Your Feedback:

3. You are a member of a project team at school and your group is presenting next week. One of the group members comes to you to show you the half-completed work. This member is responsible for preparing a visual chart to be hung up while the group speaks. Although the letters are the right size, it is messy and the colours may not show up at the back of the room. This person says to you, "Is this okay or what!"

Your Feedback:

Source: Based on material from Engleberg and Wynn (1997) and Lumsden and Lumsden (1997).

petent teams (Bergner, 1998; Ray, 1999). Leaders openly suggest and encourage the development of positive group norms such as openness, mutual concern, mutual respect, cooperation, decision making by consensus, trust and the involvement of all members (Lumsden and Lumsden, 1997).

7. **Leaders help manage conflicts among group members.** As we saw in earlier chapters, conflict is a normal process between people and between group members. Constructive conflict is welcome when it is managed with a focus on collaboration, win-win, and when the environment fosters negotiation. Leaders can help other members who are experiencing a conflict and act as a facilitator and establish common ground for the conflicting parties (Ray, 1999). Part of conflict management is also the ability to develop alternative solutions (problem solving) that satisfy the differing opinions of the group.

The leader assists in managing the conflict while still ensuring that the groups and its members continue to work and advance toward their goals and objectives (McKenna, 1998).

8. **Leaders inspire others.** Effective leaders do more than influence followers; they inspire them to new levels of achievement and growth. One way to describe this is that effective leaders *encourage the heart* (Kouzes and Posner, 1987). These leaders do so by recognizing accomplishments and contributions in such a way that members are encouraged to continue their efforts. Perhaps you have had this kind of experience. During a team meeting (for any activity), you come up with an idea. Your team leader, or manager, welcomes your idea and enthusiastically applauds your continued efforts. You leave the meeting eager and ready to try your idea with the knowledge that it has been supported.

9. **Leaders change their style to meet the needs of others.** Earlier we discussed the situational model of leadership and the finding that leaders tend to be high self-monitors. With the ability to read the social situation and ability to adapt leadership style, leaders can change their styles to meet the needs of followers. For example, a training officer notices some reluctance on the part of a rookie to do something. The training officer, reading the cues from the situation, adopts more of a telling or coaching approach to assist the rookie. According to Hersey and Blanchard (1988), good leaders are flexible in how they supervise and manage subordinates.

10. **Leaders engage in coaching and mentoring. Coaching** is encouraging someone toward a level of competency or proficiency in an area of development (McKenna, 1998). Usually the coach has superior skills in the area of competency. Mentoring is similar to coaching and involves learning a variety of skills or approaches from a senior staff member. Programs that pair rookie officers with senior officers are good examples of mentoring in the police service. The rookie officer may learn a variety of skills from the senior officer. Effective leaders can be effective coaches and mentors.

11. **Leaders stay current.** If leaders are going to inspire followers, assist in organizational change and restructuring, it is essential that they stay up to date with what is going on. This means reading, examining and questioning not only in their area of leadership but in what is going on elsewhere in the nation and in the world. For police leaders this means reading trade and professional journals, journals outside traditional law enforcement literature, local and wider perspective newspapers and books on management (Sewell, 1996). The new police leader of the twenty-first century also needs to review writings that have a futurist perspective and ideas about where the future is heading (Lunney, 1989).

12. **Leaders are ethical.** A leader in law enforcement is committed to ethics in law enforcement. "This includes the values of helping others and fighting 'bad guys' while staying within the boundaries of legal and ethical standards in his attempts to suceed" (Bergner, 1998, p. 18). Leaders are models for others and must therefore model or demonstrate the behaviour they wish to see in other organizational and team members

13. **Leaders fulfill their managerial responsibilities.** Many people do rise in the ranks of organizations and forces and take on managerial duties. While many of us would prefer to spend our time inspiring, leading, visioning and creating, legitimate leaders still have to engage in the day-to-day processes of management. Leaders who are managers are still faced with a number of things that must get done that require not only the skills above but also some additional (albeit more mundane) ones.

- **Time management skills.** An effective manager manages time efficiently and competently (Bergner, 1998). This includes coming to work on time, working independently and turning in well-written reports in a timely manner. By demonstrating these skills, he or she can expect others to do the same.

- **Effective meeting skills.** While all group members need to come to meetings prepared and ready to work, the manager must provide the framework for the meetings. Whether the individual is a manager based on formal authority or a designated team leader, he or she must plan, distribute and modify the agenda (Lumsden and Lumsden, 1997). The type of climate of the meeting is also established by the leader. For example, meetings where the leader does all of the talking or behaves defensively can quickly develop into a negative climate.

- **Planning and organization.** This managerial, or leader, function involves the ability to design the anticipated future, to develop the goals and organization for the future and to assist the team or organization in getting there (Lunney, 1989; McKenna, 1998). Organization may involve creating set meeting times, providing information in some way, goal-setting with time lines for completion and so on. Planning is often tied in with decision making in the organization.

- **Goal and objective setting.** We have covered this area before. Briefly, good leaders and managers know how to set effective goals and set effective objectives.

CANADIAN PERSPECTIVE:

The Canadian Police College and Leadership

According to a recent publication from the Canadian Police College, managing police services will become an increasingly challenging and demanding task. "Public demand for a greater variety of police services continue as do the increases in resource restrictions" (p. 6). As a result of the many societal and political changes, the CPC Advisory Committee recommended that the Canadian Police College training programs be redesigned using key competencies. One area was to identify the competencies of effective leadership and to design training to teach these competencies. Utilizing expert input from within and outside of policing (including focus groups from across the country) led to the development of six competencies that make up a teachable model of leadership. Of interest, leadership was also defined as being different from management, as we have already discussed in this chapter. Below are the six competencies of leadership with their accompanying sub-competencies. The competencies have been ranked as they should be taught.

1. *Continuous Personal Growth* includes the six sub-competencies of learning continuously, developing self-awareness/self-discipline, projecting self-confidence, demonstrating flexibility, finding the right balance and practicing stress-management.

2. *Communication Skills* includes the sub-competencies of listening in order to understand and communicating to be understood. A leader requires the ability to interact with others to promote and foster understanding, affect behaviours and achieve desired results.

3. *Relationship Building* includes four sub-competencies of demonstrating integrity, establishing credibility, developing interpersonal awareness and building on diversity. "Through trust, honest, integrity, the leader gains the respect of others, fosters mutual understanding and creates productive relationships" (p. 25).

4. *Stewardship* "is the management of others" in such a way as to create an environment that guides others towards fulfilling personal, professional and team goals (p. 28). The five sub-competencies are creating an environment for empowerment, building commitment, developing others, resolving conflicts and directing others.

5. *Critical thinking* includes the sub-competencies of recognizing patterns in multi-dependency systems, dealing with complexity and challenging assumptions/analyzing present paradigms. The leader demonstrates the ability to evaluate, question, analyze and challenge both the internal and external environment with the goal of organizational improvement.

6. *Organizational awareness and renewal* includes the leader being able to focus the attention of employees towards a vision of the future. The five sub-competencies include developing and enunciating vision, inviting, accepting and promoting change, recognizing and promoting the concept of the learning organization, being client-centred, and demonstrating a commitment to quality.

The leadership training has been organized around four themes: Mastership, Influencing with Integrity, Stewardship, and Organizational Awareness and Renewal. Courses are organized around these themes and include the competencies. Since this is new, there is currently no feedback and evaluation as to the success of this training. However, it is worth noting that the Canadian Police College is responding to the changes in society and in policing and providing the training required in a changing country.

Source: Adapted from Program Development and Evaluation Branch S/Sgt. J. M. Desrochers, Sgts. N. Duquette and G. R. Gregoire in collaboration with the Andrakon Consulting Group Raymond Labonte' (1999). Leadership Development Program: Research Findings and Analysis. Ottawa: Canadian Police College. Sgt. G. R. Gregoire (March/April 1999). Leadership competencies: The Canadian Police College model. The Mezzanine. Ottawa: The Canadian Police College.

SKILLS FOR DEALING WITH SUPERIORS

Although this may seem an odd inclusion in a chapter devoted almost entirely to leadership, part of developing leadership skills is to know how to act when around those who are senior or more skilled than you. Sometimes we are so busy trying to lead and influence, we neglect the fact that there are others who have superior leadership skills and abilities greater than our own. Second, many of us will have to work under, and be supervised by, others. Policing is still very much an organization based on a bureaucratic structure of different levels of authority. To be an effective officer, you will need to develop a constructive relationship with your superior officers. Here are some strategies for you to use to develop this type of relationship.

1. **Display loyalty to the organization.** According to Bergner (1998), loyalty means displaying a commitment to the ethics and effectiveness of the law enforcement profession. Loyalty also involves a commitment to the department and to one's superiors that supercedes personalities. If an officer sees a problem or disagrees with something, he or she speaks up out of a commitment to achieve the best outcome. Even if the final decision is not what the officer would like to have seen, the officer will support the outcome and work hard to ensure that it is done (as long as it is not something illegal or unethical). Loyalty is also expressed by defending your superior and department against outside attacks (Dubrin and Geerinck, 1998).

2. **Appreciate the strengths of your superiors.** Rather than focusing on the things that your manager or superior does wrong (at least in your eyes), appreciate what your superior can do well and learn from it. Ask yourself, "What can I learn from this person that will help me advance my career?" (Dubrin and Geerinck, 1998).

3. **Be dependable and honest.** Many workers become thorns in the sides of their managers because they are not dependable. Workers who are not dependable are not trusted by managers or co-workers as they cannot be counted on to do their share of work. Dependable workers are punctual, only miss work for legitimate reasons, do their assigned duties with minimal complaint, prepare for and attend court dates and turn in their reports on time (Bergner, 1998).

4. **Know your job responsibilities.** Managers and superiors appreciate workers who know their jobs. A good officer knows the law, works hard and demonstrates good judgment (Bergner, 1998).

5. **Respect authority.** A common complaint about our current society is that respect for authority is diminishing (Dubrin and Geerinck, 1998). While you may not always like your superior officers, they are due the respect that comes with their position.

6. **Minimize complaints.** While being open and honest are seen as virtues, to continually engage in complaining about work conditions, co-workers, the laws and so on will not endear you to your supervisor. You may also get the reputation of being a whiner or complainer, which will also not be conducive to developing relationships with co-workers.

7. **Take initiative in problem solving.** Too often, subordinates ask to see their superiors when they are having problems (Dubrin and Geerinck, 1998). Already dealing with a multitude of tasks and problems, this only adds more pressure to a heavy workload. Coming forward not only with the problem but also with some ideas for solving it will demonstrate your ability and willingness to help solve organizational problems.

8. **Demonstrate that you are a team player.** Participating actively with other team members, helping team members and working cooperatively with your supervisor and fellow officers all demonstrate your ability to be an effective team member (Bergner, 1998). Too

often officers are rewarded for individual acts and rarely for effective teamwork. As the focus in policing changes, supervisors will be more able to recognize the importance of being a team player.

9. **Engage in professional development activities.** Interested employees continue to develop skills that will enhance their performance in the workplace. Such activities are not only the ones offered through the police force itself. Professional development includes a broad range of activities including courses, reading and even sporting activities. Courses that will help you deal with the public may include language courses, courses in psychology, sociology and diversity. Many sporting activities provide opportunities to develop team and leadership skills. The key is to continue in personal growth efforts.

POLICING AND LEADERSHIP IN A CHANGING ENVIRONMENT

With all the changes that are occurring in policing in Canada, there is a strong need for effective leadership. In the next chapter the many changes and issues will be discussed in more detail. These changes include the increasing demand for aboriginal policing, increasing population diversity, community-oriented approaches in policing, new partnerships, amalgamation and changes to various federal and provincial acts that impact on policing. All of these changes are occurring within other significant social changes, such as the impact of new technology, changing national and international political scenes, unity issues and so on. All organizations, including police organizations, need strong leaders so that these changes can be managed effectively.

One of the current problems facing policing today is the "machine bureaucracy" (De Paris, 1998). Machine bureaucracies are characterized by a rigid organizational structure with a tall hierarchy. These systems are closed, have relatively narrow jobs with distinct specialization and use one-way communication from the top down to get information to the ranks. Machine bureaucracies also have an elaborate system of rules, regulations, policies and procedures. If you examine the current structures of many police services in Canada, you will see several services that have a large machine bureaucracy, such as the Ottawa-Carleton Regional Police Service and the Toronto Police Service (these organizational charts can be found in McKenna, 1998, pp.100–102). There is little lateral or horizontal communication in these structures and several layers of organization. While such structures were useful, "in today's dynamic policing environment, situations are too complex and varied for a machine bureaucracy to respond effectively" (De Paris, 1998).

Community oriented policing has emerged in response to the many environmental changes that vary from community to community. As the police mission has expanded, as the public has sought input into the policing process and as service demands continue to increase, a new structure is needed (De Paris, 1998). Machine bureaucracies were designed for stability and do not react well to change. De Paris (1998) has proposed a more "organic structure" that encourages flexibility and innovation. This structure, what he terms a "professional police bureaucracy," is more de-centralized, more open, has a flatter structure (fewer levels), less role definition, encourages and supports two-way communication, more decision making at lower levels and an environment that fosters collaboration. Police work, by its very nature, cannot permit an organizational structure without some sort of bureaucracy, but the organization can be restructured to include all of the previous characteristics, hence the term "professional police bureaucracy."

While we do not want to go into the entirety of how police structures need to change and how many forces are currently changing, there are two fundamental differences with this new structure. First, the machine bureaucracy uses a hierarchy of authority whereby people go up the ranks, sometimes based on some sort of testing system. The professional police bureaucracy relies instead on authority based on expert power or authority of a professional nature. Second, rather than relying on preprogrammed rules and so on to carry out the work, the professional police bureaucracy focuses more on facilitating and supporting the work of skilled professionals. In other words, the authority is placed in the hands of the professionals, such as police officers, rather than the administrators. In essence, the pyramid of authority is turned upside down in regards to decision making. This type of structure gives greater autonomy to its officers. Officers will have the "flexibility to be innovative in developing solutions to community problems" (De Paris, 1998, p. 70). This does not mean that policing becomes a "free for all." Officers are guided by the traditional ethics and rules, but are also guided by goals determined by the organization. The organization determines the goals through developing an organizational vision, and officers determine the processes of how these goals can be achieved. The new structure will still be based on a bureaucratic model but will be a more flexible organization that can meet the changing demands of the environment. Each police organization may structure differently. Some services are already undergoing major restructuring with specialized and cross-functional units. Also, many services have moved to flattened structures with fewer supervisors (McKenna, 1998).

If police services are going to restructure to meet the new demands, then leadership training is going to be essential. The average police manager today typically has little formal preparation for the variety of managerial and leadership tasks that he or she must undertake. The majority of management experience that police managers bring with them is the knowledge and experience gained from climbing ranks (several studies quoted in Dantzker and Mitchell, 1998, p. 99). Current structures provide little opportunity to develop leadership skills (Dantzker and Mitchell, 1998). Below is one law-enforcement author's ideas on how to develop police leaders.

LAW AND JUSTICE PERSPECTIVE:

Developing Leaders

According to Laurie Bergner, a law enforcement trainer and consultant, developing the skills and qualities for effective police leaders should start at the outset of a career in policing. Officers with potential should be recognized early and should rise to the top before promotional testing occurs. Leadership is more than passing a promotional test (as we saw from our characteristics of the effective leader). Here are some of her ideas about how police organizations can develop leaders. This involves two areas: creating conditions that encourage such qualities and providing opportunities to try out leadership roles.

Creating conditions that encourage and promote good leadership qualities:

- Respect officers who share ideas and initiate suggestions with their unit. Publicly recognizing good ideas promotes a culture in which leadership is encouraged.

- Create opportunities for participatory decision making. This will give officers practice in thinking about options, choosing the best option and practicing trying to influence others.

- Reward teamwork; discipline lack of teamwork. Too often departments re-

ward those who go it alone with individual acts of courage or a spectacular arrest. But what about other officers who help another officer on a call by sending in information by radio about the suspect's car to the officer who then makes the arrest. In sports this is called an "assist," and it is rewarded. Breaches of teamwork should be handled in a serious way.

- Recognize and reward good ethics and values; deal seriously with ethical violations.

Providing opportunities to act in supervisory and leadership roles:

Officers who are seen as having leadership potential should receive both formal and informal on-the-job training. This gives the department an opportunity to evaluate in order to see if these officers are as good as they seem.

- Use the role of Field Training Officer. This role contains several skills of supervision—teaching, assessing performance and giving feedback.

- Use temporary shift command as an important opportunity to practise a leadership role. This gives the officer

a chance to practise his or her leadership abilities.

- Assign probationers to take charge of crime scenes when they are first responders on the scene.

- Create opportunities to do training, both inside and outside the department.

According to Bergner, hoping that good leaders will surface is not a strategy that will pay off. Instead, each department should have a planned strategy that develops leadership qualities in potential leaders from the first day on the job.

Source: Laurie Bergner. Developing good leaders begins at the beginning. *The Police Chief*, November 1998, 17-23. Reprinted with the permission of the International Association of Chiefs of Police, Alexandria, VA.

A final note on leadership comes from a Canadian author. In his book, *Foundations of Policing in Canada* (1998), Paul McKenna divides the required elements of leadership into a "Leadership Grid" (see Figure 11-2). Note that this grid contains many of the skills that were discussed earlier. This grid charts the various qualities in terms of their focus.

FIGURE 11-2 Leadership Grid

Job-centred Qualities
- resourceful
- accomplishment-oriented
- decisive
- quickly processes new information

Team-centred Qualities
- leads peers and subordinates
- fosters environment that promotes growth
- deals with problems among team members
- attracts quality team members

Interpersonal Qualities
- develops and sustains strong relationships
- demonstrates compassion and sensitivity
- maintains personal composure
- deals directly with individuals and groups

Self-possessed Qualities
- balances personal life with work commitments
- demonstrates self-awareness
- makes people comfortable in a variety of settings
- demonstrates flexibility in changing situations

Source: Paul F. McKenna (1998). "Foundations of Polcing in Canada." Prentice Hall Canada Inc., p. 98.

SUMMARY

In this chapter we have explored the very large topic of leadership. First, we defined leadership and compared leadership to management. Leadership is more about personal qualities and skills whereas management is more about the actual tasks of holding a higher position in an organization.

We then explored some of the various theories of leadership including the trait approach, the behavioural approaches and the situational approaches. An important situational theory is Hersey and Blanchard's Situational Leadership theory that includes the situation, style of leadership and the ability and/or willingness of the followers. Power and the sources of power were discussed as bases and sources of power of both leaders and managers. Leaders differ in their style of leadership: authoritarian, laissez-faire, person-centred, transactional, charismatic and transformational are all styles of leadership.

Effective leaders demonstrate skills that influence and help others in the organization to reach organizational goals. Effective leaders have vision, communicate effectively, manage and know themselves, know how to get and maintain attention, recognize and encourage others to develop skills, establish positive communication climates, help manage conflicts, inspire others, adapt their leadership style, engage in coaching and mentoring, stay current, are ethical and fulfill their managerial responsibilities. As we are not all leaders, we also need to develop skills that assist us in getting along with our managers and superior officers. To develop good relations with superiors, employees should display loyalty to the organization, appreciate the strengths of superiors, be dependable and honest, know their job responsibilities, respect authority, minimize complaints, take initiative in problem solving, demonstrate team player skills and engage in professional development activities. The chapter ended by examining leadership in policing within a rapidly changing environment, which will be explored more deeply in the next chapter.

JOURNAL AND DISCUSSION QUESTIONS

1. Write down the characteristics and skills that you would want the next police chief hired in your community to possess. Identify which ones you feel are essential for effective leadership.

2. Select two or three leadership skills, abilities and characteristics that you currently feel you do not possess. Write an action plan for each one that will help you attain these identified skills.

3. In this chapter it was stated that there is not as much respect for authority as there used to be in the past. What are your ideas about this lack of respect? Where does this new disrespect come from?

WEB SITES

www.selfgrowth.com

This is a site devoted to personal growth and self-improvement. You can sign up for a free e-mail newsletter.

www.amdahl.com/ext/iacp

This is the site for The International Association of Chiefs of Police. There are several links at this site including one for The Police Chief Magazine.

www.fbi.gov/academy/academy.html

This is the site for the FBI Academy.

REFERENCES

J. E. Alcock, D. W. Carment and S. W. Sadava (1998). *A Textbook of Social Psychology.* Scarborough, ON: Prentice Hall Allyn and Bacon Canada.

B. M. Bass (Winter 1990). From transactional to transformational leadership: Learning to share the vision. *Organizational Dynamics, 19*–31.

Warren Bennis (1989). *Why Leaders Can't Lead.* San Francisco: Jossey-Bass.

Laurie L. Bergner (1998). Developing leaders begins at the beginning. *The Police Chief,* November, pp.17–23.

Robert R. Blake and Jane S. Mouton (1978). *The New Managerial Grid.* Houston: Gulf.

Kenneth H. Blanchard and Paul Hersey (1996). Great ideas revisited .... *Training and Development, 50,* p.42.

J. A. Conger and R. N. Kanungo (1987). Towards a behavioural theory of charismatic leadership in organizational setting. *Academy of Management Review, 12,* pp. 637–647.

J. A. Conger and R. N. Kanungo (1988). Behavioural dimensions of charismatic leadership. In J. A. Conger and R. N. Kanungo (eds.). *Charismatic Leadership.* San Francisco: Jossey-Bass.

J. A. Conger and R. N. Kanungo (1992). Perceived behavioural attributes of charismatic leadership. *Canadian Journal of Behavioural Science, 24,* pp. 86–102.

S. F. Cronshaw and R. J. Ellis (1991). A process of investigation of self-monitoring and leader emergence. *Small Group Research, 22,* pp. 403–420.

Mark L. Dantzker and Michael P. Mitchell (1998). *Understanding Today's Police,* Canadian edition, Scarborough, ON: Prentice Hall Canada.

Richard J. De Paris (1998). Organizational leadership and change management: Removing systems barriers to community-oriented policing and problem solving. *The Police Chief,* December, pp. 68–76.

Andrew J. Dubrin and Terri Geerinck (1998). *Human Relations for Career and Personal Success,* Canadian edition. Scarborough, ON: Prentice Hall Canada.

A. H. Eagly and B. T. Johnson (1990). Gender and leadership style: A meta-analysis. *Psychological Bulletin, 108,* pp. 233–256.

A. H. Eagly, M. G. Makijani and B. G. Klonsky (1992). Gender and the evaluation of leaders: A meta-analysis. *Psychological Bulletin, 111,* pp. 3–22.

Isa N. Engleberg and Dianna R. Wynn. (1979). *Working in Groups: Communication Principles and Strategies.* New York: Houghton Mifflin.

J. R. P. French and B. Raven (1959). The bases of social power, in D. Cartwright. *Studies in Social Power.* Ann Arbor, MI: University of Michigan Press.

Paul Hersey and Kenneth H. Blanchard (1988). *Management of Organizational Behavior: Utilizing Human Resources*, 5th edition. Englewood Cliffs, NJ: Prentice Hall.

E. P. Hollander (1985). Leadership and power, in G. Lindzey and E. Aronson (Eds.), *Handbook of Social Psychology*, 3rd edition, *Vol. 2.* New York: Random House.

James Kouzes and Barry Posner (1987). *The Leadership Challenge: How to Get Extraordinary Things Done in Organizations.* San Francisco: Jossey-Bass.

Gay Lumsden and Donald Lumsden (1997). *Communicating in Groups and Teams: Sharing Leadership.* Belmont, CA: Wadsworth Publishing.

Robert Lunney (1989). The role of the police leader in the 21st century, in Donald J. Loree *Future Issues in Policing: Symposium Proceedings.* Ottawa, ON: Canadian Police College, pp. 197–213.

Paul F. McKenna (1998). *Foundations of Policing in Canada.* Scarborough, ON: Prentice Hall Canada.

Steven L. McShane (1995). *Canadian Organizational Behaviour*, 2nd edition. Toronto, ON: Times Mirror Professional Publishing.

Stephen E. Nancoo (1993). Epilogue, The future: Trends and issues, in J. Chacko and S. E. Nancoo (eds.). *Community Policing in Canada.* Toronto, ON: Canadian Scholar's Press.

Ronald P. Phillipchalk (1995). *Invitation to Social Psychology.* Orlando, FL: Harcourt Brace College Publishers.

Robert A. Portnoy (1999). *Leadership: 4 Competencies for Success.* Upper Saddle River, NJ: Prentice Hall.

B. H. Raven (1993). The bases of power: Origins and recent developments. *Journal of Social Issues, 49,* pp. 227–251.

R. Glenn Ray (1999). *The Facilitative Leader*. Upper Saddle River, NJ: Prentice Hall.

J. B. Rosener (1990). Ways women lead. *Harvard Business Review, 68,* 119–125.

John R. Schermerhorn, Jr., James G. Hunt and Richard Osborn (1994). *Managing Organizational Behavior*, 5th edition. New York: John Wiley and Sons.

James D. Sewell (1996). The four R's for police executives. *The FBI Law Enforcement Bulletin, 65,* July 1996, pp. 9–14.

G. A. Yukl (1989). *Leadership in Organizations*. Englewood Cliffs, NJ: Prentice Hall.

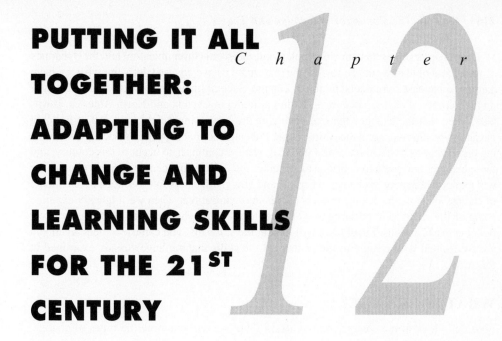

PUTTING IT ALL TOGETHER: ADAPTING TO CHANGE AND LEARNING SKILLS FOR THE 21ST CENTURY

Chapter 12

LEARNING OUTCOMES

After studying this chapter you should be able to:

1. Define change and the various types of change.

2. Explain how organizations react to change.

3. List the ways people react to change and why people may resist change.

4. Use force-field analysis to explain the process of change.

5. List the organizational and personal methods that can be used to overcome resistance to change.

6. Discuss areas of change occurring in policing today including changes in officer training and recruitment.

Person 1: *Look at this! Another meeting about reducing the number of staff sergeants and sergeants in the division and all the other restructuring.*

Person 2: *I know what you mean! Why don't they just do it and let us get on with our jobs.*

Person 3: *Well, I'm still not sure what it's all about. I could use a little more information about what is going on. Some of these changes are really baffling!*

Person 1: *Hey, just go with the flow! There's nothing you can do.*

Person 2: *And if you try, they just knock you down anyway. I gave up trying to understand what goes on in this department years ago.*

Person 3: *Well, I've only been here a few months. I thought they wanted our input and ideas.*

This chapter represents our final look at interpersonal communication and the dynamics of group and of teamwork. To review the material we have covered, let's put what we have learned to increase our understanding of change. Several times in this text we have brought up the number of changes occurring within policing in Canada and North America. It was also stated that the changes that are occurring are happening quickly not just in policing but across organizations and the entire nation. Policing does not happen in a vacuum. As policing organizations try to adapt to new changes, change continues to occur in this country, and these changes are likely to continue as we enter the twenty-first century. In this chapter we will explore the nature of change: what it is and how it affects us. We will look at one model of change and how the change process occurs in organizations. Then we'll quickly examine some of the changes in policing and attempt to see what changes will continue to effect policing organizations. Finally, we will look at the skills that you can use to help when you are confronted with change in the context of the skills that we have already examined in this text.

WHAT IS CHANGE?

First, let's look at the change process itself. Here we will examine the types of change, change agents and reactions to change.

Types of Change

Change occurs when something is not working the way it used to work. If a store that used to be very busy is no longer busy, then something has changed. If a relatively crime-free area is suddenly a crime "hot spot," something has changed. **Change** occurs when something that used to be one way is now different in some manner. When things no longer work or there have been negative occurrences, it alerts us to look more closely at what is going on. Why is there more crime in this area? Why are profits diminishing? Why are there fewer shoppers? Changes can be positive as well as negative. Usually it is the negative changes that we concentrate on, but we may also want to examine positive change to continue movement in that direction.

There are two kinds of change that occur in organizations. One type of change is **radical change** or **frame-breaking change** (Nadler and Tushman, 1988). This is a change that results in a major makeover of the entire organization or parts of the organization. This type of change is often caused by some sort of radical event. For example, a merger or takeover produces radical organizational restructuring. Many Canadian colleges experienced a sudden loss of funding several years ago, which for many colleges led to restructuring with a flatter bureaucracy, tuition hikes for students, program cuts and so on. The good news for many of us is that radical change does not occur frequently in the life cycle of an organization (Schermerhorn et al., 1994).

A more common form of change is **incremental** or **frame-bending change**. This type of change is less traumatic for an organization and can often be viewed as part of the natural evolution of an organization. These types of changes can include introducing new technology, introducing new products and developing new systems. The nature of the organization remains basically the same. Incremental change builds on the ways things are currently done and usually seeks to enhance or extend them (Schermerhorn et al., 1994). A good example of this type of change was the introduction of computer networking in organizations, including police departments. For the most part, the process was planned in advance. The changeover was messy for many of us as walls and floors were ripped apart for new wiring to be installed, professional development was arranged for the computer illiterate or computer fearful and software selected and loaded. Following quickly on the heels of networking were organizations adjusting to the Internet. For policing, this also meant training in a new area of crime and enforcement. Organizations need the capability to improve continuously through incremental change to stay in tune with today's continuing changes (Schermerhorn et al., 1994).

Change can also be planned or unplanned (Schermerhorn et al., 1994). **Unplanned change** occurs spontaneously or randomly without any initial input from the organization. Wildcat strikes, sudden closure of a major supplier or other unforeseen events can suddenly rock an organization. When unplanned change occurs, the goal is to act immediately to minimize negative effects of the change and to maximize any possible positive benefits.

Planned change comes about as a result of specific efforts to change by an organization. Usually planned change results from the perception of a **performance gap** by a person or group of people within the organization. Performance gaps are discrepancies between what is currently occurring and what the desired state is. In some ways a performance gap is similar to a problem; a deviance between what is and what you would like. For example, if the chief of a small police department notes that there are several public complaints about how officers are communicating to them, this is not the desired effect or state of how the public should be perceiving interaction with officers.

Change Agents

Change does not magically occur in organizations. Organizations are made up of people; people, therefore have to make the changes. **Change agents** are individuals or groups that take the responsibility for managing a change within an organization. They take the responsibility for changing the existing pattern of behaviour or ways of doing things or current practices of a person or social system. Using our above example, the chief and two officers examine the current communication practices of officers in the department. They also interview all of those who have made complaints. From this, new procedures and guidelines are established about communicating with the public. These three individuals were responsible for making a change; in essence, they were change agents.

Reactions to Change

In our opening dialogue, there are some reactions to changes going on within the department. Two of the people want to be left alone because they have had enough. The third person wants more information about the proposed flattening of the organization. When changes are about to happen or are already under way, people react in different ways. Let's examine some of the ways that people react to change.

1. **Inertia.** Inertia is not really reaction to change. **Inertia** "refers to a person's attitude about change" (Portnoy, 1999, p. 137). This reaction is one of doing nothing; the person is unaware of the need for change and continues to behave in the usual or routine pattern of doing things. A salesperson who continues to use high-pressure sales techniques and

is unaware of the negative impact of such techniques is an example of inertia. He or she sees no reason to change or that the current methods need revision.

2. **Supportive.** Much to the delight of many change agents, some people embrace change and welcome it. The attitude is one of, "It's about time that someone fixed that!" These individuals volunteer to help get the changes rolling, champion the changes at meetings or other gatherings and work hard to ensure positive results.

3. **Reluctant.** While understanding the need for change, these individuals will go along if given sufficient information and incentive to change their behaviour. Their reluctance may stem from being unsure about how to behave or how to actively implement the changes. For example, if the number of supervisors is being reduced, the person may be unsure of to whom they now report.

4. **Resistance.** Unfortunately, the avid supporters are few, and many organizational change efforts are resisted by employees, managers, clients and others who have vested interests in the organization (McShane, 1995). Resistance stems from a natural tendency or motivation to keep things the same or to maintain the status quo rather than to change behaviour (McShane, 1995). It is not so much the change that is resisted but the implications of the change (Conner, 1994). When people feel unwilling and/or unable to change, then change becomes difficult and is resisted (Conner, 1994).

Resistance can occur in many forms, such as passive noncompliance. For example, the person continues to do things the "old way" even though being continually reminded of the new system. Another form of resistance is complaining about current or proposed changes. As we saw in our opening dialogue, two of the people were complaining about proposed change. These two individuals may have also been trying to actively promote a negative attitude in others, another form of resistance (Conner, 1994). Other types of resistance are absenteeism, turnover, sabotage and collective action and other methods of active noncompliance.

People resist change for many reasons. Below are some of the main reasons (McShane, 1995; Nadler, 1987; Katz and Kahn, 1978):

- **Direct costs.** People resist change when they perceive that the new way will have higher costs or fewer benefits. For example, some people did not want computer training as they saw it as overly time consuming and did not perceive the long-term benefits.

- **Fear of the unknown.** Change is resisted because it involves uncertainty and risk. For example, restructuring may mean working with new people and leaving some old and familiar colleagues behind.

- **Saving face.** People may resist change to "prove" that the decision is wrong. This is often a political manoeuvre and may involve trying to have the decision-makers look wrong while making the resister(s) look right.

- **Disruption and breaking of routines.** While routine may be boring, it is also comfortable and safe. When changes occur, people may have to abandon these comfortable ways and learn new ways. People may not feel that they have the capabilities to address the change and may dig in their heels (Conner, 1994). It takes time and energy to learn new behaviours.

- **Incongruent organizational systems.** When many organizations changed over to computer networks and expected all employees to use computers, some organizational systems were not ready for the increased use. Many companies did not have enough computers, and employees were stuck sharing computers. Organizational control systems such as rewards, training and so on may not be in place and so employees become discouraged (McShane, 1995). Why learn computer skills if you cannot access a computer?

- **Incongruent team dynamics.** Characteristics of teams can also discourage people from accepting change. For example, norms that protect and ensure the status quo of the team may result in team resistance to change.

THE CHANGE PROCESS

With the knowledge that organizations face resistance to change, how do organizations go about making changes? How do change agents make changes to benefit an organization? To answer these questions, a model was developed by the behavioural scientist, Kurt Lewin, in the 1950s. This model has been adapted and changed over the years, but it has basically stayed much the same over the last 40-plus years. This model is referred to as **force field analysis** and consists of three phases or steps. Force field analysis helps change agents examine and diagnose forces that drive and restrain proposed changes in an organization. *Driving forces* are forces that push or propel the changes. *Restraining forces* are forces that resist the changes and attempt to maintain the status quo. When both types of forces are relatively equal, there is stability or equilibrium. Change occurs when the driving forces are greater than the restraining forces. This occurs by either increasing the strength of the driving forces and/or decreasing the strength of the restraining forces (Lewin, 1951). As these forces change in strength, there is a period of transition (Conner, 1994). Thus, there are three processes embedded in this model. First, effective change begins by **unfreezing** the status quo or current situation. During this period, Conner (1994) states that people go through a period of transition as they "unfreeze" and then begin to "refreeze." Unfreezing occurs as the change agent introduces disequilibrium to change the driving and resisting forces. **Refreezing** is the introduction of new systems, methods and conditions that reinforce and maintain new roles and patterns. Let's examine unfreezing, transition and re-freezing in more detail.

Unfreezing

After change agents have identified a need for change (and hopefully have developed an action plan for the change), the status quo must undergo unfreezing. Unfreezing is accomplished by strengthening the driving forces, weakening the restraining forces or some combination of both. For example, management could hold meetings to have input into the desired changes and to inform employees why change is necessary. As well, free training can be offered and so on. As part of actually using force field analysis, change agents can brainstorm what the current driving and restraining forces are that are maintaining the current situation or state. Then, the forces that could be changed (strengthened or weakened) can be identified. Try the exercise below and see if you can identify some of the forces that are maintaining a current situation.

SKILLS PRACTICE:

Using Force Field Analysis to Implement Change

One practical use of force field analysis is to identify current forces that are maintaining a situation in its present state and then to develop a strategy to overcome these forces. Let's use an example from the field of policing (although it has been somewhat fictionalized). This may be a good exercise to conduct in teams, using a brainstorming approach.

The Current Situation: Because of several changes in the nation, it is becoming apparent that recruits need more formal education and training before being accepted into services. If policing is to be viewed as a professional occupation, more formalized training and higher education is seen as necessary to take this "traditional job" into a profession.

Your Responsibilities: Your team is a provincial group of experts from a variety of fields including policing, higher educational institutions and various ministry personnel. You have been assigned to examine this issue and to come up with some strategies about how this training should be implemented.

1. As a team, you are to first identify the existing forces that will help you implement formal officer training. Second, identify the forces that will hinder your implementation of higher education standards in officer training. These are the restraining forces. Place them on the areas identified below.

Driving Forces	C	S	Restraining
	U	T	Forces
	R	A	
	R	T	
	E	E	
	N		
	T		

2. Circle the forces that you (or your team) feel could most easily be used to change the current state or status quo. In other words, what driving forces could you increase to help implement the change? What restraining forces could you decrease to help you implement the change?

3. Choose two of the forces that you have chosen and develop a plan that would increase that force or decrease a force. Ideally, choose one restraining and one driving force. You may want to use the models for goal setting, decision making or problem solving for this process.

4. Identify potential problems with your action plan, solution or decision.

Often change agents work on strengthening driving forces only, and this is usually ineffective as the restraining forces often increase to meet the challenge (McShane, 1995). For example, if employees are threatened with being fired for not taking new training, they may counter such efforts by launching union grievances or sitting sullenly and learning nothing during the forced training.

Transition or Change

The second stage in Lewin's model is the change or transition. From the stage of unfreezing to refreezing, people are affected by what is happening in the organization. During a change process, whether organizational or personal, individuals go through a transition process where old ways are discarded and new ways adopted. This is rarely an easy process. According to William Bridges, in his book *Managing Transitions: Making the Most of Change* (1991), the starting point for a transition is not the end or goal of the transition but the ending of what you are leaving behind. A major problem with organizational changes is the failure of change agents to think through what people will be letting go when the change occurs. For example, learning new computer skills means leaving behind my multi-coloured markers, the fun of designing and drawing on overheads and so on. There are now computer software packages that do all this too, but it takes time and effort to learn these new things.

According to Bridges (1991), the transition is the psychological process that people go through during change. He views it as a three-part process of endings or letting go of the "old ways" and so on, a neutral zone characterized by disorientation, confusion, and uncertainty and new beginnings where there is discovery of establishing new relationships, developing new skills and competencies and making new plans. While the process is much more complex than what is stated here, the real key is for you to understand that people have to make a transition from a current state to a new state, and people will vary in how quickly or appropriately they make that transition. The role of change agents is not only to identify what changes are required and how they should be implemented but also to assist those affected by the changes to adapt to the "new order."

Refreezing

Refreezing is the implementation of systems and conditions that maintain the new changes and prevent slippage back to the old way of doing things. For example, if a minimum of a college diploma is the new requirement for becoming a police officer after a specific year, then new hiring and recruiting policies will have to reflect that change. Colleges and universities will need to be informed, potential candidates will have to be informed and other activities carried out to assure that this policy will be carried out. Internal changes that need to be implemented, such as offering similar opportunities for current officers or other training initiatives, will also likely occur. See Figure 12-1 below for an illustration of these three processes.

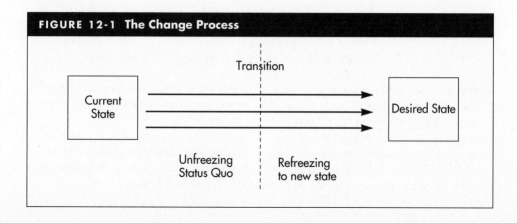

FIGURE 12-1 The Change Process

Transition

Current State

Desired State

Unfreezing Status Quo

Refreezing to new state

METHODS TO OVERCOME RESISTANCE TO CHANGE AND EASE TRANSITION

If you are going to become a change agent in the future (and you most likely will) or experience change (you most definitely will), you will need an understanding of the methods that you can use to help others and yourself cope with change and the transition process. Although used by both organizations and individuals, we will discuss methods under the headings of organizational and personal methods. Organizational methods refer to the methods and strategies that change agents within organizations used to effect planned change. Personal methods will refer to the skills and strategies that you can personally use to help you cope with organizational changes (and personal changes).

Organizational Methods

Organizations may use one or several methods to go from unfreezing to refreezing. Below are some of these methods (adapted from McShane, 1995):

- **Communication.** Communicating the change effort through all levels of an organization is an important strategy to reduce resistance. Organizational change requires a top-down approach (De Paris, 1998), and the ranks should be kept informed as to what is occurring, why it is occurring and what the implications are for them personally. By being well informed, there is less fear of the unknown.

- **Employee involvement.** When the individuals and teams that are going to be most affected by the change are given opportunities for decision making and planning around the change, they are more likely to support the change. Having had input into the changes, there will likely be more commitment to the change (Pollock and Colwill, 1987). Teams and groups of employees can use problem-solving and decision-making strategies to develop goals and action plans to carry out proposed changes.

- **Training.** One of the reasons for resistance was the fact of perceived costs as a result of the change. One of the ways to ease transition is to ensure that employees have the skills to handle the new ways. By increasing comfort levels and expertise levels, employees will experience reduced costs of changing and are less likely to resist the change. See the Canadian Perspective box below to see how New Brunswick is responding to changes in community-based policing.

CANADIAN PERSPECTIVE:

Community-Based Policing in New Brunswick

As are the other provinces, New Brunswick is shifting towards community policing. While the province is undergoing significant changes throughout its services, one interesting area is some of the information referred to in a recent framework document about changing management and empowering front line officers (1997).

In this comprehensive report with significant planning for change, the police leader will now be a facilitator or coach rather than a rule enforcer. The basic role of this facilitator is to empower the front line officers so that they may effectively address local crime and problems that have been identified and prioritized through consultation with the community. As facilitators, management will create and maintain an environment or climate that is conducive and supportive of community policing. Managers will also have to trust that people and groups inside and outside of the organization can make good decisions and solve problems. This means that some of the traditional control will have to be loosened so that groups are responsible for their decisions and productivity.

This report also discusses a tier model for policing based on four levels and other significant changes in policing in New Brunswick. Police organizations across the country are changing and will continue to do so as new structures are adopted, revised and implemented.

Source: Adapted from New Brunswick Department of the Solicitor General. *Community Based Policing in New Brunswick Framework Document.* December 19, 1997. View the entire document at: www.gov.nb.ca/solgen/english/framewrk.htm

- **Introduce changes slowly using a planned approach.** Successful change is introduced slowly and incrementally (De Paris, 1998). Organizations need to develop action plans that introduce change in a logical sequence of steps until the new vision has been attained.

- **Negotiation.** At times, organizations may need to negotiate other benefits for employees to offset some of the costs of a change.

- **Coercion.** Although not highly recommended, coercion may be required to overcome resistance and to obtain the necessary compliance to implement the change. The major problem with coercion is that it produces adverse emotional effects. For example, a manager who is forced to follow new procedures may start complaining to others about how angry he as at the unfair treatment.

Personal Methods

Whether we are for it or against it, whether we like it or do not like it, if we are not the change agents we will be on the receiving end of change many times in our lives. Sometimes we react unfavourably, even inappropriately (like throwing a temper tantrum), when change knocks on our own doors. So rather than looking foolish or stressed out or seething quietly (or perhaps not so quietly) with anger, there are ways to manage change. Below are just a few strategies:

- **Manage your stress.** Change can be very stressful. Among several ways to manage stress, two strategies may be very helpful in assisting you with managing stress due to change. One strategy is to develop competence. Competence refers to both job skills and social skills, including being able to solve problems effectively, to manage conflict and to control anger (Cowen, 1991). Many of the interpersonal skills from the first part of this text will help you gain competence in your social skills. Being able to tell people how you feel, expressing your perceptions of a new situation using such skills as I-language and perception checking, using the conflict and problem-solving strategies are just a few of the skills that will help you achieve the competency to manage change.

A second strategy is to develop **resilience**, the ability to withstand pressure and stress and to emerge from the experience stronger than before (Cowen, 1991). Learning how to manage stress will help you develop resilience and to bounce back from a number of stressful events, including major organizational changes.

- **Talk to others.** Talking to others can also help you cope with change. If you are a new employee, talking to "veterans" can be extremely helpful. Most long-term employees have probably experienced several changes in their careers and can help you gain some perspective. A veteran officer can tell you of the turmoil in the sixties and the number of legislative changes that have occurred as a result of acts such as the Human Rights Act.

    You can also ask questions to clarify the change. Ask your supervisors or others who are implementing the change these questions. Co-workers may not always be the best source for some of your questions as they, too, may be unsure of the change. They also may be feeling negatively about the change and not give you accurate information.

- **Realize that adjustment takes time.** Change takes time. According to De Paris (1998), successful strategic change in law enforcement agencies is a prolonged process. "Accordingly, an incremental approach— in which personnel are able to identify with the new vision and internalize with the new vision and behaviours necessary for its attainment—is essential" (p.73). Unfortunately, many organizational changes may not be as well planned as they should have been, leaving the employees rushing to behave in new roles. When this does happen, realize that it will take time for you to adjust, and do not be too hard on yourself if you cannot remember everything and do everything new all at once.

- **Change your perceptions.** Another way to manage change is to review your current perceptions and change them. Although it may be difficult seeing challenges as opportunities, this change in viewpoint may benefit you in the long run. You can engage in such strategic thinking as, "What can this change do for me now and later?" or "What skills do I have that I will be able to shine at this time?" You can see the change as something that is beneficial for you in the long term. For example, if yearly physical fitness testing becomes a reality, view it as a way to ensure that you may actually live longer rather than as some sort of grueling torture test. If you are already in top shape, this is a chance for you to show your superiors that you take care of your health and ask if there is anything you can do to help out or coordinate such testing (an opportunity to practice and demonstrate your leadership ability?).

CURRENT CHANGES AND POLICING

The skills, abilities, strategies and knowledge in this text will help you in many ways with a career in law enforcement. While managing yourself daily on and off the job, these skills will also help you to cope with the challenges of changing police practices across the nation. While not a complete list, below is a summary of some of the major changes in our society that are effecting current practices. Some issues not discussed below include the impact of globalization, changes in the RCMP and various legal and law changes. As we have seen earlier in this chapter and in earlier chapters, police services are undergoing major and minor changes to cope with these new challenges.

Demographic and Population Changes

As was discussed in previous chapters, the Canadian population is changing. There is more ethnic and cultural diversity, a continuing increase of visible minorities especially in large urban areas, increased representation of women in the workforce and an aging general population. These changes are impacting on all organizations including policing organizations. In response to these changes, police services are making efforts to increase representation of minorities to reflect the demographic make-up and to provide services to some of these more crime-vulnerable groups (such as the elderly and women). There is also a continued potential for ethnic and racial violence that is transplanted from homelands to Canada (McKenna, 1998). This will require specialized forms of police intervention. These will not be easy tasks. "There will be a continuing need to ensure that the criminal justice system and, in particular, the front-line officer are in tune with the expectations and requirements of Canada's diverse population" (McKenna, 1998, p. 25).

In this text, many of the skills required for you to be effective when dealing with those from cultures different from your own have been discussed.

Aboriginal Policing

In 1996 the federal government endorsed a new First Nations Policing Policy that supports the ongoing development of law enforcement services that meet the different law enforcement needs of aboriginal communities. The policy has led to ongoing negotiations of tripartite agreements involving the federal government, provincial or territorial governments and band councils. The policy is directed towards self-policing for the First Nations and Aboriginal peoples (Canada, Solicitor General, 1996).

As a result of this policy, there will continue to be changes as new agreements are entered into for new policing services for First Nations and Aboriginal peoples. For example, in February 1999 two new agreements were announced for new policing services for the Tsawwassen, Semiahmoo and Spallumcheen First Nations in British Columbia. The two agreements were finalized in the respective communities in informal signing ceremonies attended by federal, provincial and First Nations officials (Canada, Solicitor General, 1999).

Changes Due to Legislation

In the last 20 years there have been significant legislative changes in Canada. The North American Free Trade Act, the Human Rights Act and several other legislative changes have greatly influenced Canadian society. Revisions and amendments to the Police Services Act, the Regional Municipalities Act and the District Municipality of Muskoka Act have had major impact in Ontario. Municipalities must now pay for their policing, which resulted in a flurry of restructuring, amalgamations and even competition between provincial and local services as to who would be the police organization in a given area. Police services found themselves in a unique position: competing for a local market share. While the general public expects top-of-the-line service, such service has become more difficult given the current financial status of many areas.

With many new amalgamations and major restructuring of forces, it is too early to assess their effectiveness. There will continue to be restructuring and reorganization as police services deal with a changing political climate.

Focus on Community Policing

"In a relatively short time, community policing has replaced professional crime control policing as the dominant ideology and organizational model of progressive policing in Canada" (Murphy, 1993, p. 13). Several times in this text we have discussed community policing, perhaps without a really clear idea why there was a change to this approach. Community policing emerged during an atmosphere of dislike and distrust in the late 1980s. "Faced with accusations of incompetence and inadequacy, public police in large urban centres across Canada ... responded by deploying 'community policing' programs" (Stansfield, 1996, p. 193). Community policing emphasizes the use of directed foot patrols, mini-stations or storefront stations such as in Toronto and Victoria, teams and zones-policing (police service based on a geographical area). The goal of this approach is to proactively identify and solve problems to maintain peace rather than to simply respond to calls after the peace has been broken (Stanfield, 1996). According to Stansfield (1996), the real key of community policing is the use of teams that are responsible for working in an identified zone or in team areas. These teams work with members of the community that may represent population diversity. Teams or zones can be identified based on the unique characteristics of the area or zone.

Changes in Recruitment, Selection and Training

Community policing is thus very different from traditional policing and therefore calls upon a different and expanded skill set of officers. A substantial amount of research has been undertaken in recent years to try to determine what the precise knowledge, skills and abilities are required for effective policing duties (McKenna, 1998). In Ontario, the Ministry of the Solicitor General's Strategic Planning Committee on Police Training and Educations identified twenty areas of knowledge, skills and abilities that more closely align policing to a profession with complex skills. Such skills are analytical skills and problem-solving ability, communication skills, a knowledge of human behaviour, interpersonal and sensitivity skills and the ability to serve victims (Ontario, Ministry of the Solicitor General, 1992a). Skills in conflict resolution, interpersonal communication, problem solving, crisis management, managing diversity and team skills are essential for you to work effectively in this new type of policing environment. Traditionally, once an individual has applied to a force, there is some sort of assessment process including a physical skills test. There is also a background and reference check that usually takes place after an interview with the potential candidate.

The most noticeable changes have occurred in assessment and training prior to police service application and assessments. This area has undergone some massive research and changes as a result of the implementation of community policing and in response to changes in society. Since we have not covered much in this area, let's examine this one area a little more closely. With new emphasis on community policing, how can services attract the best candidates to fill this new role and what are the skills/training required for this role? In other words, how can services attract recruits and then assess them for suitability for the responsibilities of being a community police officer?

Recruitment and selection include more than just attracting applicants. What services want to do is to attract those who are qualified and make selection based on criteria that determine an individual's ability to be a good officer. Most police agencies employ several criteria and methods to ensure as good a selection as possible (Dantzker and Mitchell, 1998). Many forces are using a variety of tests including aptitude tests like the G.A.T.B (see box below), personality tests such as the Minnesota Multiphasic Personality Inventory (MMPI-2) and physical skills and ability testing (McKenna, 1998). In Ontario, there is ongoing development of the Police Qualifying Examination (PQE), which may be implemented in May of 2000 (Ontario, Minister of the Solicitor General, March 30, 1999). The PQE will be a comprehensive test of the learning outcomes of Police Foundations Training that has been implemented across the province in many areas including community colleges. You may be using this text for one course in the Police Foundations Training. If so, there will be questions on the PQE that will reflect the learning outcomes of this course. Are you ready?

LAW AND JUSTICE PERSPECTIVE:

Using The General Aptitude Test Battery (G.A.T.B.)

The Police Constable Selection Project in Ontario (Ontario. Ministry of the Solicitor General, 1992) established a number of competencies that would be required at the entry level for officers. The General Aptitude Test Battery was researched as part of this project and has been deemed as a reliable and valid testing tool that can be used in the process of selecting police constables. For use as a test in policing, three of the eight aptitudes are tested. These three aptitudes make up the "G score," or General Learning Ability. Each of the three sub-tests is timed although individuals are not penalized for wrong answers. The questions get more difficult, and individuals are not expected to complete all the questions. A score that is above average for the "G score" has been identified for police recruits.

The three aptitudes used from the G.A.T.B. are:

- **Numerical aptitude.** A person's ability to perform arithmetic operations quickly including addition, subtraction, division and multiplication.

- **Spatial aptitude.** This part of the test measures an individual's ability to select what shape a flat object will look like when it is folded in a specific way.

- **Verbal aptitude.** This part of the test measures an individual's ability to understand the meaning of words and to use them effectively, as well as verbal comprehension.

There is some controversy about the use of this type of testing and at what point in training it should be used. For example, should it be used as part of recruitment to determine who can go further in training or who cannot proceed? Should colleges use it as a screening tool to identify who can be admitted into Police Foundations? As well, there are diversity issues here. Learning-disabled individuals and others with special needs, those with English as a second language and Native Canadians with poorer educational opportunities may not do as well as those without these differences. Should the results be used to recommend further training for retesting in the future as other training continues? It will be interesting to see what changes will occur in regards to testing in the next few years.

An Increased Concern with Ethics

There has been an increasing concern on the part of police leaders about ethics in policing as a result of serious questions raised by the public. These questions centre around standards of police accountability, the excessive use of force and the proper use of police discretion. As a result, many services are reviewing their current programs in the training of ethical standards of policing (McKenna, 1998). As part of new selection and training procedures, police organizations will be making increasing attempts to ensure that they are attracting people who will operate at high moral and ethical levels.

Ethics and morals can be tied into our earlier chapters on perception and diversity. Raised in different families and cultures, we may have different morals and values in some areas. For example, some cultures have a closer knit family structure than other cultures. While some cultures do have different values and display them in different ways, police need to attract candidates from diverse cultures that hold high moral and ethical values in such areas as protecting the weak and valuing human life. As well, how we perceive an event or how we are influenced by others may change our behaviour. Therefore, it is important that police not only hire those with strong moral and ethical values, but current officers behave in ways that display these values and ethics.

Technological Changes

Technology is changing our lives and workplaces at a dizzying speed (McShane, 1995). "Because policing relies so heavily on the latest developments in technology, it is important that we have a good understanding of this area" (McKenna, 1998, p. 36). Computer technology, weapons, identification techniques, equipment, the Internet are just a few of the technological areas of advancement. Unfortunately, these same changes have also provided new opportunities for the misuse of such advancements. For example, the use of the Internet for purposes of fraud and other types of "cybercrime" will continue to increase. Another recent report also pointed out the usage of encryption technology and software that allows terrorists to send virtually unbreakable coded messages across the Internet (United Press, 1999). Often such crimes continue until new statutes can be put into place for legitimate law enforcement.

The police officers themselves are confronted with a wide array of new technology to master personally. New car equipment, new office computers, new e-mail packages and so on can be bewildering for any person even with professional development training. Police leaders will need to be aware of the stress that change can create among officers and develop long-term and ongoing strategies to introduce change at levels that can be managed.

SUMMARY

In this chapter we have explored change by first defining what change is and the types of change that occur within organizations. Change agents are individuals or groups within organizations that can facilitate the change process. Organizations undergo restructuring; the people really undergo the changes. People react differently to change, ranging from inertia, support, reluctance to various types of resistance. People resist change for several reasons, including direct costs of the change, fear of the unknown, saving face, disruption and breaking of familiar routines, incongruent organizational systems and team dynamics that do not promote acceptance of the changes.

Change is a process that occurs in three stages according to force field analysis: unfreezing, transition and refreezing. The model of force field analysis can actually be used to assist change agents in managing organizational changes. There are several methods that can be used to overcome resistance to change. Organizations can use communication, employee involvement, training opportunities, introduce change at an appropriate pace, use negotiation to move ahead, and although it should be avoided, coercion can also be used to facilitate change. Because change happens to people, we also need to use strategies to help us cope with change. Some strategies included managing stress, talking to others, realizing that adjustment to change takes time and changing our perceptions.

The last part of the chapter concluded with exploring current changes that are having significant impact on policing in Canada. The changes discussed were demographic and population changes, aboriginal policing, changes as a result of legislation, the focus on community policing, changes in recruitment, selection and training of constables, an increased concern with ethics, the impact of technological changes.

Equipped with the knowledge and skills from this text, you are well on your way to developing the skills and abilities that will assist you in becoming an effective community policing officer.

JOURNAL AND DISCUSSION QUESTIONS

1. What are some significant changes that have occurred in your life in the past two to three years? What was your reaction to these changes?

2. Organizations do not always manage change very well. Examine a company in your area that is managing change well and one that is not. How do these two organizations differ?

3. Is community policing here to stay? Why or why not? It is just a label, or are there real changes going on in policing today?

WEB SITES

www.sgc.gc.ca

This is the site for the Solicitor General of Canada. This site has links to recent agreements with First Nations and other information on changes in policing.

www.gov.nb.ca/solgen

This is the web site for the Department of the Solicitor General in New Brunswick.

www.gov.on.ca/opp/english/about/learn/default.htm

This is a paper about the OPP becoming a learning organization in response to changes in the last five years.

www.acsp.uic.edu/oicj/pubs/cjintl/1306/130607.shtml

This is the Office of International Criminal Justice's online journal, Crime and Justice International. This article is about community policing.

REFERENCES

William Bridges (1991). *Managing Transitions: Making the Most of Change.* Don Mills, ON: Addison-Wesley.

Canada. Solicitor General Canada (1996). *Outlook.* Ottawa: Solicitor General of Canada.

Canada. Solicitor General Canada (Feb 17, 1999). News Release, Victoria, B. C.

Daryl R. Conner (1994). *Managing at the Speed of Change: How Resilient Managers Succeed and Prosper Where Others Fail.* New York: Villard Books.

Emory L. Cowen (1991). In pursuit of wellness. *American Psychologist.* April, p. 406.

Mark L. Dantzker and Michael P. Mitchell (1998). *Understanding Today's Police.* Toronto, ON: Prentice Hall Canada.

Richard J. DeParis (1998). Organizational leadership and change management: Removing systems barriers to community-oriented policing and problem-sovling. *The Police Chief,* December pp. 68–76.

D. Katz and R. L. Kahn (1978). *The Social Psychology of Organizations,* 2nd edition. New York: Wiley.

Kurt Lewin (1951). *Field Theory in Social Science.* New York: Harper and Row.

Paul F. McKenna (1998). *Foundations of Policing in Canada.* Toronto, ON: Prentice Hall Canada.

Steven L. McShane (1995). *Canadian Organizational Behaviour,* 2nd edition. Toronto: Times Mirror Professional Publishing Ltd.

Chris Murphy (1993). The development, impact and implications of community policing in Canada, in James Chacko and Stephen E. Nancoo (Eds.), *Community Policing in Canada.* Toronto, ON: Canadian Scholar's Press.

D. A. Nadler (1987). The effective management of organizational change. In J. W. Lorsch (Ed.), *Handbook of Organizational Behavior.* Englewood Cliffs, NJ: Prentice Hall, pp. 358–369.

David Nadler and Michael Tushman (1988). *Strategic Organizational Change.* Glenview, IL: Scott, Foresman.

Ontario. Ministry of the Solicitor General (1992a). Strategic Planning Committee on Police Training and Education. *A police learning system for Ontario: final report and recommendations.* Toronto: The Ministry.

Ontario. Ministry of the Solicitor General. (1992b). *Report on high impact learning methodologies.* Toronto: The Ministry.

Ontario. Ministry of the Solicitor General and Correctional Services (March 30, 1999). *Changes to the police recruit system of education, selection, and training in the province of Ontario.* Toronto: The Ministry.

M. Pollock and N. L. Colwill (1987). Participatory decision making in review. *Leadership and Organizational Development Journal, 8(2),* p. 710.

Robert A. Portnoy (1999). *Leadership: 4 Competencies for Success.* Upper Saddle River, NJ: Prentice Hall.

John R. Schermerhorn, Jr., James G. Hunt and Richard N. Osborn (1994). *Managing Organizational Behavior,* 5th edition. New York: John Wiley and Sons.

Ronald T. Stansfield (1996). *Issues in Policing: A Canadian Perspective.* Toronto, ON: Thompson Educational Publishing.

United Press International (January 15, 1999). *Report: Terrorists use latest cybertech.* Ottawa: United Press International.

Glossary

A

Abstract A representation of an object, thing or concept such as the word "chair," which represents a specific piece of furniture.

Acculturation The process whereby one culture is modified by contact with another culture.

Achievement norms Norms that determine the quality and quantity of work expected from group/team members.

Active listening An active process whereby the listener tries to understand exactly what the speaker is saying and feeling by reflecting both feelings and content back to the speaker.

Actor-versus-observer bias Tendency to view others' behaviour as caused by internal factors while viewing our own behaviour as caused by situational factors.

Aggressive behaviour Behaviour whereby an individual gets what he or she wants without concern for others.

Ambiguous Something that is not clear or well understood.

Artifacts Personal objects that announce who we are and that are used to personalize our environments.

Assertive behaviour Behaviour whereby an individual communicates in a straightforward and honest manner while still maintaining the rights of others.

B

Beliefs The things that you hold as true or false.

Body language The postures, movements and gestures that nonverbally communicate information to others.

Brainstorming A process for encouraging creative thinking by generating "free-wheeling" ideas and alternatives.

C

Central traits Primary traits to which other traits are attached or grouped.

Change When something is different from what it used to be or is different in some manner.

Change agents Individuals or groups that take responsibility for managing a change within an organization.

Charisma A quality that inspires followers to attain the goals of the leader.

Chronemics The study of how we perceive and use time.

Closure The process of filling in missing information.

Coaching Encouraging someone to a higher level of competency or skill in an area in which the coach already has greater skill.

Co-culture A culture that exists within a larger culture.

Cognitive complexity The level of ability to develop a sophisticated set of personal constructs.

Cohesiveness Extent to which members are attracted to, and want to be part of, a group/team.

Communication climate A condition or environment that is created within a team or group by the interaction of its members.

Communication continuum A range of communication that varies from not knowing the existence of a person to intimate communication with another. We vary our communication along this continuum with others to manage relationships.

Community Policing Delivery of police services based on a partnership with the community. The community and police jointly identify issues and work together to resolve these issues to mutual satisfaction.

Compliance An attempt to influence behaviour by making a direct request.

Confirming responses Responses that indicate that both the listener and the speaker are valued and that also demonstrate respect for individuals.

Conflict A condition that occurs when two sets of demands, goals or motives are incompatible.

Conformity Going along with the norms or rules of a group or team due to perceived pressure.

Connotative level of meaning The subjective and personal level of the meaning of a word.

Consensus Agreement by all members of a group about a decision or solution.

Constructive controversy Conflict whereby team or group members debate their different opinions about an issue without involving personal issues.

Constructs A set of specific qualities

Covert conflicts Conflicts that are not expressed openly but are hidden and expressed indirectly.

Creative thinking The ability to process information that results in a product that is new, original and meaningful.

Crisis An event that goes beyond an individual's ability to cope at that period of time when the event is occurring.

Crisis prevention A set of strategies that can be used to avoid a crisis or to prevent a crisis from escalating.

Culture A learned and shared system of knowledge, beliefs, values, attitudes and norms.

Cultural values A set of central and enduring goals in life and ways of life that are important to a specific culture.

D

Decentring The ability to think about another person's thoughts and feelings.

Decision The selection of one option from a set of options or alternatives.

Decision making The process of developing and selecting from a set of options or alternatives.

Decoding The process whereby a receiver interprets a message into meaningful information.

Defensive behaviour When people feel threatened, they act in ways to protect themselves.

Delphi technique A method of receiving input from a group of experts on a particular issue or problem.

Denotative level of meaning The literal level of meaning of a word that is shared by a large group or culture.

Disconfirming responses Responses that devalue another person and do not project respect towards that individual.

Discrimination Unjustifiable negative behaviour directed towards members of a group.

Dissensus Lack of consensus in a group. The group cannot reach a mututally agreeable conclusion or decision.

E

Empathizing To be able to put yourself in another person's "shoes," to "feel" what another person is feeling.

Encoding The process of organizing ideas or thoughts into a series of symbols to communicate with a receiver.

Enculturation The process whereby culture is transmitted from one generation to another.

Ethnocentrism A belief or conviction that the way that your culture does things is superior to another culture's ways.

Explicit Norms Norms that are made clear to all members verbally or in written form.

Extroversion An attitude characterized by outgoing behaviour of interacting and mingling with others.

F

Feedback Information that tells you how well you have performed.

Feminine cultures Cultures that stress more traditional feminine values such as valuing relationships, caring for others and emphasizing the quality of life.

Force field analysis A model of change that consists of unfreezing, transition and re-freezing. The model consists of driving and restraining forces that drive or restrain proposed changes.

Fundamental attribution error Overestimating and attributing another's behaviour as being caused by dispositional or internal factors.

G

Goal An event, circumstance, object, condition or purpose for which an individual strives.

Group Two or more people who are aware of each other, who both influence and are influenced by each other, who are engaged in an ongoing and relatively stable relationship, who share common goals and who view themselves as belonging to the group.

Group polarization The group's decision is more extreme, either more conservative or more risky, than the decision group members would have made by themselves.

Groupthink A process of faulty decision making by a cohesive group.

Groupware Software that is designed for use by teams or groups to aid in problem solving and decision making.

H

Halo effect Attributing a set of positive characteristics to someone we like.

Hearing The physiological process of sound waves entering the ear and hitting the eardrums.

Heterogeneous team A team composed of people with a diversity of characteristics, interests, cultures and values.

Hidden agenda Personal goals or motives that an individual hides from the rest of the group.

Hierarchy The structure of a group based on power and status differences.

Homogeneous team A team composed of people who share things in common, such as expertise, characteristics, culture and values.

Horn effect Attributing a set of negative characteristics to someone we dislike.

Human communication Sharing observations with others as we try to make sense of the world.

I

Impersonal communication A type of communication whereby we treat the other person as an object or whereby we respond only to his or her role.

Implicit norms Unwritten and unstated norms that are adhered to by all members. Usually develop as a result of group/team interaction over time.

Impression formation The process of forming an impression of someone based on a collection of perceptions.

Incremental change (frame-bending change) Change that occurs in series of steps over time.

Inertia A reaction to change whereby the individual does nothing.

Inferences Guesses, opinions and ideas about a person, object or event that are not necessarily true or factual.

Interaction norms Norms that determine how group/team members will communicate with each other.

Internalize Taking external information and making this information part of who you are or part of your psychological make-up.

Interpersonal communication A form of human communication between two people that occurs simultaneously where there is mutual influence and where it is used for the purpose of managing the relationship.

Interpersonal perception The process of selecting, organizing and interpreting others' actions and behaviour.

Interference Noise that interferes with the transmission or reception of a message.

Interpersonal attraction The factors that bring people together at the early stages of a relationship.

Intimacy The degree of closeness we feel with another.

Intimate distance A range of distance from touching to about 18 inches that is reserved for intimate communication.

J

Jargon Abbreviations or short forms of a word or phrase that is shared by a specific group, which may not be understood by others outside of the group.

L

Lateral thinking Another term for creative thinking, or the ability to process information that results in a new idea or product.

Leader The person with the skills or abilities to influence others towards obtaining organizational and/or personal goals.

Leadership The ability or process to influence people towards attaining goals of the organization or team.

Listening An active process of trying to understand exactly what the speaker is saying in interpersonal communication.

M

Masculine cultures Cultures that value more traditional masculine characteristics such as material wealth, assertiveness, achievement and heroism.

Management The technical tasks of a prescribed position within an organization.

Matching hypothesis We are attracted to others similar to us in physical appearance.

Monopolizing An ineffective listening strategy where the speaker continually re-focuses the conversation on himself or herself.

Myers-Briggs type indicator (MBTI) A psychological instrument used to help identify personality preferences.

N

Nominal group technique (NGT) A method of decision making that involves both individual and group decision making.

Nonassertive behaviour Behaviour whereby an individual does not stand up for his or her rights nor lets his or her feelings be known.

Nonverbal communication Behaviour that communicates meaning to another person and is not a written nor verbal language.

Norms Shared beliefs about what constitutes acceptable and unacceptable behaviours within a group or team.

O

Obedience Complying with a request given by someone perceived to be of higher authority.

Overt Conflicts Conflicts that are expressed openly between individuals. Issues and differences are expressed and discussed between parties.

P

Paralanguage Vocal communication that does not include actual words. It includes sounds, voice volume, pitch, tone and intensity.

Paraphrasing Repeating the feeling and/or content of what a speaker has said in different words as part of active listening.

Perception The process of selecting, organizing and interpreting stimuli to make sense of the world.

Perception-checking A process of soliciting feedback to confirm the accuracy of a perception.

Performance gap A discrepancy between what is currently occurring and what should be occurring.

Peripheral traits Traits that do not appear to be related to other traits.

Personal constructs Specific qualities that we use to categorize people.

Personal distance A distance between people ranging from 18 inches to four feet that is reserved for friendly relations.

Personality clash An antagonistic relationship between two people that results from differences in characteristics and attributes, preferences, interests, values and personal styles.

Personality traits Enduring characteristics of an individual.

Physical noise External noise that interferes with the transmission or reception of communication, such as loud music or traffic noise.

Planned change Change that occurs as a result of specific efforts.

Polarization In language and communication, describing events, people or objects in terms of extremes.

Positive reinforcement Rewarding a behaviour to increase the likelihood that the behaviour will be repeated or maintained.

Power The ability to get someone to do what you want them to do.

Prejudice An unjustifiable negative attitude toward a group and its members.

Private acceptance Conformity as a result of changed beliefs.

Problem A gap between what currently exists and the desired state.

Problem solving A complex decision-making process that involves the analysis of the problem and develops a plan to correct the problem or reduce its effects.

Procedural norms Norms that determine how the group/team operates.

Prototypes Cognitive structures that represent the best or clearest example of a category.

Proxemics The study of spatial communication or how we use space to identify relationship intimacy.

Proximity Physical nearness to others.

Pseudo listening Pretending to listen to another person when in reality you are attending to other things or focused on internal thoughts.

Psychological noise Internal noise that interferes with the transmission or reception of communication, such as hunger or distraction by other thoughts. Any internal interference that reduces an individual's capacity to send or receive a message.

Public compliance Conforming to a behaviour publicly without truly believing the behaviour to be correct or appropriate.

Public distance A distance between people ranging from 12 to 25 feet and beyond that is maintained for very impersonal interpersonal contact.

R

Radical change (frame-breaking change) Change that results in a major make-over of an organization.

Reflected appraisal Your view of yourself based on the assessment of others.

Refreezing After a change has been implemented, re-establishing equilibrium.

Relational level of meaning The level of meaning that defines our identity and relationships with others on three levels: interest, responsiveness and power.

Reinforcement affect model People are attracted to others who are associated with pleasurable events or stimuli.

Resilience The ability to withstand pressure and stress and emerge stronger from stressful or taxing experiences.

Restricted code A set of words or phrases that are developed and used by a small group, such as a family.

Role A position or place held in society; a set of attitudes and behaviours attributed to a position or place in society.

Role conflict Conflict that is caused by competing demands or expectations.

S

Scripts A series of actions or behaviours that serve as guides in various daily activities.

Self-disclosure The process of revealing your inner self to another.

Self-concept What you think of yourself and who you think you are.

Self-esteem The positive or negative evaluation of your self-concept.

Self-handicapping strategy Setting up an external reason for possible failure.

Self-presentation The process of conveying who we are to others.

Self-monitoring The degree to which people change their behaviour according to their perception of the demands of a situation.

Self-sabotage Behaviours, including negative self-talk, that interfere with or stop change efforts.

Self-serving bias Attributing success to internal factors and blaming failure on external factors.

Selective attention The process of attending to a limited amount of stimuli.

Semantic noise Interference that arises from differences in the perception of the meaning of a transmitted message, such as not knowing the meaning of a word.

Similarity Grouping stimuli together based on common characteristics.

Simplification Organizing stimuli in the easiest way possible.

Social affiliation Association with others; being with others in a group or team context. One of the reasons we join groups.

Social comparison By observing others around us, we try to present ourselves and see ourselves in a favourable light.

Social distance From four to 12 feet, this distance is used to conduct more impersonal interaction.

Social exchange theory In relationships, people measure their social, physical and other assets against those of a potential partner.

Social identification Defining ourselves in relation to those around us.

Static evaluation Maintaining the same evaluation of something without recognizing the changes that may have occurred.

Status norms Norms that determine the status and relative power and influence of group/team members.

Stereotypes Placing people or situations into separate and distinct categories based on broad generalizations and assumptions.

Strategic self-presentation The process of conveying a certain image to others to obtain specific goals.

Supportive behaviour Behaviour that encourages openness, trust and self-disclosure.

Symbols Representations for concepts, thoughts, ideas and objects.

Synergy Energy that results from the combined efforts and contributions of individual team members.

T

Tactical communication A standardized communication system used by law enforcement personnel.

Team A group of diverse people who share leadership responsibility for creating a group identity in an interconnected effort to achieve a mutually defined goal within the context of other groups and systems.

Team building A formal intervention process directed towards improving the functioning and development of a team.

Team culture A shared system of beliefs, values and ways of behaving within a team or group.

Team effectiveness The extent to which a team achieves its objectives, meets the needs and objectives of members and maintains itself over time.

Theory of reasoned action One theory that discusses the link between attitudes and behaviour.

Tolerance Being aware of and understanding that cultural differences do exist and being able to actively cope with these differences through understanding and empathy.

Trait approach The theories that suggest that leaders have unique qualities or traits that qualify them to lead.

Transmission The sending of a message through a chosen medium, such as verbal or written communication.

U

Ultimate attribution error Attributing internal causes for positive behaviour of people we like while attributing external causes for their negative behaviour. Attributing external causes for positive behaviour of people we dislike while attributing internal causes for their negative behaviour.

Unfreezing Changing the status quo or current state to prepare the organization for change.

Unplanned change Change that occurs spontaneously or randomly.

V

Values A set of central and enduring goals in life and ways of living that you feel are important, right and true.

Vertical thinking Traditional thinking style that is logical, sequential and analytical.

W

Win-lose The notion that in the outcome of a conflict there must be a winner and a loser.

Win-win The notion that in a conflict both sides can get what they want and both sides win.

Index

D